IMPROVING BEHAVIOUR AND ATTENDANCE AT SCHOOL

IMPROVING BEHAVIOUR AND ATTENDANCE AT SCHOOL

Susan Hallam and Lynne Rogers

Open University Press

Open University Press
McGraw-Hill Education
McGraw-Hill House
Shoppenhangers Road
Maidenhead
Berkshire
England
SL6 2QL

email: enquiries@openup.co.uk
world wide web: www.openup.co.uk

and Two Penn Plaza, New York, NY 10121—2289, USA

First published 2008

A catalogue record of this book is available from the British Library

ISBN-10: 0-33-522242-0 (pb) 0-33-522241-2 (hb)
ISBN-13: 978-0-33-5222421 (pb) 978-0-33-5222414 (hb)

Typeset by Kerrypress, Luton, Bedfordshire
Printed and bound in the UK by Bell & Bain Ltd, Glasgow

The *McGraw·Hill* Companies

Contents

Section 1
The context

1 Background

This chapter sets out the issues relating to behaviour and attendance at school providing a theoretical framework for tackling problems. It describes how the key elements of the Behaviour Improvement Programme and the Primary Behaviour and Attendance Pilot operated within this framework and the extent to which they were successful.

Introduction

Throughout the world policy makers have increasingly acknowledged the importance of education for promoting economic development and the social and personal welfare of individuals. The right to education is recognized by international human rights conventions and primary education is legally guaranteed in most countries. Despite this, it is estimated that something in the order of 18 per cent of the world's 650 million primary-aged children are not in school (UNESCO 2005).

In the developed world the issue is not access to school but rather disaffection from it. For instance, in the USA, a student drops out of education every nine seconds (Lehr et al. 2004) with rates being particularly high among minority students (Orfield 2004) and in urban areas (National Research Council 2003). In the UK, Ofsted suggests that there may be as many as 10,000 pupils missing from school on any given day (Home Office Research 2004), while NACRO (2003) estimates that the figure may be closer to 100,000. This book focuses on the issues faced by the developed world in sustaining the interest of children in formal education, improving their attendance at school, and their behaviour and motivation when they are there.

Attendance at school

It is difficult to obtain accurate information regarding attendance at school. While in most developed countries schools are required to keep records of attendance, not all distinguish between different types of absence, legitimate (for instance illness) or illegitimate (truancy), and many schools do not keep records of attendance at individual lessons. Even where schools are required to distinguish between different types of attendance, distinctions are not always applied consistently between or even within schools, particularly when high levels of unauthorized absence reflect badly on the reputation of the school. There are reported differences in the extent to which schools are willing to authorize absence for holidays (Malcolm et al. 2003) and teachers sometimes have difficulty in assessing whether attendance should be authorized or not (Munn & Johnston, 1992).

A useful categorization of non-attendance is set out in Table 1.1 (Carlen et al. 1992). It draws attention to the possibility that schools and teachers may officially disapprove of absence but yet unofficially condone it, for instance, where pupils are disruptive in class. It distinguishes between absence from school and absence from lessons (post-registration truancy), and acknowledges the role of parents in condoning absence, currently a major issue in the UK, where the Audit Commission in 1999 estimated that at least 50,000 of the pupils who officially missed school did so with the knowledge and support of their parents.

Table 1.1: Categories of absence from school

Officially induced	Absences forced on pupils by schools, e.g. closures, disciplinary action, exclusions
Officially approved	Absences officially recognized as being attributable to personal or family reasons, e.g. illness, bereavement, religious observance
Officially illicit but unofficially condoned	Absence which is officially illicit but which tends to be ignored by teachers, e.g. absence of disruptive pupils, pupils staying at home to complete examination coursework
Officially illicit but parentally approved	Absences instigated by parents, e.g. getting a child to help at home or undertake paid work
Officially illicit but parentally condoned	Absences which parents do not approve but where they feel unable or willing to enforce attendance
Officially illicit and parentally disapproved	Absences where officials and parents disapprove
Internal and illicit	Absence from lessons, even though the pupil is in school

Incidence of non-attendance at school

Although there are difficulties in accurately assessing the extent of non-attendance at school, in the developed world it is perceived to have reached epidemic proportions particularly in urban settings. In the USA, thousands of students truant each day (US Department of Education 1996) with a 96 per cent increase since 1988 (Puzzanchera et al. 2000). In much of Europe, national monitoring of attendance is relatively new, but such evidence as there is indicates increases in recent years (*Morgan 2001, Schropfer 2002* and *Schreiber-Kittl*), while in England, on any single day about 450,000 pupils (about 7 per cent of the total school population) are absent and of these about 50,000 pupils (about 0.7 per cent) are unauthorized absentees (National Audit Office 2005). Overall, since 1996/97, there has been a small decrease in overall absence but unauthorized absence has remained at about 0.48 per cent in primary schools and just over 1 per cent in secondary schools (Department for Education and Skills (DfES) 2006). However, there is variation related to individual schools, location, time of year and day of the week (Reid 2002).

In England, schools with higher proportions of Asian, Black African or Black Caribbean pupils are associated with lower absence rates despite the fact that some of these children may be absent on long trips abroad to visit relatives (NAO 2005). Absence seems to be a particular problem with White pupils from more deprived areas (Morris and Rutt 2004). There are higher absence rates in primary schools where pupils have a first language which is not English (NAO 2005) and the highest overall rates of non-attendance are in special schools. Recent data suggest that at least 2 per cent of pupils are persistent truants (Morris and Rutt 2004; Scottish Executive 2005).

Another source of data regarding attendance at school, particularly in relation to post-registration truancy is that derived from surveys of students. Research in Germany revealed that a third of pupils reported skipping school at least once in their school career, with a higher incidence among boys, and an increase between the ages of 13 and 17. Truancy was more common among the less academically able (Wagner et al. 2004). In the UK, the most extensive research exploring post-registration truancy surveyed 38,000 pupils aged 14–16 (O'Keeffe 1994). Overall, levels of truancy, including post-registration, were around 30 per cent. The majority of cases were occasional truants (less than once a month) but 8.2 per cent of all students truanted once a week or more. A more recent study which included data relating to primary-aged children found that truanting was more extensive than previously thought with 27 per cent of children admitting truanting without their parents' knowledge, 17 per cent reporting that they were able to leave school without detection (Malcolm et al. 2003). An analysis of data from primary Oftsed reports also suggests an increase in non-attendance in some primary schools (Reid 2006). The schools with the greatest problems tended to have high levels of deprivation, a high proportion of pupils with Special Educational Needs (SEN) or high proportions from minority ethnic groups. This is a worrying trend as a significantly high proportion of secondary pupils report starting to truant in primary school and there has already been a reported increase in the number of pupils in Years 7, 8 and 9 missing school (Ofsted 2004).

Trends in non-attendance

Drawing on a range of research evidence (O'Keeffe 1994; Hallam 1996; Malcolm et al. 2003; Department for Education and Skills (DfES) 2006; Scottish Executive 2006) it is possible to identify the following trends:

- there is an increase in absenteeism as pupils transfer from one phase of education to another;
- children with significantly higher-than-average absence at one school are likely to continue to be poor attenders at the next;
- there is a general increase in absenteeism as pupils progress through secondary schools with the highest level of unauthorized absenteeism in Year 11;
- in all phases girls are absent more than boys, although there is little difference in their rates of unauthorized absence;
- absence by girls is more often parentally condoned;
- there are differences in absenteeism during the school year. It is likely that each school has its own particular pattern;
- any break in routine can precipitate increases in absenteeism (holidays, INSET days, other breaks);
- absenteeism is greater in inner-city and deprived areas;
- attendance varies between minority ethnic groups;
- children with SEN, 'looked-after' children and those with multiple risk factors have higher-than-average absence rates; and
- even within the same catchment area, schools have different levels of attendance.

Exclusion from school

Since the 1980s, there has been an increase in the rates of exclusion from school in the UK, the USA and Australia, with a substantial minority of children experiencing long periods without education. This trend has not been replicated in other areas in Western Europe where exclusion is extremely rare (Parsons 1999). This may be because in many European countries, if a child is to be excluded from school, it is the headteacher's responsibility to find another placement for the child before the exclusion occurs (Panayiotopoulos and Kerfoot 2007).

In England, there was a huge rise in exclusions in the 1990s. A major cause of this was the 1988 Education Reform Act which introduced the publication of league tables and widened the concept of parental choice. The rise of a quasi-market in education made certain pupils more desirable to some schools (Glennerster 1991). Children became commodities and each school, as a producer, was in competition with other schools to attract consumers (parents and children). The media, government and Ofsted focus on overall performance of schools measured through results in national tests and examinations faced schools with disincentives to retain children at risk of poor attainment or exclusion (Wright et al. 2000). Increased exclusions were also the result of parental pressure from those who did not want their children's education disrupted by lower-performing or difficult pupils.

In the mid-1990s, in response to the increase in exclusions, the then DfEE set up a series of projects which had the reduction of exclusion and indiscipline as their principal aim. They were successful in raising awareness of the importance of reducing exclusion and succeeded in slowing the rate of increase to 2 per cent during 1996/97. Further reductions occurred with the rate stabilizing at under 10,000 by 2004/05 representing 0.12 per cent of the number of pupils in schools, 85 per cent from secondary schools, 12 per cent from primary schools and 3 per cent from special schools. In 2004/05 there were also 389,560 fixed-period exclusions, 85 per cent from secondary schools, 11 per cent from primary schools and 4 per cent from maintained special schools. The most common point for exclusion is age 13–14. Almost 3 per cent of pupils had one or more fixed-term exclusion, the majority 63 per cent being excluded on one occasion only. The average length of a fixed-period exclusion was 3.6 days, the majority lasting one week or less.

Official statistics are generally thought to be a significant underestimate of the true numbers of children excluded. Concerns have been raised about the accuracy of record keeping (Webb and Vulliamy 2004) and that many school exclusions occur outside formal channels with little or no clear recourse to legal procedures or established support mechanisms (Ofsted 2004). Schools have widely different exclusion rates, the attitudes of staff, and in particular those of the senior management team and headteacher, being the most important factors in explaining differences between similar schools (Munn et al. 1997).

In 2004/05 the permanent exclusion rate for boys in England was nearly four times higher than that for girls representing around 80 per cent of the total number of permanent exclusions each year. The trend for fixed-period exclusions was similar. Boys are also more likely to be excluded at a younger age. Girls are more likely to exclude themselves either by parentally condoned absence or by withdrawing more subtly from classroom learning (Lloyd 2005).

In 2004/05 around 26 in every 10,000 pupils of Mixed Ethnic origin were permanently excluded from school, a similar rate to that for Black pupils, about twice that for White pupils. Permanent exclusion rates were highest in Traveller of Irish Heritage children (78 in every 10,000) and White and Black Caribbean (41 in every 10,000). Almost 8 in every 100 pupils of Black and Mixed Ethnic origin were excluded for a fixed period in 2004/05. This compares with almost 6 in every 100 pupils of White Ethnic origin and around 2 in every 100 Asian pupils.

Pupils with statements of SEN are around three times more likely to be permanently excluded than the rest of the school population, although these rates have decreased steadily over the last three years. In 2004/05, 37 in every 10,000 pupils with statements of SEN and 40 in every 10,000 pupils with SEN without statements were permanently excluded from school. This compares with 6 in every 10,000 with no SEN. There may be a relationship between the extent of inclusion of children with special educational needs in mainstream education and exclusion, although differences in policy and practice may also play a part (Slee 1995).

There is a positive relationship between eligibility for free school meals and exclusion rates. However, schools with the highest rates of exclusion do not always have high rates of free school meal eligibility, although they do tend to have higher proportions of pupils with SEN and low levels of pupil attainment.

Reasons for exclusion

Many excluded pupils have experienced several fixed-period exclusions prior to a permanent exclusion which suggests that the troublesome behaviour is persistent, although there are some permanent exclusions where pupils are excluded for one-off serious incidents of bad behaviour which are unpredictable in nature, for instance, violence, sexual abuse, assault, supplying illegal drugs or carrying an offensive weapon. In 2004/05, 31 per cent of permanent exclusions and 27 per cent of fixed-period exclusions were due to persistent disruptive behaviour. Around 12 per cent of permanent and 23 per cent of fixed-period exclusions involved verbal abuse or threatening behaviour against an adult. Around 19 per cent of permanent and 21 per cent of fixed-term exclusions involved physical assault against a pupil. Overall, the most common reason for permanent exclusion is persistent disruptive behaviour (Office of National Statistics 2005). The type of behaviour that warrants exclusion varies enormously from school to school despite government guidelines. Official reasons may overdramatize the actual incident –

assault may simply mean pushing or playground fighting. A relatively minor incident is often the final straw in a series of unacceptable behaviours.

In 2004/05, around 1090 appeals were lodged by parents against the permanent exclusion of their child. This represented a 4 per cent decrease from the previous year. Just over 20 per cent were determined in favour of the parents.

Behaviour in schools

In recent years, there has been increasing concern in the developed world that pupil behaviour has deteriorated. The evidence to support this assertion has been drawn largely from data on exclusions (as the ultimate sanction for poor behaviour), despite the fact that these data are unreliable as schools vary in the extent to which they exclude pupils, even for the same kinds of behaviour. Developments in computer software are enabling schools more easily to record and categorize instances of poor behaviour but it will be some time before sufficient data have been collected for long-term trends to be identified.

Despite the rhetoric, in the UK there seems to have been some overall improvement in behaviour in schools since 2001. Fewer teachers identify behaviour as a major problem now than at the beginning of the decade (Smithers and Robinson 2001, 2005) and this is reflected in parents' views and overall in Ofsted judgements (Reed 2004; Wiseman and Dent 2005). Some teachers remain anxious about behaviour but much of this concern is concentrated in a minority of schools with challenging intakes and poor exam results (Bush 2005). The number of schools failing an Ofsted inspection because of unsatisfactory behaviour has fallen and violent incidents are rare. Behaviour is only a significant problem in about 1 in 10 schools (Ofsted 2005), although in these schools poor behaviour may lead to a high staff turnover thus exacerbating the problem (in some challenging schools up to 25 per cent annually) creating difficulties for maintaining consistent behaviour policies and practices. Of those teachers leaving the profession, 45 per cent cite poor behaviour as one of the reasons for doing so (Smithers and Robinson 2003).

Despite the reported improvements in behaviour, low-level disruption continues to be a problem (Munn et al. 2004; Scottish Executive 2006). The most concerning behaviours for teachers are those that involve minor violations of rules and regular disruption to the smooth running of the classroom. Violent behaviour in schools is not a major concern of most teachers, although extreme incidents of school violence are a global phenomenon and growing (Infantino and Little 2005).

The role of disadvantage and prejudice in social exclusion

There is extensive evidence throughout the developed world that patterns of exclusion, dropout and non-attendance mirror the wider picture of disadvantage and prejudice. For instance, Slee (1995) cites the vulnerability to exclusion from school of Maori pupils in New Zealand and Aboriginal children in Australia. In the USA, there is an over-representation of minorities in the statistics for dropouts (Lehr et al. 2004), while in the UK, high proportions of children from some minority ethnic groups are excluded from school (Department for Education and Skills (DfES) 2006). The impact of membership of disadvantaged minority groups, however, can be ameliorated by higher socio-economic status.

Why it is important to retain all pupils in education

There is considerable evidence that those who are not in school regularly for whatever reason, have limited lifetime opportunities, socially, professional and economically (Reid 1999). They are more likely to experience unemployment, underemployment, and long-term dependency on social services (Coley 1995). There are strong associations between exclusion from school, unemployment and homelessness (MORI 2004; Office of National Statistics 2005) and between truancy, exclusion and crime (DfES 2006). Success in school acts as a protective factor against these long-term risks particularly for boys aged 12–16 (McCarthy et al. 2004).

There is also a relationship between educational attainment and poor health (Hammond and Feinstein 2006). Truants and excluded pupils, in the short term, are more likely to be sexually active, smoke, drink and take drugs (McAra 2004). They are also more likely to experience marital breakdown, psychological problems and have more children at an earlier age. Female truants are more likely to be single parents, have children when they are relatively young and in early adulthood be depressed. These differences remain after controlling for social background and prior educational attainment (Hibbett and Fogelman 1990).

Poor attendance is a major source of discontent among teachers and hinders teaching and learning (MacBeath et al. 2004). Teachers are often frustrated by the persistent non-attendance of certain pupils, particularly as helping them to catch up takes time and distracts from teaching the remainder of the class. Pupils who have missed school fall behind in their work and frequently have difficulties with friendships.

The costs to society, financially and in terms of social cohesion, of educational failure through poor behaviour and attendance are high. The financial costs to health and social services of a range of conduct disorders are up to ten times higher than for children without difficulties (Scott et al. 2001), and Boyle and Goodall (2005) suggest that over their lifetime each truant costs society at least £250,000. Behaviour and attendance problems can be detected early and action taken to address them. Where this does not happen young people are placed at high-risk for a wide range of problems in later life (Fergusson et al. 2005). Governments have increasingly acknowledged the importance of maintaining children in full-time education and have developed a range of policies to support this.

Government initiatives

In England, a range of initiatives have been developed with the aim of maintaining children in full-time education. The Green Paper, *Every Child Matters* (DfES 2003), identifies five outcomes expected for children and young people:

1. Being healthy: enjoying good physical and mental health and living a healthy lifestyle.
2. Staying safe: being protected from harm and neglect.
3. Enjoying and achieving: getting the most out of life and developing the skills for adulthood.
4. Making a positive contribution: being involved with the community and society and not engaging in antisocial or offending behaviour.
5. Economic well-being: not being prevented by economic disadvantage from achieving their potential in life (HM Government 2003).

The Children Act 2004 enhanced the protection of children at risk of harm or neglect, by improving professional support and ensuring that they do not fall between the boundaries of different services. Increased support for parents and carers has led to earlier intervention, and there is more accountability and integration between services at local, regional and national levels. Schools' contributions to pupils' well-being are assessed under new inspection arrangements and some schools and their facilities are open all year and for an extended day becoming the epicentre of their community for all children perceived to be at risk.

In Scotland, the Education (Additional Support for Learning) (Scotland) Act 2004 embraced all children experiencing difficulties in learning, including those with behaviour problems with the intention of ensuring that a wider range of children than previously was eligible for a Co-ordinated Support Plan. A wide range of initiatives have been undertaken to promote positive behaviour in school.

Initiatives have also been undertaken to address issues relating to attendance at school. In Wales, the Welsh Assembly (2002, 2003) established a task force to produce a report on reducing truancy and absenteeism, while in England, the DfES set a target for the total absence rate to be reduced to 8 per cent by 2008. Initiatives to assist in this process include fast-track prosecutions, fixed-penalty notices, parenting contracts, parenting orders and truancy sweeps (see Chapter 12).

A framework for thinking about improving behaviour and attendance at school

The recent policy emphasis on multi-agency initiatives in addressing issues relating to disaffection from school reflects theoretical approaches which focus on the complex interactions between a variety of environmental systems affecting human behaviour (Bronfenbrenner 1979) (see Figure 1.1). Bronfenbrenner conceptualized a micro-system, consisting of an individual in his/her immediate environment at the centre, interacting with meso-systems involving the individual's interactions in a wider group of settings, for instance, at school or with peers. The individual might also be influenced by activity in an exo-system, a system within which someone close to the individual interacts, for instance, the influence of a parent's working life on a child. All of these systems are nested within a macro-system which is defined as a particular subculture in which the particular beliefs, values and ideologies of the lower-order systems are embodied. Within the model an individual's behaviour and development may be profoundly affected by events which occur in parts of the overall system within which they do not interact.

Working in Australia, De Jong (2005) has recommended a set of core principles to underpin the development of educational interventions based on understanding student behaviour from an eco-systemic perspective. These emphasize the importance of:

- embracing a health-promoting approach to creating a safe, supportive and caring environment;
- inclusiveness;
- incorporating a student-centred philosophy that focuses on the whole student (personal, social and academic);
- acknowledging that student behaviour is inextricably linked to the quality of the learning experience; and
- positive relationships between student and teacher.

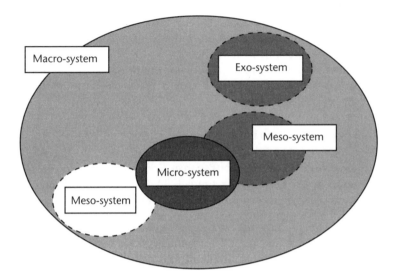

Figure 1.1 Eco-systemic model

Similarly, in the USA, McPartland (1994) has suggested that effective programmes aimed at promoting continuing engagement with education must include:

- opportunities for success in school work;
- creating a caring and supportive environment;
- communicating the relevance of education to future endeavours; and
- helping with students' personal problems.

School structures and climate, the academic curriculum offered, and the relationships between students and teachers play a crucial role in keeping students engaged in school (Lee and Burkam 2003). Caring school environments enhance opportunities for engagement by developing supportive relationships and by increasing opportunities for success in various aspects of the school experience (academic, extra-curricular, peer relations) (Bryk and Thum 1989).

Programmes adopting multidimensional approaches to improving behaviour and attendance in England

In England, the government has developed a number of initiatives aimed at improving behaviour and attendance at school. Notable among these are the

Behaviour Improvement Programme (BIP) and the Primary Behaviour and Attendance Pilot. This book draws on findings from these projects and other research to set out ways in which schools, Local Authorities (LAs), and other agencies can work together to improve the educational outcomes of the most vulnerable pupils.

The Behaviour Improvement Programme

In 2002, as part of the Government's Street Crime Initiative, the Department for Education and Skills (DfES) funded 34 LAs to support measures to improve pupil behaviour and attendance in two to four selected secondary schools and their feeder primary schools. Over 700 schools were involved in Phase 1 of the programme from LAs which were selected on the basis of an indicator combining truancy and crime figures. LAs selected from a menu of measures set out by the DfES based on existing good practice. They were also allowed to develop their own ideas. The menu included:

- the development of whole-school approaches to promote good behaviour;
- support for individual pupils at risk of developing behaviour problems;
- innovative approaches to teaching and learning to meet the needs of pupils at risk of disaffection;
- measures to identify pupils who were not attending school regularly and support them in improving attendance;
- extending the use of school premises to provide a range of services, activities and additional learning opportunities for pupils, their families and the wider community;
- the development of Behaviour and Education Support Teams (BESTs) to draw together the full range of specialist support for vulnerable young people and their families;
- basing police on the school site working alongside school staff; and
- providing a key worker to support or broker the necessary help for pupils who had or were at risk of developing, significant behaviour problems.

The evaluation of Phase 1 was undertaken in three stages. In Stage 1, all LAs engaged with BIP were contacted, telephone interviews undertaken, and information collated regarding the way in which the programme was implemented. From these data 18 LAs were selected for fieldwork to reflect the different types of interventions and those combinations of them which had been most commonly implemented. Meetings were arranged with the coordinating officers of these LAs and interviews undertaken with individuals or teams involved in the implementation of BIP. In some cases the focus was within the school, for example, the development of whole-school approaches to promote good behaviour, extending the use of school premises to provide a range of services, in others it was with LA-led teams (e.g. truancy sweeps, BESTs). Evidence from the interviews, and the data collected regarding exclusions, attendance and behaviour (taking account of contrasts with comparator schools) were used to select 10 secondary schools and a selection of their feeder primary schools for extended field visits. Interviews were undertaken with teachers not directly involved with the implementation of the project, classroom assistants, pupils and parents.

Phase 2 of BIP included 26 LAs involving 99 secondary schools and 446 primary schools. All of these LAs were contacted in 2004 and information about the way in which they were implementing BIP was gathered. From these LAs, 16 were selected for visits providing examples of different types of LAs, with different school populations, adopting different approaches to the implementation. The visits were focused at LA level and interviews were undertaken with LA personnel. No visits were made to schools.

The schools participating in Phase 1 of the BIP had high levels of children with SEN both statemented and without statements, high proportions of children in receipt of free school meals and high percentages of children for whom English was not the first language. Control schools were selected to enable comparison of performance indicators and were matched on SEN, free school meals and proportions of children for whom English was believed not to be a first language.

To provide an indication of the way that behaviour changed as a result of the programme, case study examples of individual and groups of pupils were collected in the school visits. School and LA staff also provided insights into the impact of the programme during interviews undertaken with them. There were perceived positive changes in: the status of behaviour and pastoral issues in school; school policies and practices; school ethos; the way that schools supported families; children's behaviour, well-being and learning; relationships with parents; staff stress; and a reduction in time spent managing poor behaviour.

The secondary and primary schools participating in Phase 1 of the BIP made greater improvements over a two-year period in attendance than the comparator schools and those in Phase 2 of BIP. In secondary schools there was a statistically significant reduction in overall absence from 11.89 per cent in 2001/02 to 10.13 per cent in 2003/04. At primary level there was a statistically significant reduction in overall absence from 7.65 per cent in 2001/02 to 6.74 per cent in 2003/04. These data suggest that the programme had a major impact on pupils' experiences in school leading them to want to attend. This is of particular importance as relatively little funding was targeted at measures to specifically improve attendance, such as electronic registration.

There was a reduction in fixed-term exclusions in the BIP Phase 1 secondary schools in relation to both the number of incidents and the number of days of exclusions accompanied by a small but significant increase in permanent exclusions, reflecting national trends, compared with matched schools, those in Phase 2 BIP, and Excellence in Cities (EiC) (non-BIP) schools. There was considerable variability between schools with 50 per cent showing a reduction in permanent exclusions and 16 per cent no change. Phase 2 BIP secondary schools showed a statistically significant reduction in permanent exclusions. There were no statistically significant changes in exclusions at primary school (fixed or permanent) which, given their normally low levels, is unsurprising.

An examination of the way that BIP was implemented and the funding allocated to its various elements in those LAs where there had been the greatest overall improvements in relation to attendance and attainment suggested that they:

- offered support at the level of the individual, the school and the community;
- focused on preventative initiatives;
- were proactive rather than reactive in relation to behaviour issues; and
- adopted a multi-agency approach.

The Primary Behaviour and Attendance Strategy Pilot

The Primary Behaviour and Attendance Strategy Pilot took place from 2003/05 and involved 25 LAs. The four strands of the pilot included:

1. A universal element providing professional development opportunities for all schools (the Continuing Professional Development (CPD) strand).
2. A targeted element providing focused support for schools where behaviour and attendance had been identified as key issues (the school improvement strand).
3. A universal element providing curriculum work focusing on the social and emotional aspects of learning for all children in pilot schools (the curriculum materials or Social and Emotional Aspects of Learning (SEAL) strand).

4. A targeted element providing group work for children needing extra help and their parents/carers (the small group intervention strand).

For the CPD strand, LAs were provided with funding to free school-based 'leading teachers' to work with teachers visiting to observe their practice, and to provide supply cover for all schools to send a representative to termly cluster/network professional development meetings. For the school improvement strand, LAs were funded to employ a 'teacher coach' to work with existing services (educational psychology and behaviour support) in schools experiencing difficulty, using a systematic process of audit, action plan, and professional development that included on-the-job solution-focused coaching. Funding for supply cover was provided for ten schools in each LA to receive training and have time for planning their use of the curriculum materials in the SEAL strand. For the small group interventions strand each LA was funded to appoint a specialist professional (usually a mental health worker) to work with children and families.

The evaluation consisted of:

- analysis of each LA's plans for the implementation of the pilot;
- telephone/email interviews with the 25 LA pilot coordinators;
- selection of 10 LAs for more detailed evaluation work. This involved sending questionnaires to school staff on their perceptions of the impact of the pilot and interviews with LA and project staff. Schools/LAs which were self-evaluating their pilot work were also able to fill in and return these questionnaires;
- visits to 16 schools which were identified as exemplars of good practice. This involved interviews with school staff, pupils and parents/carers;
- pre- and post-intervention completion of questionnaires by children in schools involved with SEAL or the small group work to assess change in their social, emotional and behavioural skills;
- case studies, where parental, teacher and children's self-assessments were used to assess the impact of the small group work; and
- analysis of attainment and attendance data in the pilot schools between 2002/03–2004/05 to assess levels of change. These data were compared to data for all primary schools.

The pilot had a significant impact on behaviour in the participating schools. The coaching was highly successful and valued by teachers. The supportive, collegial, non-judgemental model gave teachers confidence to admit to problems and be open and reflective about finding solutions to them. Leading teachers provided valuable role models particularly for Newly

Qualified Teachers (NQTs). The majority of headteachers believed that the coaching had improved the skills and confidence of teachers in promoting positive behaviour. Ninety-five per cent of teachers believed that it had improved their skills and 100 per cent their confidence. There was a perceived positive impact on children's behaviour, the working climate in the school, children's well-being, confidence, communication skills, social skills and control of emotions. Some impact was reported on learning and home–school relationships.

The SEAL programme increased staff understanding of the social and emotional aspects of learning helping them to understand their pupils better. This changed their behaviour, enhanced their confidence in their interactions with pupils, and led them to approach behaviour incidents in a more thoughtful way. All staff perceived a positive impact on the children's behaviour and well-being. Classrooms and playgrounds were calmer and children's confidence, social, communication, negotiating skills and attitudes were perceived to have improved. There were positive perceptions of the impact on the children's work. Overall 90 per cent of teachers indicated that the SEAL programme had been at least relatively successful. Analysis of the responses to the children's questionnaires revealed a range of complex relationships between age, gender, questionnaire responses made prior to the pilot, and school factors which all contributed to children's perceptions of their emotions, self-esteem, social skills, attitudes towards school and academic work. Overall, the programme had a positive impact on the children's social skills and relationships and their awareness of emotions in others. School ethos was an important contributory factor to children's personal and social development.

The children included in the small group work were selected because of poor behaviour, risk of exclusion, lack of response to rewards or sanctions, withdrawn behaviour, social difficulties in relation to other children, or fears of attending school. Groups were balanced across these difficulties. Teachers welcomed the small group work as an additional resource learning from the expertise of the group workers. Although there were difficulties in engaging parents in the group work, when they did participate, they reported that it was worthwhile and of benefit to the whole family. Assessment using the Goodman Strengths and Difficulties Scale showed statistically significant improvements in emotional symptoms and the pro-social behaviour of participating children depending on the particular problems that they were exhibiting initially. Eighty-two per cent of parents perceived that the programme had helped their child.

There was a statistically significant reduction in authorized absence across the programme as a whole over the period of the implementation of the pilot but no significant reduction in unauthorized absence. The largest statistically significant decrease in unauthorized absence was seen for those schools which implemented the SEAL programme, the school improvement strand and the small group interventions together.

At KS1, across the programme as a whole there were no statistically significant changes in relation to scores in reading, writing or mathematics in national tests. However, there were statistically significant differences between the various strands of the programme in relation to improvement in writing. The writing scores for schools implementing the small group work and the school improvement strand increased more than those for the other strands.

At KS2, across the programme as a whole there were statistically significant improvements in national test scores in English and mathematics. These reflected national trends. Schools participating in the school improvement strand appeared to make significantly greater improvements than CPD-only schools and non-pilot primary schools. This may have been because of their lower levels of performance at the start of the programme. Schools implementing SEAL and small group interventions together, and those implementing SEAL, the school improvement strand and small group interventions together made consistent improvements across all subjects from 2003/05.

The way forward

The success of the two programmes described earlier suggests that what is required to bring about improvement in behaviour and attendance at school is an approach which acknowledges their multifaceted nature and causes, and addresses issues in relation to society, particular groups within it, the school, the family and the individual child. Chapter 2 explores theories of behaviour and individual and environmental factors which contribute to it. Chapter 3 considers the evidence regarding the whole-school management of behaviour while Chapter 4 explores issues relating to pupil behaviour within and around the school and the way that it can be improved, particularly at break and lunch times. Chapters 5 and 6 continue the focus on the wider community considering home–school relationships and supporting parents respectively, while Chapters 7 and 8 focus on behaviour within the classroom, and the provision of alternative curricula. Chapter 9 addresses ways in which children identified as at-risk can be supported and Chapter 10 outlines alternative approaches to excluding children from school. Chapters 11 and 12 focus on ways of improving attendance for all pupils and persistent absentees, and the final chapter draws together the various strands covered in the book providing an overview of the ways in which policy makers, communities, schools, families and children can assist in reducing disaffection.

Chapter summary

- Education is important for promoting economic development and the social and personal welfare of individuals.
- In the developing world the challenge is to provide education for all. In the developed world the challenge is to raise standards and reduce disaffection.
- There are difficulties in accurately assessing and categorizing absenteeism from school.
- There is concern in the developed world about the high incidence of absenteeism from school particularly in the later stages of education.
- In recent years there has been an increase in exclusions from school. A range of initiatives has succeeded in reducing levels.
- There has been little rigorous assessment of the incidence of poor behaviour in schools. Most poor behaviour consists of low-level disruption, although there has been an increase in violence in some schools.
- Some children are particularly at risk of exclusion and disaffection (boys, those of low economic status, those with SEN, some minority ethnic groups, looked-after children).
- The long-term consequences of poor educational outcomes are many and carry a high cost for society.
- Governments worldwide are developing initiatives to improve behaviour and attendance at school.
- Eco-systemic approaches to intervention are the most likely to be successful in improving behaviour and reducing disaffection.

Further reading

Hallam, S., Castle, F., Rogers, L., Rhamie, J., Creech, A. and Kokotsaki, D. (2005) *Evaluation of the Behaviour Improvement Programme. Research Report 702.* London: DfES.

Hallam, S., Shaw, J. and Rhamie, J. (2006) *Evaluation of the Primary Behaviour and Attendance Pilot. Research Report 717.* London: DfES.

References

Boyle, D. and Goodall, E. (2005) *The Financial Cost of Truancy and Exclusion.* London: New Philanthropy Capital.

Bronfenbrenner, U. (1979) *The Ecology of Human Development*. Cambridge, MA: Harvard University Press.

Bryk, A. and Thum, Y. (1989) The effects of high school organization on dropping out: An exploratory investigation. *American Educational Research Journal*, 26: 353–83.

Bush, A. (2005) *Choice and Equity in Teacher Supply*. London: IPPR.

Carlen, P., Gleeson, D. and Wardaugh, J. (1992) *Truancy: The Politics of Compulsory Schooling*. Milton Keynes: Open University Press.

Coley, R.J. (1995) *Dreams Deferred: High School Dropouts in the US*. Princeton, NJ: Policy Information Center, Educational Testing Service.

De Jong, T. (2005) A framework of principles and best practice for managing student behaviour in the Australian education context. *School Psychology International*, 26(3): 353–70.

Department for Education and Skills (DfES) (2006) *Pupil Absence in Schools in England 2004/05*. London: DfES.

Department for Education and Skills (DfES) (2003) *Every Child Matters*. Norwich: HMSO.

Dockrell, J., Peacey, N. and Lunt, I. (2002) *Literature Review: Meeting the Needs of Children with SEN*. London: Institute of Education, University of London.

Fergusson, D., Horwood, L. and Ridder, E. (2005) Show me the child at seven: The consequences of conduct problems in childhood for psychosocial functioning in adulthood. *Journal of Child Psychology and Psychiatry*, 46: 837–49.

Glennerster, H. (1991) Quasi-market for education? *The Economic Journal*, 101(408): 1268–76.

Hallam, S. (1996) *Improving School Attendance*. London: Heinemann.

Hammond, C. and Feinstein, L. (2006) *Are Those Who Flourished at School Healthier Adults? What Role for Adult Education? Wider Benefits of Learning. Research Report 17*. London: Institute of Education, University of London.

Hibbett, A. and Fogelman, K, (1990) Future lives of truants: Family formation and health-related behaviour. *British Journal of Educational Psychology*, 60: 171–9.

Home Office Research, Development and Statistics Directorate (2004) *The Role of Education in Enhancing Life Chances and Preventing Offending*. London: Home Office.

Infantino, J. and Little, E. (2005) Students' perceptions of classroom behaviour problems and the effectiveness of different disciplinary methods. *Educational Psychology*, 25(5): 491–508.

Lee, V.E. and Burkam, D.T. (2003) Dropping out of high school: The role of school organization and structure. *American Educational Research Journal*, 40(2): 353–93.

Lehr, C.A., Johnson, D.R., Bremer, C.D., Cosio, A. and Thompson, M. (2004). *Essential Tools: Increasing Rates of School Completion*. Minneapolis, MN: National Center on Secondary Education and Transition.

Lloyd, G. (ed) (2005) *Problem Girls, London*: Routledge Falmer.

McAra, L. (2004) *Truancy, Exclusion and Substance Misuse*. Centre for Law and Society, No 4. The Edinburgh Study of Youth Transitions and Crime.

MacBeath, J., Galton, M., Steward, S. and Page, C. (2004) *A Life in Secondary Teaching: Finding Time for Learning*. London: National Union of Teachers and Cambridge University Press.

McCarthy, P., Laing, K. and Walker, J. (2004) *Offenders of the Future? Assessing the Risk of Children and Young People Becoming Involved in Criminal or Antisocial Behaviour. Research Report 545*. London: DfES.

McPartland, J.M. (1994) Dropout prevention in theory and practice, in R.J. Rossi (ed.) *Schools and Students at Risk: Context and Framework for Positive Change*, pp. 255–76. New York: Teachers College Press.

Malcolm, H., Wilson, V., Davidson, J. and Kirk, S. (2003) *Absence from School: A Study of Its Causes and Effects in Seven LEAs. Report 424*. London: DfES.

Morgan, S. (2001) *Truancy and Exclusion in France: Report of a Conference*. London: Franco-British Council.

MORI (2004) *Youth Survey*. London: MORI.

Morris, M. and Rutt, S. (2004) *Analysis of Pupil Attendance Data in Excellence in Cities (EiC) Areas: An Interim Report*. London: DfES.

Munn, P. and Johnston, M. (1992) *Truancy and Attendance in Scottish Secondary Schools*. Edinburgh: Scottish Council for Research in Education.

Munn, P., Cullen, M.A., Johnstone, M. and Lloyd, G. (1997) *Exclusions and In-school Alternatives. Interchange No 47*. Edinburgh: Scottish Office Education and Industry Dept, Research and Intelligence Unit.

Munn, P., Stead, J., McLeod, G. et al. (2004) Schools for the 21st Century: The national debate on education in Scotland. *Research Papers in Education*, 19(4): 433–52.

NACRO (2003) *Missing Out*. London: NACRO.

National Audit Office (NAO) (2005) *Improving School Attendance in England*. London: The Stationery Office.

National Research Council (2003) *Engaging Schools: Fostering High School Students' Motivation to Learn*. Washington, DC: The National Academies Press.

Office of National Statistics (ONS) (2005) *Permanent and Fixed Period Exclusions from Schools and Exclusion Appeals in England* (2003/04). London: The Stationery Office.

Ofsted (2004) *Out of School: A Survey of the Educational Support and Provision for Pupils Not in School*. London: Ofsted.

Ofsted (2005) *Managing Challenging Behaviour*. London: Ofsted.

O'Keeffe, D.J. (1994). *Truancy in English Secondary Schools*. London: HMSO.

Orfield, G. (2004) *Dropouts in America: Confronting the Graduation Rate Crisis*. Cambridge, MA: Harvard Education Press.

Panayiotopoulos, C. and Kerfoot, M. (2007) Early intervention and prevention for children excluded from primary schools. *International Journal of Inclusive Education*, 11(1): 59–80.

Parsons, C. (1999) *Education, Exclusion and Citizenship*. London: Routledge.

Pasteror, R.N. and Reuban, C.A. (2000) Attention Deficit Disorder and learning disability: United States 1997–98. *Vital Health Statistics*, 206: 1–12.

Puzzanchera, C., Stahl, A.L., Finnegan, T.A., Snyder, H.N., Poole, R.S. and Tierney, N. (2000) *Juvenile Court Statistics, 1997*. Pittsburgh, PA: National Center for Juvenile Justice.

Reed, J. (2004) *Toward Zero Exclusion: Beginning to Think Bravely*. Presentation for the Launch of the IPPR Project, 21 June 2004.

Reid, K. (1999) *Truancy and Schools*. London: Routledge.

Reid, K. (2002) *Truancy: Short and Long Term Solutions*. London: Routledge-Falmer.

Reid, K. (2006) An evaluation of Inspection Reports on primary school attendance. *Educational Research*, 48(3): 267–86.

Schreiber-Kittl, M. and Schropfer, H. (2002) *Abgeschrieben? Ergebnisse einer empirischen Untersuchung uber Schulverweigerung*. Ubergange in Arbiet, Bd.2 Opladen: Leske + Budrich.

Scott, S., Knapp, M., Henderson, J. and Maughan, B. (2001) Financial cost of social exclusion: Follow-up study of antisocial behaviour in clinical practice. *British Medical Journal*, 323: 191–4.

Scottish Executive (2005) *Attendance and Absence in Scottish Schools 2004/05.* Edinburgh: Scottish Executive Education Department.

Scottish Executive (2006) *Attendance and Absence in Scottish Schools 2005/06.* Edinburgh: Scottish Executive Education Department.

Slee, R. (1995) *Changing Theories and Practices of Discipline.* London: Falmer.

Smithers, A. and Robinson, P. (2001) *Teachers Leaving.* London: NUT.

Smithers, A. and Robinson, P. (2003) *Factors Affecting Teachers' Decisions to Leave the Profession. Research Report 430.* London: DfES.

Smithers, A. and Robinson, P. (2005) *Teacher Turnover, Wastage and Movements between Schools.* London: DfES.

Steer Report (2006) *Learning Behaviour: The Report of the Practitioners' Group on School Behaviour and Discipline.* London: DfES.

UNESCO (2005) *Children Out of School: Measuring Exclusion from Primary Education.* Montreal: UNESCO Institute for Statistics.

United States Department of Education National Center for Education Statistics (1996) *Annual Report.* Washington, DC: Department of Education.

Wagner, M., Dunkake, I. and Weiss, B. (2004) *Truancy in Germany: A Theoretical and Empirical Analysis.* Paper presented at the Euro conference on the 'Causes and Consequences of Low Education in Contemporary Europe', Granada, Spain, 18–23 September.

Webb, R. and Vulliamy, G. (2004) *A Multi-agency Approach to Reducing Disaffection and Exclusions from School. Research Report 568.* London: DfES.

Welsh Assembly (2002) *The Attendance Task and Finish Group: Final Report.* Cardiff: National Assembly for Wales.

Welsh Assembly (2003) *The Attendance Task and Finish Group: Final Report.* Cardiff: National Assembly for Wales.

Wiseman, J. and Dent, R. (2005) *London Challenge: Third Survey of Parent and Carers 2005. Research Report 698.* London: DfES.

Wright, C., Weekes, D. and McGlaughlin, A. (2000) *Race, Class and Gender in Exclusion from School.* London: Falmer Press.

2   Theoretical underpinnings and the causes of poor behaviour and attendance

This chapter outlines theories which address how behaviour is learned and sustained and presents a model of the way that behaviour is determined through interactions between the individual and his/her perceptions of the environment. Evidence relating to societal, community, family, school, peer group, and individual factors contributing to poor behaviour and attendance are considered.

Introduction

The particular systems affecting poor behaviour and attendance at school include those operating at the level of society, subgroups within it, the family, the school, peer groups and the individual (Reid 1999; Edward and Malcolm 2002). It is now generally accepted that the causes are complex and multifaceted and that behaviour depends on interactions between the various systems.

Theories of how behaviours are learned and sustained

Historically, theorists have attempted to explain human behaviour from three main perspectives: those which emphasize behaviour as deriving from within the individual, those where the individual is perceived to be motivated to behave in particular ways by environmental factors, and those where behaviour is seen as a complex interaction between the individual and the various systems in the environment mediated by cognition.

Behaviourists suggest that the behaviours that we exhibit are shaped by the responses we receive from the environment. Positive reinforcement for particular behaviours leads to their repetition and is the most powerful way of bringing about change, the most effective rewards being those based on social approval and praise. For those children who seek attention, being given it even through punishment will be rewarding. The principles of behaviourism are particularly relevant in school settings. Systems with clear rules, acknowledged by pupils to be fair, consistently applied by all teachers with a focus on rewarding good behaviour, are effective in maintaining appropriate behaviour in most children most of the time. Where poor behaviour occurs it should, if possible, be ignored with an immediate focus on rewarding good behaviour. This is clearly problematic in situations where other children may observe such behaviour, see it go unpunished, and thus learn that it is acceptable. For this reason, many schools adopt systems where poor behaviour is dealt with by the isolation of the offending individual for a short time. This does not provide the immediate reward of attention, allows for a cooling-off period, and also indicates to other pupils that the particular behaviour exhibited is unacceptable. Where children find particular situations consistently unrewarding they may avoid them. This explains some non-attendance at school. In extreme cases, where the child experiences high levels of anxiety in relation to school attendance, or being separated from a parent, phobias can develop.

Social learning theory further developed behaviourist principles to take account of the importance of modelling (Bandura 1977). Human beings learn from observing others. Whether what they learn is enacted will depend on whom they have observed, whether they have high status, and whether the behaviour that they have observed has been rewarded. Role models are important influences on the 'possible selves' that we envisage for ourselves in the future and the goals which we set in order to attain those selves. Society determines those who have high status and it is inevitable that many young people aspire to their values and emulate their behaviour. Society as a whole therefore bears responsibility for setting the standards of behaviour which are deemed acceptable and rewarding those who meet those standards. All too often, those who have high status behave in ways which do not present good role models. In some youth cultures alienation from society has become so great and the rewards attained by the majority of people so unattainable that high status models and perceived rewards reflect reversed values. Within such a culture, being excluded from school can be viewed as rewarding and a means of enhancing status. The need for peer approval can encourage non-attendance and the exhibition of poor behaviour.

Psychoanalytic theories explain behaviour in terms of the human being as an energy system, driven by sexual and aggressive drives and operating in the pursuit of pleasure (tension reduction). Behaviour is determined by the way in which we pursue these drives or their more acceptable alternatives. In contrast, humanistic theories emphasize the individual's freedom to choose a particular course of action. Motivation to behave in particular ways is viewed as a striving towards self-fulfilment through self-actualization, maturity and socialization. Self-actualization explains human creativity, our constant attempts to improve and change, and our attempts to maintain and enhance our self-esteem. These self-developments are influenced strongly by environmental factors in the form of feedback given by others.

Modern theories have evolved from these major meta-theoretical positions taking much greater account of cognition, the way our perceptions of events are determined by our construction of them, and the ways in which our interpretations of them subsequently influence the constantly changing perceptions we hold of ourselves and our behaviour. They acknowledge the capacity of the individual to determine their own behaviour, while also recognizing the role of the environment in rewarding or punishing particular behaviours and influencing the individual's thinking and subsequent actions. This process is influenced, in part, by the extent to which the individual perceives that they have control over situations. Where learners believe that there is nothing that they can do to improve their situation learned helplessness can result.

Our self-concept, self-esteem and self-efficacy develop through our interactions with others and are influenced by the way that we attribute our success or failure in particular situations to causes which will allow us to maintain a consistent view of ourselves (Weiner 1986). The causes of success or failure can be seen as stable or unstable; controllable or uncontrollable; or internal or external. If we attribute outcomes to an unstable source, for example, bad luck, expectations about what will happen in the future are likely to be unaffected. However, if failure in a particular situation is attributed to a stable factor (e.g. I am a naughty child), there will be an expectation of continued failure. Some causes are perceived to be within our control (e.g. the effort we make), while others (e.g. the behaviour of peers or teachers), are not. Some are perceived to be internal (e.g. hyperactivity, learning difficulties), others are not (e.g. the social climate within the school). In explaining the outcomes of particular situations these three elements interact with each other.

Figure 2.1 presents a model setting out the key elements which in interaction determine our behaviour. Personality, self-concept, self-esteem and self-efficacy are developed, in part, through feedback from the environment. We are motivated to behave in particular ways because we desire social approval, particularly from those we admire and respect. Such praise is internalized, raises self-esteem and enhances confidence. Individuals set themselves goals which determine their behaviour. These goals are influenced by individual characteristics including personality, ideal and possible selves as well as environmental factors. Behaviour is the end link in the chain but at the time of enactment it too can be influenced and changed by environmental factors. There is interaction between the environment and the individual at every level and in the long and short term. Individuals can act upon the environment to change it, or seek out new environments more conducive to their needs.

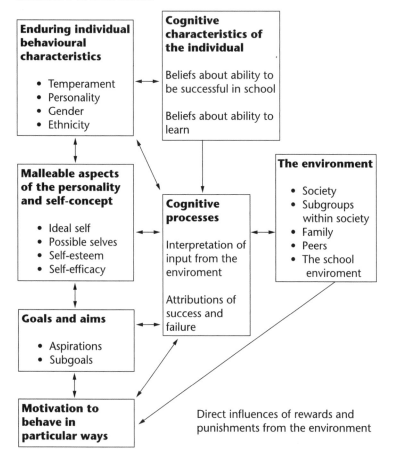

Figure 2.1 Interactions between individuals and environmental factors in determining behaviour

The following sections will outline what we know about the societal, subgroup, family, and peer factors which interact with individual characteristics to determine behaviour.

Societal factors

In the global knowledge economy high levels of educational attainment are viewed as national imperatives for economic success and governments have invested considerable time and money in ensuring that their education systems are capable of delivering high standards to meet the requirements of employers, particularly those operating worldwide. The value that society attaches to education inevitably has an impact on the attitudes to it held by parents and children with a subsequent impact on attendance and behaviour at school. However, the messages communicated by society about the value of education are sometimes conflicting. Those with considerable wealth and prestige often have relatively low-level qualifications, while those who have spent many years training may not be held in high esteem. Even in cultures where qualifications are valued and rewarded, education systems may be constructed in such a way that some young people are denied the opportunity to attain them. Those having high-level qualifications may be unable to find employment that utilizes their expertise, or young people may live in an area where there is no prospect of work. In such locations many young people simply drop out of education (Wilkinson 1994). For some, involvement in crime and antisocial behaviour is their only means of establishing their status and worth, particularly among their peers.

In the UK, the gap between the rich and poor is widening (Mortimore and Whitty 1999) and many children live in poverty, a situation which has been exacerbated by the breakdown of the traditional family (Pritchard and Cox 2005). Britain also faces a significantly greater problem of teenage pregnancies than the rest of Europe (Social Exclusion Unit 1998), an outcome that is more common among teenagers who are disaffected from school (Bonnell et al. 2005).

Subgroups and communities within society

Within society, the socio-economic status and social class of particular communities impact on life chances and children's educational opportunities (Smith and Farrington 2004). There is considerable evidence that there is a link between eligibility for free school meals and pupils' non-attendance at school (Zhang 2003; Kendall et al. 2004). Official statistics in Wales show that in secondary schools, where more than 30 per cent of pupils have free school meals, unauthorized absence rates are as high as 4.6 per cent, over six times the national average (National Assembly for Wales 2004). In Scotland, the rate of exclusions among pupils accessing free school meals is almost four times higher than their peers (Scottish Executive 2005).

At the community level there are links with a range of delinquent behaviours from vandalism to criminal violence (Miller and Plant 1999). A range of background factors are important in determining future criminal activity, poverty, poor parental supervision, parental neglect and conflict, a parent with a criminal record, or a mother receiving psychiatric help. These have more influence on whether a child becomes an offending youth than schools or attendance at school (Collins 1998).

As we saw in Chapter 1, the data for exclusions from school indicate that some minority ethnic groups are over-represented. However Black excluded pupils are not characterized by the same negative home and social problems as frequently as White excluded pupils (Ofsted 1996a), suggesting that the high exclusion rates among this group are linked to institutional factors (Ofsted 1999; Wright et al. 2000). The evidence from the USA also shows that school dropout is related to social class and ethnicity (Lee and Burkam 1992). Blacks and Hispanics show higher dropout rates than average, although Black females are much more likely to stay in school than males.

Despite the differences in exclusions, ethnic minority pupils are less likely to truant than their White peers (NAO 2005). Sasson (1993/2000) argues that their parents may insist on school attendance. The same does not apply to the children of travellers who in England have an attendance rate of below 50 per cent in secondary school (Social Exclusion Unit 1998) and limited engagement with education, with up to 12,000 traveller children not registered at any school (Ofsted 1996b, 1999, 2003; Derrington and Kendall 2004). Even where traveller children live on established plots or in housing only 38 out of 44 successfully achieve the transfer to secondary school and of those only 20 complete the first three years of secondary education (Derrington and Kendall 2004). Ofsted estimates that less than 1 in 5 traveller students access school in Key Stage 3 (Ofsted 1996b).

Family factors

A range of family factors affect children's behaviour and attendance at school. For some children the demands and traumas of family life are so great that the impact on their attendance and behaviour at school is profound. Schools have a vital role to play in such circumstances, providing a stable and supportive environment for the child. As children spend a relatively small proportion of their time at school, it is unrealistic to ignore family influences.

Children missing from school

Estimates suggest that there are as many as 10,000 children in England who are absent from school rolls. Their families tend to be characterized by disadvantage and school disengagement including lone female parenting, poor housing, dependency on state benefits, a history of domestic violence, mental health problems, and at least one child with emotional and behavioural difficulties or a disability. Such families are most likely to be living in the private rented sector and often have a history of homelessness and bed and breakfast accommodation. Broadhurst and colleagues (2005) found that in about half of the families in their sample, at least one child had spent a period of more than 12 months missing from school registers and for a small number of children this extended to four years. Three distinct life course groups emerged. In the first group, parents and children were active participatory agents who opted for a temporary period of non-participation in schooling, in the second group some mothers were fleeing from domestic violence and their need for safety was more important than schooling. For these families engagement with education was discontinuous, depending on other life events, and their priority was reinstating stability. The third group were the most problematic with continuous multidimensional disengagement, and an almost total withdrawal from social systems often characterized for the parents by a life lived indoors. School was not relevant or important and the children often adopted alternative and occasionally criminal lifestyles.

Child carers

Some children have primary caring responsibilities for parents who have profound physical disabilities, are terminally ill or have psychiatric problems. The impact of caring in relation to a child's education can be immense. Substance abuse is another risk factor both among family members and pupils themselves. It is estimated that as many as 250,000 to 350,000 children are living with parental drug abuse while 920,000 are living with parental alcohol abuse. In such environments there is a risk of neglect, abuse and the development of emotional and social problems in later life (Bancroft et al. 2004). Children can find themselves caring for their parents in these circumstances which can lead to poor attendance.

'Looked-after' children

Although families can be the cause of difficulties for children, those who are 'looked-after' are at greater risk. Forty per cent of 'looked-after' 10–15-year-olds have clinically significant conduct disorders compared with 6 per cent in private households (Meltzer and Gatwood 2000). 'Looked-after' children are over-represented in the exclusion and truancy figures. One in four 'looked-after' children over the age of 14 does not attend school (McCarthy et al. 2004). In Scotland 'looked-after' pupils are five times as likely as their peers to be excluded from school (Scottish Executive 2005). These most disadvantaged young people are let down by the system.

The impact of stressful family life

Where families are under stress the children are most at risk of exclusion (McCarthy et al. 2004). Many excluded children have dysfunctional, chaotic, or stressful home lives, death and illness also being risk factors (Wilkin et al. 2005). Children often experience emotional difficulties when their parents separate or divorce (Butler 2003a, 2003b). Excluded children frequently come from families where there has been a change in partner. Only 25 per cent of excluded children live with both parents, compared with 60 per cent of non-excluded peers (Prince's Trust 2002). A range of behaviour problems also tends to develop in the context of harsh, inconsistent parenting and low levels of positive parenting (Gardner et al. 2003). In these situations children tend to perceive unthreatening situations as threatening and respond to them aggressively (Dodge and Somberg 1987).

Parental influences on education

Parental involvement and interest in their child's education has a positive impact on its outcomes (Flouri and Buchanan 2004). Even where the family is not intact this association is strong, providing that the separated parents continue to take an interest in the child. Parents/carers living in deprived areas need considerable help to support their children. Poor language and basic skills often act as barriers and many parents lack a fundamental understanding of how the school system works. However, the majority do want their children to do well at school, even if they themselves underachieved (McCarthy et al. 2004), and they have positive attitudes towards their child's school (Woodward and McVie 2001). In contrast, those children who are excluded tend to have parents who show little interest, tending not to help with homework, rarely attending parent–teacher evenings, rarely praising their children, and being less likely to discipline their children at home (Prince's Trust 2002).

Family influence and parenting styles tend to be transmitted across generations (Smith and Farrington 2004). If parents have been alienated from education often their children are too. In households headed by women the mother's attitude and expectations of education are the key to the children's educational response. This commitment can compensate for the absence of a father (Zhan and Sherraden 2003). Teenage mothers when supported by the child's father have fewer difficulties (Roye and Balk 1996), although depression in lone and isolated mothers impacts on their child's psychosocial development (Pritchard 2006), boys being particularly vulnerable, especially if exposed to domestic and community violence and a high rate of background crime (Ingoldsby and Shaw 2002).

The role of the family in attendance at school

The influence of the family, positive or negative, in relation to attendance and performance at school cannot be underestimated. Although family circumstances can contribute towards absenteeism, families also contribute to its reduction. Many children do not truant because they are afraid of their parents finding out (O'Keeffe 1994). However, some families take their children on extended holidays during the school year, indicating a low value placed on formal education (Atkinson et al. 2000). Over 10 per cent of primary school pupils believe that their parents/carers would condone an absence, the most common reason being 'having something more important to do' (Malcolm et al. 2003). Most parents believe that it is unacceptable to miss school to allow access to services at home, earn money, go shopping, or look after someone who is ill, although visiting the doctor is seen as more acceptable and opinion is divided about taking a child on holiday during term time (Dalziel and Henthorne 2005). The parents of truants tend to hold different attitudes (Malcolm et al., 2003). Table 2.1 sets out the details. Ofsted (2001) found that a small proportion of parents/carers of pupils at secondary school were very uncooperative and their attitudes whether confrontational or passive served to reinforce their children's negative attitudes towards school.

Table 2.1 Parents' beliefs about and attitudes towards school attendance

---

Most parents believe that:
- poor attendance leads to poor school work;
- good attendance is necessary for children to get qualifications;
- children could be at risk if they are not in school;
- missing school occasionally does not harm a child's education;
- it is more acceptable to use school time for doctor's appointments than dental appointments.

Where there are issues with children's attendance parents:
- identify problems with teachers, bullying and peer pressure;
- believe school attendance is less important, is unrelated to attainment and do not value qualifications to the same extent as other parents;
- are more likely to think that children might have something more important to do at home than school;
- are more likely to keep their children away from school for illness, family holidays, and medical or dental appointments.

Source: Derived from Malcolm et al. (2003).

The families of children with poor attendance tend to be those experiencing multiple and complex problems (Dalziel and Henthorne 2005). Reid (2002) identified five types: anti-education, laissez-faire, frustrated, desperate or adjusting. Frustrated parents were those who were unable to ensure that their child attended school despite having appealed to a range of other services and resources. In some cases the child absconded having been taken to the school gate.

Parents tend to lay most of the blame for poor attendance on schools (Malcolm et al. 2003). They believe that children misbehave and play truant because they are bored and the National Curriculum is failing to address their needs. They also blame their own shortcomings as parents, peer pressure, a breakdown in pupil–parent relations, bullying, boredom at home and lack of school discipline (Kinder and Wilkin 1998).

The role of the school in promoting good behaviour and attendance

In England, political policies which have promoted a quasi-market in schooling have created a climate where some schools are reluctant to admit or maintain pupils who threaten their image or performance (Parsons 1999). Where schools have adopted a competitive culture, the response to alienating and alienated behaviour is to view excluded pupils as culprits rather than victims who have little entitlement to education (Abbots and Parsons 1993; Lloyd-Smith 1993).

In general, the increased focus on attainment has reduced the role of the teacher in developing 'the whole child' and led to less emphasis on pastoral care. The National Association of Schoolmasters and Union of Women Teachers carried out a study of indiscipline in schools and found that pupils perceived that the greatest impact on the behaviour of their peers was the amount of quality time teaching staff spent getting to know and value pupils as individuals (Wright and Keetley 2003). Ofsted (1996a) has suggested that appropriate pastoral support is the key to reducing exclusions. However, there is a shortage of staff trained in behaviour management, counselling and social work in UK schools (Ofsted 2005). In addition, many newly qualified teachers feel that their training has not adequately prepared them to deal with disruptive pupils or to cope with the challenges presented by bullying and harassment in the classroom (Wright and Keetley 2003).

Other factors contributing to disaffection for some children are the perceived irrelevance of the curriculum and the unlikelihood of achieving in examinations (Wright et al. 2000). Early success in school is needed to engage students (Slavin 1999), as attitudes towards school become increasingly more negative as children get older (Armstrong et al. 2005).

School characteristics, poor behaviour and exclusion

Each school has its own ethos and social climate which impacts on exclusion and discipline policies and practices (Hallam et al. 2005). There is great disparity in exclusion rates between schools. For instance, in 2001, 40 per cent of secondary schools did not exclude any pupils while 100 schools were responsible for around 10 per cent of all permanent exclusions (Ofsted 2001). The attitudes of the headteacher are crucial in determining the levels of exclusion.

Appropriate and flexible curriculum organization and provision, distributed leadership, shared beliefs, positive relations with the world outside school, and good relationships between teachers and pupils based on mutual respect are key features of schools likely to have few behavioural problems (Munn et al. 2000; Kane et al. 2004). Praise-and-reward systems and peer support can promote positive behaviour (Naylor and Cowie 1999), including assertive discipline procedures (Swinson and Cording 2002), and systems of restorative justice (Hopkins 2004). Participation of the pupils in the decision-making processes within a school can also mitigate violent and aggressive behaviour in pupils (Carter and Osler 2000).

Schools with high levels of disruptive behaviour often have mobility of pupils and staff as powerful undermining factors (Reed 2005). Taking pupils, some with disruptive backgrounds excluded from other schools, throughout the school year can destabilize the social dynamics of existing classes. Also, many of the most vulnerable schools face significant problems with recruitment and retention of staff. Over 60 per cent of challenging schools have a staff turnover of greater than 12 per cent and 1 in 4 have more than double this rate (Bush 2005). These schools depend heavily on supply teachers who pupils report to be less engaged and committed and poorer at keeping order (Reed 2005). Staff commitment to the school is a major factor underpinning school pride and pupils' sense of responsibility.

Attendance at school

In the UK, school circumstances, the physical environment of the school and school procedures, for instance, rules regarding uniforms, can all discourage attendance. Other influential factors include bullying, inability to cope with school work, peer group pressure, poor relations with teachers, the content and delivery of the curriculum, the classroom context, not having completed homework, and tiredness (O'Keefe 1994; Kinder et al. 1995, 1996; Atkinson and Hornby 2002).

The peak times for the onset of persistent absenteeism are the last two years of primary schooling, and the first and third years of secondary schooling, the grouping of pupils into different ability groups being important at secondary school. The reasons given for initially missing school are set out in Table 2.2. The majority of children cited school factors as initiating non-attendance (Reid 1999).

Table 2.2 Reasons for first missing school

Factors	Reasons	Number of students	Percentage of students
Social (28%)	Domestic	20	15.6
	Peer group influences	13	10.2
	Entertainment	2	1.6
	Employment	1	0.8
Psychological (16%)	Illness	11	8.6
	Psychosomatic	7	5.5
	Laziness	3	22.3
Institutional (56%)	School transfers	21	16.4
	Bullying	19	14.8
	Curriculum and examinations	13	10.2
	School rules and punishment	7	5.5
	The teachers	6	4.7
	Desire to leave	5	3.9
Total		128	

Source: Derived from Reid (1999).

Similar findings emerged in a study of 17 persistent absentees. In just over half of the cases a precipitating event or series of connected events could be identified as the immediate explanation for a significant episode of truancy, for instance, a change of school which led to being bullied, dislike of the poor behaviour of classmates. Other precipitating factors were refusing to return to school after a health-related absence or after suspension. In some cases this was the first time that the young person had missed school. Other cases reflected a major escalation in what had previously been fairly low-level truancy related to general disillusionment with school. All of the participating students had poor relationships with teachers, but responses relating to the curriculum were relatively positive. A key factor was the lack of an orderly environment in school and a tense and disruptive atmosphere (Attwood and Croll 2006).

School and Local Authority perceptions of the causes of truancy

Generally, teachers do not believe that schools contribute to pupil absence (Malcolm et al. 2002). They attribute poor attendance to individual, family and community factors although at secondary level some school-related issues are acknowledged, including poor management, the ease at which some pupils can slip away unnoticed, poor relations with teachers and peers, and the perceived irrelevance of some aspects of the school curriculum (Kinder et al. 1995). In addition form tutors recognize that they have insufficient time to undertake their role in relation to attendance and lack training particularly about the role of outside agencies (Reid 2006).

Post-registration truancy and children's attitudes towards school

While the majority of children report being happy at school and valuing their education, relatively high numbers of pupils skip individual lessons. While exact figures are difficult to obtain, O'Keeffe (1994) found that 67 per cent of all truants were absent from school in order to avoid particular lessons that were deemed irrelevant or because of dislike of a teacher or a particular subject. Schools which engender positive attitudes in their pupils are perceived as having a positive ethos, a good reputation, well maintained premises, clear rules of behaviour, firm discipline, good teaching practices and high expectations. Pupils see themselves as being praised frequently and their work being marked regularly (Keys and Fernandes 1993).

Those who frequently miss school tend to feel that school is a waste of time, dislike school, are uninterested in school work and bored in class, dislike certain teachers or types of teachers, resent school rules, believe that school cannot improve their career prospects and has done little to prepare them for life, have low educational aspirations, and lack confidence (Keys and Fernandes 1993).

For many pupils the main reason for attending school is being with their friends (Bealing 1990). This is particularly true in Years 10 and 11. The most favoured activities for pupils in the early years of secondary school are social, working with friends, making something together, and being involved in discussions (O'Keeffe 1994). Motivation towards school and learning is only weakly associated with the type of catchment area, school type, the percentage of pupils receiving free school meals, the reading age of the intake and GCSE results (Keys and Fernandes 1993).

Generally, pupils have a utilitarian view of school. They see the main function as helping them to do well in examinations, acquire qualifications and get jobs. Related to this they hope that they will be supported in acquiring life skills, making decisions about careers, work and other options, and doing as well as they possibly can. Even those reporting unauthorized absence seem to share these aspirations. Many indicate that they value education and wish to continue in formal education after leaving school. They are not alienated from education they just want to miss particular classes from time to time.

Teacher–pupil relationships

Teachers who are supportive of students promote better attendance (Barth 1984). There are clear relationships between pupil motivation and teachers' interpersonal behaviour (Den Brok et al. 2004). Teacher behaviour which is perceived as helpful, friendly and understanding is related to students' enjoyment, confidence, effort, and the perceived relevance of work (Brekelmans et al. 2002). Negative relationships occur when teachers are punitive, dissatisfied with work and strict (Van Amelsvoort 1999). One of the single most reported reasons for missing individual lessons is that the teacher is unpleasant; very few students report missing lessons because the teacher is unhelpful or uninterested (O'Keeffe 1994).

The role of peers

Children have a sophisticated culture which has its own rules and social conventions (Troyna and Hatcher 1992). Successful negotiation within this culture requires considerable social competence (Measor and Woods 1984). In schools the formal culture encompasses the goals and values connected with the school organization and is specified by the staff, but the values and aims of the informal culture are expressed through the peer group and include 'unofficial' adaptations to the formal organization of the school (Cullingford 1991). Children's perceptions of their own identity are related to their friendship groups (Pollard 1985). Friends help children cope with life outside the classroom providing practical help, support and reassurance (Fine 1989). Broad groupings of pupils have been identified in a range of studies (Sluckin 1981; Pollard 1985). 'Good' groups see themselves as kind, quiet and friendly. 'Jokers' see themselves as clever, good fun and sensible while 'gangs' regard themselves as tough and rough, and outside the normal official life of the school. Although these groups hold different sets of values they evaluate themselves by comparison with their peers and by how they are judged by them (Sluckin 1981; Pollard 1985; Cullingford 1996).

Parental influence decreases during adolescence as the influence of peers rises (O'Brien and Bierman 1988). Reference group orientation shifts from parents to the peer group. In adolescence, for some children, the peer group acts in many respects as a surrogate family (Besag 1989). For boys, where there is an absence of positive parental relationships, adolescents may depend more on peers for support and run the risk of developing negative behaviours (Feldman and Wentzel 1990). Developing associations with deviant peers is one of the strongest predictors of adolescent deviant activity (Silbereisen et al. 1989). Confidence and high levels of self-esteem can provide a positive defence against negative peer pressure (Connor 1994).

In an interview study with young offenders, Cullingford and Morrison (1997) established that most had experienced some form of exclusion from school, often preceded by some form of psychological exclusion by peers or teachers. Once their deviant identity was established, changing it was difficult. Their involvement in crime occurred through a series of events, often as the result of being unable to resist peer pressure. The desire to gain peer approval was so strong for some that rebelling against an anonymous social system was irrelevant. The influence of peers could be mediated through the counter influences of home and family. Where these were weak the peer group was more significant.

Peer pressure can have positive or negative effects on attendance at school. Many pupils want to be at school to be with their friends, but if their friends are skipping school they may want to join them. Sixty to seventy per cent of truants are estimated to skip school with others, usually in groups of two to six (Reid 1999). Truancy may be perceived as a way of being part of the crowd. Parents certainly perceive that a key cause of truancy is peer pressure (Malcolm et al. 2003) and this perception is supported by children (Kinder et al. 1996).

Bullying

Bullying in school is a serious problem worldwide (Smith et al. 1999). Victims may exhibit low self-esteem, depression, poor psychosocial health, drug addiction or suicidal behaviour (Wild et al. 2004), and are at increased risk of underachievement and later unemployment (Woodward and Fergusson 2000). A substantial proportion of children have at some time been afraid of attending school because of bullying (DfEE 1999). Girls are more likely to be involved in sustained psychological and verbal bullying, whereas boys are more likely to resort to actual violence (Ofsted 2001). Two main types of bullying have been identified: serial bullying, where a single child bullies a great many children, and multiple victimization, where more than one bully converges on one victim (Chan 2006). Serial bullies bully children in different classes and grades, can have many victims, and are responsible for a sizeable percentage of bullying problems. Bullies have a positive attitude towards violence, tend to be impulsive, have a desire to dominate others, and have little empathy with their victims. Bullying is one component of a more generally antisocial and rule-breaking behaviour pattern with the probability of later deviance increasing if a child is involved in bullying at a young age (Kumpulainen and Rasanen 2000).

Bullies seem to have had negative emotional experiences with their prime caregiver in infancy, alongside a permissive attitude towards aggressive behaviour. The child rearing methods of the parents of bullies tend to be based on power, accompanied by physical punishment, and violent emotional outburst. Too little care and affection alongside too much freedom seems to contribute to the development of an aggressive reaction pattern (Olweus 1997).

Typical bullying victims are more anxious, cautious, sensitive, quiet and insecure than other pupils and frequently react to bullying by crying and withdrawal (Olweus 1997). They suffer from low self-esteem, have a negative view of themselves and their situation, often look upon themselves as failures and feel stupid, ashamed and unattractive. Olweus describes these as passive or submissive victims. A small number of victims are provocative. They are characterized by a combination of anxious and aggressive reaction patterns, often have problems with concentration, or hyperactivity and behave in ways that may cause irritation, tension and negative reactions from the whole class. These victims are often isolated children who dislike others and may frequently be absent from school. Some may become bullies themselves (Smith et al. 2004).

Individual characteristics contributing to poor behaviour and attendance

Children with social, emotional and behavioural difficulties

There are no agreed international definitions of what constitute behavioural difficulties in children so being classified as having Emotional and Behavioural Difficutlies (EBD) is somewhat haphazard (Kelly and Gray 2000). In 2001, the Department for Education and Employment (DfEE) indicated that where schools were pursuing statutory assessment of EBD for a child, identifiable factors that could impact on learning outcomes should include:

> Evidence of significant emotional or behavioural difficulties, as indicated by clear recorded examples of withdrawn or disruptive behaviour; a marked and persistent inability to concentrate; signs

that the child experiences considerable frustration or distress in relation to their learning difficulties; difficulties in establishing and maintaining balanced relationships with their fellow pupils or with adults; and any other evidence of a significant delay in the development of life and social skills.

(DfEE *2001: 83*)

Partly because of the issues relating to definition, epidemiological surveys of children in a number of countries have found varying prevalence rates for conduct disorder between 4 and 12 per cent in the general population (Visser 2003). The number of children in the UK identified with EBD (Dockrell et al. 2002; Scottish Executive 2005) and designated with ADHD (Lloyd 2005a) appears to be increasing with many more boys than girls in EBD schools and Pupil Referral Units (Lloyd 2005b). These changes may be due to the increasing demands made of children in school and society more widely, and the breakdown of traditional family life in many homes. It has been estimated that 15 per cent of children exhibit oppositional and defiant behaviour when they begin primary school, although this decreases to just over 7 per cent at age 14 (Sutton et al. 2004). In inner-city areas the percentage may be as high as 25 per cent (Rutter et al. 1979).

The role of communication skills

Difficulties with verbal expression may be an important contributory factor in poor behaviour in young boys (Ripley and Yuill 2005). Children with poor expressive language skills have poor social relationships and engage in fewer social interactions than their peers. Language competence may be a key factor in the development of emotional literacy which supports successful self-regulation and relationships, and social encounters with both peers and adults at school (Strauss 2001).

Gender differences

As we saw in Chapter 1, boys account for most of the exclusions from school. However, there is evidence that girls' behaviour is changing. A growing number of girls, 'ladettes', are exhibiting challenging behaviour, disengaged from school work, and share experiences of drinking and sexual behaviour in order to gain credibility with their peers (Jackson 2006). Teachers, particularly male teachers, often underestimate the extent of poor behaviour in girls.

Transience

Problem behaviour is frequently transient. A recent study showed that 15 per cent of 5-year-olds demonstrated behaviour that was oppositional and defiant, and viewed as inappropriate by their parents. Around 20 per cent of these children moved out of this high-risk category between the ages of 5 and 8, although another 10 per cent joined it. This pattern was repeated. Only about half of the children whose behaviour was routinely troublesome at age 8 were likely to be rated as antisocial by age 17 (DfES 2003). Although most antisocial adults have almost always been antisocial as children, most children assessed as antisocial do not go on to become antisocial adults (Robins 1978). Within education settings, however, children can become labelled as 'difficult' and minor misdemeanours, which in other children would be dismissed as trivial, are frequently interpreted as supporting the label and add to the 'difficult' reputation. Once established, the label tends to persist.

Characteristics of persistent absentees

Persistent absentees tend to have lower academic self-concepts, lower general levels of self-esteem, greater patterns of alienation from school, and higher levels of neuroticism. They also tend not to be liked by other children (Reid 1999). Truancy can also be associated with a complex network of problems such as emotional maladjustment (Reid 1986), poor academic achievement, substance abuse (Miller and Plant 1999), and teenage pregnancy (Hibbett and Fogelman 1990).

Anxiety and absenteeism

Most children at some time will experience anxiety at school as a result of difficulties with relationships, academic work or the environment (O'Keeffe 1994). Bullying can be particularly anxiety provoking and even when reported to staff may not be managed effectively by the school. Where pupils retaliate for being called names (particularly where racisim is involved) schools often apportion blame equally to both parties. This can lead to some children feeling that they are being treated unfairly. Sexual harassment is also distressing and is not restricted to girls. Boys who are homosexual or appear effeminate are particularly vulnerable and school staff do not always know how to deal with this (Trenchard and Warren 1987). Some students find examinations and the pressure of meeting deadlines for course work particularly stressful (Rogers 2005), while transfer from primary to secondary school can be traumatic as pupils adapt to the frequent changes of location and the complexities of different lessons. Inadequate toilet facilities, having to change and shower for Physical Education, and disruptive behaviour in the classroom can also be anxiety provoking. While some of these anxieties may seem trivial to adults, for those experiencing them they are very real. High levels of anxiety can lead to school phobia or school refusal (Elliott 1999). This will be discussed in Chapter 12.

Child employment

Nowadays, many young people engage in part-time employment. A TUC/ MORI poll in 2001 reported that nearly half a million school-aged children were engaged in illegal work. Of these approximately 100,000 truanted from school on a daily basis in order to be able to do so (Reid 2002). Undertaking paid employment may contribute to non-attendance directly or indirectly. The child may miss school to go to work, because they are too tired, or because they have not completed homework or coursework. If children are employed for more than 10 hours each week their education is adversely affected (Clwyd 1994).

Predicting disaffection

Some research has suggested that potential dropouts, excludees and persistent absentees can be identified with reasonable accuracy in the primary phase of education (Barrington and Hendricks 1989), or even prior to entering school (Jimerson et al. 2000). Identifying risk factors is complex as they rarely operate alone but alongside other risk or preventative factors. Barrett (2003) identified a number of risk and protective factors. These are set out in Table 2.3. The extent to which each comes into play depends on their relative strength, and potential stresses or triggers.

No particular combination of risk, protective or stress factors has been found to be linked with negative outcomes. The more risk factors the greater the likelihood of disaffection from school and antisocial behaviour, although some resilient children develop into responsible and well-adjusted adults despite high levels of risk (Rende and Plomin 1993; Werner 1993).

Table 2.3 Risk and protective factors for disaffection from school

Risk factors	Protective factors
Major risk factors at birth:	
chronic poverty	
mother with little education	
moderate-to-severe perinatal complications	
low birth weight	
developmental delays or irregularities	
genetic abnormalities	
Parental:	
psychopathology/pathology/ criminality	
parents' family upbringing	
intellectual ability/disability	
difficult temperament	
Additional risk factors (within child)	**Protective factors (within child)**
Being male	Birth order (first)
Attention/concentration problems	Central nervous system integrity, good physical health
Excessive risk taking	
Lack of self-control/impulsivity	Positive self-concept
Early onset of violent/aggressive behaviour	Responsiveness to people
	Good-natured, affectionate
	Positive social orientation, good social skills
	Good problem solving skills
	Good relationship with one parent
	Free of distressing habits (e.g. tantrums, poor feeding or sleeping)
	Advanced self-help skills
	High IQ
	High activity (though not overactive)
	Special interests and hobbies or talents
	Desire to improve self, achievement motivation
	Age appropriate sensorimotor and perceptual skills

Additional risk factors (within environment)	Protective factors (within environment)
Community disorganization	Four or fewer children spaced two or more years apart
High crime rate	
Opportunities to offend (e.g. easy availability of drugs)	A lot of attention paid to infant in first year
Low parental supervision	Positive parent–child relationship in early childhood
Harsh and inconsistent parental discipline	
Delinquent peer group in adolescence	Additional caretakers besides mother
	Care by siblings and grandparents
	Wider network of social support (family/community)
	Good relationship with school
	Mother has steady employment outside the home
	Access to special services (health/education/social services)
	Structures and rules in household
	Close supportive peer relationships with non-delinquent peers
	Religion

Source: Derived from Barrett (2003).

Endnote

While individual characteristics can predispose some children to be poorly behaved or drop-out from school, the environment can operate to ameliorate or increase their impact. These include factors at the level of society, sub-groups within it, the family, the school, and peer groups. These interact in complex ways. To improve behaviour and attendance requires that interventions address each of these while focusing on the particular aspects that may be relevant in individual cases.

Chapter summary
- The causes of poor behaviour and attendance at school are complex and based on interactions between factors operating at the level of society, communities, families, schools and individuals.
- Societal factors include educational policies, pressures on schools to perform, poverty and unemployment.

- Community factors include socio-economic status and ethnicity.
- Family factors include levels of family dysfunction and stress that may be related to single parenting, poor health or addiction, and issues relating to debt or housing. Particularly vulnerable groups are child carers and 'looked-after' children.
- School factors include ethos, the physical, social and learning environment, the curriculum, the level of pastoral support, relationships with teachers and peers, and bullying.
- Individual factors which may affect behaviour and attendance include: gender, learning difficulties, hyperactivity, emotional and behavioural difficulties, personality, anxiety and child employment.
- To improve behaviour and attendance requires that interventions address all of the above while focusing on the particular aspects that may be relevant in individual cases.

Further reading

Barrett, H. (2003) *Parenting Programmes for Families at Risk: A Source Book.* London: National Family and Parenting Institute.

Osler, A., Watling, R., Busher, H., Cole, T. and White, A. (2001) *Reasons for Exclusion from School. Research Report 244.* London: DfES.

Reed, J. (2005) *Toward Zero Exclusion: Classroom Lessons for Policy Makers.* London: Institute for Public Policy Research.

References

Abbots, P. and Parsons, S. (1993) Children's rights and exclusion from primary school. *Therapeutic Care and Education*, 2(2): 416–21.

Armstrong, D., Hine, J., Hacking, S., Armaos, R., Jones, R., Klessinger, N., and France, A.. (2005) *Children, Risk and Crime: the On Track Youth Lifestyles Surveys. Home Office Research Study 278.* London: Home Office.

Atkinson, M. and Hornby, G. (2002) *Mental Health Handbook for Schools.* London: RoutledgeFalmer.

Atkinson, M., Halsey, K., Wilkin, A. and Kinder, K. (2000) *Raising Attendance 2: A Detailed Study of Education Welfare Service Working Practices.* Slough: NFER.

Attwood, G. and Croll, P. (2006) Truancy in Secondary School Pupils; Prevalence, trajectories and pupil perspectives. Research Papers in Education 21, 4, 457–484.

Barrington, B. L and Hendricks, B. (1989) Differentiating characteristics of high school graduates, dropouts and nongraduates, *Journal of Educational Research* 89, 309–319.

Bancroft, A., Wilson, S., Cunningham-Burley, S., Backett-Milburn, K. and Masters, H. (2004) *Parental Drug and Alcohol Misuse*. York: Joseph Rowntree Foundation.

Bandura, A. (1977) Self-efficacy: toward a unifying theory of behavioural change. *Psychological Review*, 84: 191–215.

Barth, R. P. (1984) Reducing non-attendance in elementary schools, *Social Work in Education*, 6(3): 151–66.

Barrett, H. (2003) *Parenting Programmes for Families at Risk: A Source Book*. London: National Family and Parenting Institute.

Bealing, V. (1990) Inside Information: Pupil perceptions of absenteeism in the Secondary School. *Maladjustment of Therepeutic Education* 8(1): 19–34

Brekelmans, M., Wubbels, T. and Creton, H.A. (1990) A study of student perceptions of physics teacher behaviour. *Journal of Research in Science Teaching*, 27: 335–50.

Brekelmans, M. Wubbels, Th and Den Brok, P. (2002) Teacher experience and the teacher-student relationship in the classroom environment. In S. C. Goh and M. S. Khine (Eds) *Studies in Educational Learning Environments: An International Perpesctive* (pp 73–100) Singapore: New World Scientrie.

Besag, V.E. (1989) *Bullies and Victims in Schools*. Milton Keynes: Open University Press.

Bonnell, C.P., Allen, E., Strange, V. and Johnson, A. (2005) The effect of dislike of school on risk of teenage pregnancy. *Journal of Epidemiological and Community Health*, 59: 223–30.

Broadhurst, K., Paton, H., and May-Chahal, C. (2005) Children missing from school systems: exploring divergent patterns of disengagement in the narrative accounts of parents, carers, children and young people. *British Journal of Sociology of Education*, 26(1): 105–19.

Bush, A. (2005) *Choice and Equity in Teacher Supply*. London: IPPR.

Butler, I. (2003a) *Social Work with Children and Families*. London: Jessica Kingsley.

Butler, I. (2003b) *Divorcing Children: Children's Expereince of the Parent's Divorce*. London: Jessica Kingsley.

Carter, C. and Osler, A. (2000) Human rights, identities and conflict management: A study of school culture as experienced through classroom relationships. *Cambridge Journal of Education*, 30(3): 336–56.

Chan, J.H.F. (2006) Systematic patterns in bullying and victimization. *School Psychology International*, 27(3): 352–69.

Clwyd, A. (1994) *Children at Risk: An Analysis of Illegal Employment of Children in Great Britain, Labour Party Report*. London: Ann Clwyd.

Collins, D. (1998) *Managing Truancy in Schools*. London: Cassell.

Connor, M. (1994) Peer relations and peer pressure. *Educational Psychology in Practice*, 9: 207–15.

Cullingford, C. (1991) *The Inner World of the School*. London: Cassell.

Cullingford, C. (ed.) (1996) *The Politics of Primary Education*. Milton Keynes: Open University Press.

Cullingford, C. and Morrison, J. (1997) Peer group pressure within and outside school. *British Educational Research Journal*, 23(1): 61–80.

Dalziel, D. and Henthorne, K. (2005) *Parents'/Carers' Attitudes Towards School Attendance. Research Report 618*. London: DfES.

Den Brok, P., Brekelmans, M. and Wubbels, T. (2004) Interpersonal teacher behaviour and student outcomes. *School Effectiveness and School Improvement*, 15(3–4): 407–42.

Department for Education and Employment (DfEE) (2001) *SEN Code of Practice on the Identification and Assessment of Pupils with Special Educational Needs*. London: DfEE.

Department for Education and Skills (DfES) (2003) *London Challenge: First Survey of London Parents' Attitudes to London Secondary Schools*. London: DfES.

Derrington, C. and Kendall, S. (2004) *Gypsy Traveller Students in Secondary Schools: Culture, Identity and Achievement*. Stoke-on-Trent: Trentham Books.

Dockrell, J., Peacey, N. and Lunt, I. (2002) *Literature Review: Meeting the Needs of Children with SEN*. London: Institute of Education, University of London.

Dodge, K.A. and Somberg, D.A. (1987) Hostile attributional biases among aggressive boys are exacerbated under conditions of threat to self. *Child Development*, 58: 213–24.

Edward, S. and Malcolm, H. (2002) *The Causes and Effects of Truancy.* Edinburgh: SCRE.

Elliott, J.G. (1999) Practitioner review: School refusal – issues of conceptualization, assessment and treatment. *Journal of Child Psychology and Psychiatry*, 40(7): 1001–12.

Feldman, J. and Wentzel, K. (1990) Relationship between parenting styles, self-restraint, and peer relations in early adolescence. *Journal of Early Adolescence*, 10: 439–54.

Fine, G.A. (1989) The natural history of preadolescent friendship groups, in H. Foot, A. Chapman and J. Smith (eds) *Friendship and Social Relations in Children.* New York: Wiley.

Flouri, E. and Buchanan, A. (2004) Early father's and mother's involvement and child's later educational outcome. *British Educational Psychology*, 74: 141–53.

Gardner, F., Ward, S., Burton, J. and Wilson, C. (2003) The role of mother–child joint play in the early development of children's conduct problems: A longitudinal observational study. *Social Development*, 12: 361–79.

Hallam, S., Castle, F. and Rogers, L. with Creech, A., Rhamie, J. and Kokotsaki, D. (2005) *Research and Evaluation of the Behaviour Improvement Programme. Research Report 702.* London: DfES.

Hibbett, A. and Fogelman, K. (1990) Future lives of truants: Family formation and health-related behaviour. *British Journal of Educational Psychology*, 60: 171–9.

Hopkins, B. (2004) *Just Schools: A Whole School Approach to Restorative Justice.* London: Jessica Kingsley.

Ingoldsby, E.M. and Shaw, D.S. (2002) Neighbourhood contextual factors and early starting antisocial pathways. *Clinical Child and Family Psychological Review*, 5: 21–55.

Jackson, C. (2006) *Lads and Ladettes in School.* Milton Keynes: Open University Press.

Jimerson, S., Egeland, B., Sroufe, A., and Cartson, B. (2000) A Prospective longitudinal study of high school dropouts examining multiple predictors accross development, *Journal of School Psychology*, 38: 528–549.

Kane, J., Head, G. and Cogan, N. (2004) Towards inclusion? Models of behaviour support in secondary schools in one education authority in Scotland. *British Journal of Special Education*, 31(2): 68–74.

Kelly, D. and Gray, C. (2000) *Educational Psychology Services (England) Current Role, Good Practice and Future Directions*. London: DfEE.

Kendall, S., White, R., Kinder, K., Halsey, K. and Bedford, N. (2004) *School Attendance and the Prosecution of Parents: Effects and Effectiveness*. Slough: NFER/LGA.

Keys, W. and Fernandes, C. (1993) *What Do Students Think about School? Research into the Factors Associated with Positive and Negative Attitudes Towards School and Education*. Slough: NFER.

Kinder, K. and Wilkin, A. (1998) *Where Parents Lay the Blame for Truancy*. Slough NFER.

Kinder, K., Harland, J., Wilkin, A. and Wakefield, A. (1995) *Three to Remember: Strategies for Disaffected Pupils*. Slough: NFER.

Kinder, K., Wakefield, A. and Wilkin, A. (1996) *Talking Back: Pupils Views on Disaffection*. Slough: NFER.

Kumpulainen, K. and Rasanen, E. (2000) Children involved in bullying at elementary school age: Their psychiatric symptoms and deviance in adolescence. An epidemiological sample. *Child Abuse and Neglect*, 24(12): 1567–77.

Lee, V.E. and Burkam, D.T. (2003) Dropping out of high school: The role of school organization and structure. *American Educational Research Journal*, 40(2): 353–93.

Lloyd, G. (2005a) International critical perspectives on ADHD, in G. Lloyd, D. Cohen and J. Stead (eds) *New Critical Approaches to ADHD*, pp. 385–410. London: Routledge.

Lloyd, G. (ed.) (2005b) *Problem Girls*. London: Routledge Falmer.

Lloyd-Smith, M. (1993) Problem behaviour, exclusions and the policy vacuum. *Pastoral Care*, 11(4): 19–24.

McCarthy, P., Laing, K. and Walker, J. (2004) *Offenders of the Future? Assessing the Risk of Children Becoming Involved in Crime and Antisocial Behaviour*. London: DfES.

Malcolm, H., Wilson, V. and Davidson, J. (2002) *Out of School Care*. Glasgow: Scottish Research in Education Centre, University of Glasgow.

Malcolm, H., Wilson, V., Davidson, J. and Kirk, S. (2003) *Absence from School: A Study of Its Causes and Effects in Seven LEAs. Report 424*. London: DfES.

Measor, L. and Woods, P. (1984) *Changing Schools: Pupil Perspectives on Transfer to a Comprehensive*. Milton Keynes: Open University Press.

Meltzer, H. and Gatwood, R. (2000) *The Mental Health of Children and Adolescents in Great Britain. Summary Report.* London: Office of National Statistics.

Miller, P. and Plant, M. (1999) Truancy and perceived school performance: an alcohol and drug study of UK teenagers. *Alcohol and Alcoholism*, 34: 886–93.

Mortimore, P. and Whitty, G. (1999) School improvement: A remedy for social exclusion, in A. Hayton (ed.) *Tackling Disaffection and Social Exclusion.* London: Kogan Page.

Munn, P., Lloyd, G. and Cullen, M.A. (2000) *Alternatives to Exclusion from School.* London: Paul Chapman.

National Assembly for Wales (2004) *Absenteeism from Secondary Schools in Wales*, 2003/04. Cardiff: HMSO.

National Audit Office (NAO) (2005) *Improving School Attendance in England.* London: The Stationery Office.

Naylor, P. and Cowie, H. (1999) The effectiveness of peer support systems in challenging school bullying: The perspectives and experiences of teachers and pupils. *Journal of Adolescence*, 22: 467–9.

O'Brien, S. F. and Bierman, L. L. (1988) Conceptions and perceived influence & peer groups *Child Development* 57, 1360–1365. 1988

Ofsted (1993) *Education for Disaffected Pupils.* London: Ofsted.

Ofsted (1996a) *Exclusions from Secondary Schools 1995/96.* London: HMSO.

Ofsted (1996b) *The Education of Travelling Children.* London: Ofsted.

Ofsted (1999) *Raising the Attainment of Minority Ethnic Pupils.* London: Ofsted.

Ofsted (2001) *Improving Attendance and Behaviour in Secondary Schools.* London: HMSO.

Ofsted (2003) *Provision and Support for Traveller Pupils* (HMI 455). London: Ofsted.

Ofsted (2005) *Managing Challenging Behaviour.* London: Ofsted.

O'Keeffe, D.J. (1994) *Truancy in English Secondary Schools.* London: HMSO.

Olweus, D. (1997) Bully/victim problems in school: Facts and intervention. *European Journal of Psychology of Education*, XII (4): 495–510.

Parsons, C. (1999) *Education, Exclusion and Citizenship.* London: Routledge.

Pollard, A. (1985) *The Social World of the School.* London: Holt, Rinehard and Winston.

Prince's Trust (2002) *The Way It Is: Young People on Race, School Exclusion and Leaving Care: Research Summary.* London: The Prince's Trust.

Pritchard, C. (2006) *Evidence-based Mental Health Social Work.* London: Routledge.

Pritchard, C. and Cox, M. (2005) *Behaviour and Attitudes of 10th and 11th Year Secondary School Pupils.* Poole: Poole Drug Advisory Team.

Reed, J. (2005) *Toward Zero Exclusion: An Action Plan for Schools and Policy Makers.* London: Institute for Public Policy Research and Centre for British Teachers.

Reid, K. (1986) Truancy and school absenteeism: The state of the art, Maladjustment and therapeutic education s 4(3), 4–17.

Reid, K. (1999) *Truancy and Schools.* London: Routledge.

Reid, K. (2002) *Truancy: Short and Long Term Solutions.* London: Routledge-Falmer.

Reid, K. (2006) The views of education social workers on the management of truancy and other forms of non-attendance. *Research in Education*, 75: 40–57.

Rende, R. and Plomin, R. (1993) Families at risk for psychopathology: Who becomes disaffected and why? *Development and Psychopathology*, 5: 529–40.

Ripley, K. and Yuill, N. (2005) Patterns of language impairment and behaviour in boys excluded from school. *British Journal of Educational Psychology*, 75: 37–50.

Robins, L.N. (1978) Sturdy childhood predictors of adult antisocial behaviour: Replications from longitudinal studies. *Psychological Medicine*, 8: 611–22.

Rogers, L. (2005) *Students' Perceptions of Studying for GCSE and Their Relationship with Attainment.* Unpublished PhD thesis, Institute of Education, University of London.

Roye, C. F. and Balk, S. J. (1996) The relationship of partner support to outcome for teenage mothers and their children: a review: *Journal of Adolescent Health* 19: 86–93.

Rutter, M., Ouston, J., Maughan, B. and Mortimore, P. (1979) *15,000 Hours.* London: Open Books.

Sasson, D. (1993/2000) The Price of banishment, education, 181 (6), in C. Wright, D. Weekes and A. McGlaughlin (eds), *Race, Class and Gender in Exclusion from School.* London: Falmer Press.

Scottish Executive (2005) *Exclusions from Schools, 2003/04.* Edinburgh: Scottish Executive.

Scottish Executive (2006) *Exclusions from School 2005/06.* Edinburgh: Scottish Executive.

Silbereisen, R., Peterson, A., Albrecht, H. and Kracke, B. (1989) Maturational timing and development of problem behaviour. *Journal of Early Adolescence,* 9: 247–68.

Slavin, R. E. (1999) Educating young students at risk of school failure: Research practice and policy in R. Stevens (ed.) *Teaching in American Shools* (pp. 103–119) Upper Saddle River, NJ: Prentice Hall

Sluckin, A. (1981) *Growing up in the Playground.* London: Routledge.

Smith, C.A. and Farrington, D.P. (2004) Continuities in antisocial behaviour and parenting across three generations. *Journal of Child Psychology and Psychiatry,* 45: 23–47.

Smith, P., Morita, Y., Junger-Tas, J., Olweus, D., Catalanot, E. and Slee, P. (1999) (eds) *The Nature of School Bullying: A Cross Cultural Perspective.* London: Routledge.

Smith, P.K., Talamelli, L., Cowie, H., Naylor, P. and Chauhan, P. (2004) Profiles of non-victims, escaped victims, continuing victims and new victims of school bullying. *British Journal of Educational Psychology,* 74: 565–81.

Social Exclusion Unit (1998) *Truancy and School Exclusion.* London: The Stationery Office.

Strauss, D. (2001) *Depression and the development of cognitive coping.* Unpublished thesis, University of Sussex.

Sutton, C., Utting, D. and Farrington, D. (2004) *Support from the Start. Research Report 524.* London: DfES.

Swinson, J. and Cording, M. (2002) Assertive discipline in a school for pupils with emotional and behavioural difficulties. *British Journal of Special Education,* 29(2): 72–5.

Trenchard, C. and Warren, H. (1987) Talking about school: The experiences of young lesbians and gay men, in G. Weinder and M. Arnot (eds) *Gender Under Scrutiny: New Inquiries in Education.* London: Open University/ Hutchinson.

Troyna, B. and Hatcher, R. (1992) *Racism in Children's Lives.* London: Routledge and Kegan Paul.

TUC/MORI Poll (2001) Half a million kids working illegally, 21 March.

Van Amelsvoort, J. (1999) *Perspective on Instruction, Motivation, and Self-regulation.* Nijmegen: Nÿmegen University Press.

Visser, J. (2003) *A Study of Children and Young People who Present Challenging Behaviour.* London: Ofsted.

Weiner, B. (1986) An attributional theory of motivation and emotion. New York: Springer-Verlag.

Werner, E. E. (1993) Risk, resilience and recovery. Perspectives from the Kanai longitudinal study, *Developement and Psycopathology* 5, 503–515.

Wild, L.G., Fisher, A.J., Bhana, A. and Lombard, C. (2004) Associations among adolescent risk behaviours and self-esteem in six domains. *Journal of Child Psychology and Psychiatry,* 45: 1454–67.

Wilkin, A., Archer, T., Ridley, K., Fletcher-Campbell, F. and Kinder, K. (2005) *Admissions and Exclusions of Pupils with Special Educational Needs. Research Report 608.* London: DfES.

Wilkinson, G. (1994) *Young People: A Chance to be Heard – A Study of School, Training and Dropping out in Sunderland, with Particular Reference to the Ford and Pennywell Area.* A research project funded by the Employment Service and the Ford and Pennywell Advice Centre.

Woodward, L.J. and Fergusson, D.M. (2000) Childhood peer relationship problems and later risks of educational under-achievement and unemployment. *Journal of Child Psychology and Psychiatry,* 41(2): 191–201.

Woodward, R. and McVie, S. (2001) *Summary of Findings 2: Summer 2001.* Edinburgh Study of Youth Transitions and Crime.

Wright, C. and Keetley, K. (2003) *Violence and Indiscipline in Schools: Research Study Commissioned by NASUWT.* Perpetuity Research and Consultancy International (PRCI) Ltd.

Wright, C., Weekes, D. and McGlaughlin, A. (2000) *Race, Class and Gender in Exclusion from School.* London: Falmer Press.

Zhan, M. and Sherraden, M. (2003) Assets, expectations, and children's educational achievement in female headed households. *Social Service Review,* 77: 191–211.

Zhang, M. (2003) Links between school absenteeism and child poverty. *Pastoral Care in Education,* 21(1): 10–17.

Section 2
Improving behaviour

3   Management and whole-school policies

In this chapter recent national and international research considering how schools successfully manage behaviour issues is considered, including the use of behaviour audits, the appointment of Lead Behaviour Professionals and the work of Behaviour and Educational Support Teams (BESTs) in developing appropriate policies which address whole-school issues. Policies and practices relating to transition between primary and secondary schools are addressed where they are relevant to whole-school policies.

Background

The Elton Report (1989) signalled a major shift with regard to the management of behaviour in schools with a move towards whole school approaches to behaviour and discipline. Pupil behaviour was no longer perceived as an issue of control but was regarded as relating to the partnership between staff and students (Rowe 2006). Schools were advised to adopt clear, planned and coherent systems of standards and sanctions that pupils could understand and acknowledge as fair and reasonable. It was suggested that clear boundaries should be put in place and that teachers should be consistent across the school in the standards they expected from students. Policies needed to be reviewed regularly as part of a whole-school approach. Furthermore, the report suggested that teachers should be more aware of the possible causes of poor behaviour, particularly for pupils with learning and behavioural difficulties, and that greater attention should be paid to the quality of teaching. In 1997, the Education Act (Great Britain Statutes 1997) required all state schools to have a policy on the promotion of good behaviour and discipline including developing self-discipline and proper regard for authority among all pupils.

Since then concerns over behaviour in schools have continued. Further guidance has been issued (DfES 2003a) which encouraged schools to take account of students' views through the discussion of behavioural issues in school councils (Macbeath et al. 2003; DfES 2004). The Steer Report (2006) reiterated the need for schools to have a coherent whole-school approach to promoting good behaviour based on effective relationships between all members of the school community.

Despite the evidence that whole-school approaches to behaviour result in positive outcomes, difficulties with implementation remain (Ofsted 2006; Steer Report 2006). While the principles are well established not all headteachers or school staff put them into practice. Particularly problematic are lack of consistency in the application of school behaviour policy; staff being insufficiently familiar with the policy; and inadequate attention paid to its regular review and monitoring (Ofsted 2001, 2006; Turner 2003; Steer Report 2006).

In a review of the behaviour policy of a mixed comprehensive school in England, the detrimental impact of the inappropriate implementation of a behaviour policy is apparent:

> The lack of consistent enforcement of the behaviour policy by staff has led to a significant difference in pupils' behaviour, with a general deterioration of positive attitude and respect from the main body of pupils. It is a concern that the decline in good behaviour has led to a deterioration in learning and motivation to learn for an increasing number of pupils.
>
> (*Turner 2003: 8*)

School policies need to be coherent and understood by all staff and applied consistently (Ofsted 2001, 2006; Turner 2003; Steer Report 2006).

Concern with poor and disruptive behaviour extends beyond schools in England. In Queensland, Australia, the Minister for Education and the Arts announced the establishment of the Ministerial Advisory Committee for Educational Renewal (MACER) in 2004 and highlighted behaviour and behaviour management as a priority for the work of the committee (MACER 2005). In Scotland, Local Authorities (LAs) have rolled out, and piloted, a range of initiatives and strategies including Staged Intervention/Framework for Intervention (FFI); and Solution-oriented Schools and Restorative Practices (Wilkin et al. 2006). In Norway, anti-bullying prevention and intervention programmes have been adopted in most schools nationally (Stephens et al. 2005). In America, whole-school Positive Behaviour Support (PBS) interventions have sought to address student discipline problems and academic performance with some success (Luiselli et al. 2005).

Emerging is a consensus surrounding the need for coherent behaviour policies or codes. In Australia the Ministerial Council on Education, Employment, Training and Youth Affairs' (MCEETYA) suggested that best practice related to addressing student behaviour issues should be based on a clearly articulated and comprehensive behaviour management policy at a system, district/community, school and classroom level (De Jong 2004). In Scotland the HM Inspectorate of Education (HMIE) (2005) emphasized the need to establish coherent links between policy and behaviour management. Evidence from a recent survey suggested that pupils, too, felt that schools could do more to ensure fair treatment from teachers (Wilkin et al. 2006). In America, the American Federation of Teachers (2003) urged that district-wide discipline codes be enacted and fairly enforced.

Thinking about whole-school behaviour

Before focusing on specific projects, it is useful to consider what aspects of practice might make a positive difference to improving and maintaining behaviour in schools. Watkins and Wagner (2000) provide a model for reflecting on improving school behaviour that operates at three levels: the organization, the classroom and the individual (see Figure 3.1). They propose that each level requires different approaches for understanding and intervening, reflecting the approach adopted in this book. Table 3.1 outlines the differences between proactive and reactive policies.

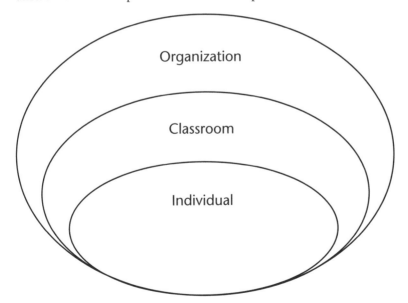

Figure 3.1 Levels for considering school behaviour

Source: Derived from Watkins and Wagner (2000).

Improving school behaviour requires work at the level of the whole school, the classroom and the individual. When whole-school policies are working effectively, some specific classroom issues may remain. When behaviour is good at the whole-school and classroom level there will still be individual pupils who require additional, sometimes specialist, support. Proactive rather than reactive approaches to behaviour management are more effective in relation to pupil behaviour in the classroom and around the school. The same is true of whole-school policies. In this context it makes sense to consider in detail what is understood by a proactive approach (see Table 3.1).

Table 3.1 Proactive versus reactive approaches to school policies

Proactive approaches	Reactive approaches
A set of principles that guide action	A set of rules
Principles that underlie any rules are clarified	Procedures and enforcement rules are tightened up
A stimulus to learn	A statement made to the public
Appreciation of what is currently helpful and an anticipation of possible future difficulties	A focus on what is not working and reacting to difficulty
Reviews current rules and their effects	Institutes new rules
Builds coherence and harmonization while recognizing and allowing for variation	Seeks consistency and uniformity
Outlines how to improve in relation to: ● school facilities and grounds ● curriculum focus on behaviour ● classrooms and their management ● staff systems for learning and development ● engaging pupils' views	Outlines what teachers are to do if pupils do X
Phrased to engage everyone	Phrased to apply to pupils
Promotes the handling of difficulties close to where they occur (e.g. in the classroom or the playground)	Promotes referral to, for instance, the Headteacher, the Deputy Head or Head of Year
Problem solving is based on conceptual analysis and understanding	Problem solving is based on trial and error

Attempts to understand 'causes' close at hand	Attempts to implement 'cures' from any source
Uses teamwork to address difficulty and promotes collaboration	Uses isolated individuals with separated responsibilities
Problem solving is organization-wide and problem centred	Problem solving is compartmentalized and hierarchical
Total school approach considers all three levels: the organization, the classroom and the individual	Fragmented strategies that cover the administrative level
Promotes and reflects the school goals, other school policies and cultures	Stands alone
Specifies review systems	Does not consider a review

Source: Derived from Watkins and Wagner (2000).

Proactive approaches look towards managing behaviour. They are distinguished by a collaborative approach to problems whereby staff are able to share practice and discuss issues with colleagues rather than working in isolation. They include a commitment to continuing professional development. It is important that all staff are involved in the development of school policy. Where this is not the case and there is a lack of ownership policy will not be effective (Turner 2003). The involvement of pupils in the development of school policies is also critical. Research indicates that where students are involved in active participation relationships are strengthened and there is the potential for pupils to feel more independent, responsible, and trusted with a sense of ownership of school policies (Osler 2000; Pearce and Hallgarten, 2000; Reed 2005). Unfortunately, pupil participation is not the norm within school cultures (Ofsted 2003; Kerr et al. 2004; Wilkin et al. 2006). Important, too, is an understanding that behaviour has to be learned and that staff need to model good behaviour for their pupils (Steer Report 2006). Pupils also need to understand any systems that are put in place.

Behaviour audits

The circumstances which affect each school's behaviour are specific to that school. In an attempt to identify good practice and those areas which warrant further attention, schools in the UK have been encouraged to make use of behaviour audits. Indeed one recommendation from the Steer Report

(2006) was that all schools should undertake an audit of pupil behaviour to include ten aspects of school practice that, when effective, contribute to the quality of pupil behaviour:

- a consistent approach to behaviour management, teaching and learning;
- school leadership;
- classroom management, learning and teaching;
- rewards and sanctions;
- behaviour strategies and the teaching of good behaviour;
- staff development and support;
- pupil support systems;
- liaison with parents and other agencies;
- managing pupil transition; and
- organization and facilities.

In both the Behaviour Improvement Programme (BIP) and the Primary Behaviour and Attendance Pilot (PBAP), the use of behaviour audits played a crucial role in school improvement (Hallam et al. 2005, 2006). While staff expressed concerns that the audits were long, they were recognized as extremely valuable. Interviewees indicated that it was important that all staff were engaged in the process, to ensure that the senior management team took seriously any challenges to make changes. The audits also needed to be undertaken with real commitment to be useful:

> In the first three schools it was just poor timing. They did do the full school audit, but it did not flag up anything helpful. If it is not identifying some priority areas for development then what is the point? I have to question whether they have been really honest with themselves. In every other sense they were committed to the programme, but I did not feel that they got an awful lot out of doing the audit. I couldn't see why because it is a great tool, well structured and thought out and should be highly informative to identify areas for action.
>
> (*Teacher coach, PBAP*)

Where behaviour audits were undertaken effectively they led to well developed action plans to address whole-school issues. An action plan could focus on a range of issues. Box 3.1 provides an example case study of the implementation of a behaviour audit.

Box 3.1   Use of a behaviour audit

Case study: Primary Behaviour and Attendance Pilot – Positive use of the behaviour and attendance audit in one Local Authority (LA)

In one LA, all schools were reported to have responded well to the audit materials. Officers were very positive about the audits and supported the schools in using them. This paved the way for the work of the teacher coach. The bench-marking criteria helped schools to establish where they were and where they were trying to go. This helped action planning. In one school, the Continuing Professional Development (CPD) summary gave clear indications of what people wanted. About 110 people in the school, including pupils, were consulted. The plan included coaching for the teachers, training for the governors on critical friend observations in the classroom and the role of social and emotional learning in school, and for the pupils developing the school council. Another element considered the way that the school gave feedback, and issues relating to communication. The Ofsted report did not identify behaviour as a key issue, but the Head recognized that there were key aspects of classroom-level work which needed addressing, in particular the relationships between teachers and children, the learning environment, and how that was set up to promote higher standards in the school. The behaviour and attendance audit helped teachers reflect on what they were actually doing and the impact that might have on the children in their classrooms (Hallam et al. 2006).

Although some audits identified specific staff development needs, there was an emphasis on emerging principles being adopted and modelled throughout the school. An important issue to emerge was consistency:

> Schools are developing action plans as a result of the audits. The theme of the action plans seems to be looking at the quality of teaching and learning and what seems to come out in nearly every audit is not the quality of practice but the consistency of practice. So the audits are bringing out that there is good practice around, but it is not consistent across the school. The action plans are looking at ways to share good practice.
>
> (*Teacher coach, PBAP*)

Where LAs and schools are planning to undertake behaviour audits it is important that time is allocated to explaining the purpose of the audit, that effective support is offered for its implementation, and that school staff are offered training in relation to undertaking it.

In the Behaviour Improvement Programme (BIP) the behaviour audits were undertaken in a variety of different ways. Some LAs were careful to ensure that there would be comparability across schools by using a small team to undertake the audits; in other cases it was treated as a joint venture and in some cases the responsibility was given to the schools. Overall, the process was perceived as particularly useful and generally schools were enthusiastic about it. There was general agreement that the behaviour audits had been beneficial to schools in providing:

- information to stimulate self-analysis;
- data to support the development of behaviour improvement plans;
- a baseline for monitoring progress; and
- a means of making comparisons with other schools.

Schools included key actions from the audit within their BIP action plan. In one secondary school, which had a considerable number of fixed-term exclusions, it had been possible to analyse who were repeat offenders, in which year group, in which lessons, and which day of the week or time of day, seemed to be risk times. Specific subjects, teachers and issues were identified, and this succeeded in shifting the school management's thinking and making the problem more manageable. The school had an influx of many difficult and challenging children and the data were enormously helpful. Other schools found the audit helpful in analysing where and why their problems occurred:

> The secondary behaviour audit in one LA was described as 'lengthy' but 'fantastic'. The graphs from the analysis had been presented to both students and management groups within the schools. The student questionnaire was regarded as particularly valuable, as was the facility for central collation of the data. However, the primary audit was less highly regarded. It had been expected that it would be different from the secondary one but in practice was very similar. It did not, therefore, seem appropriate to use the whole audit in primary schools and specific instruments were therefore selected for use e.g. the teacher questionnaire. Use of the audit in the LA highlighted a range of issues and working parties had been established to develop action plans. Another working party was established to plan how to roll out the training packages, although in schools where training programmes had already been planned for the year this was difficult. The role of the Lead Behaviour Professional (LBP) enabled more time to be spent collating and analysing the data that had been collected and more time to prepare this and provide it for use by other staff. For example, in one school, scrutiny of the data identified the most vulnerable children but also high-

lighted the fact that only seven required additional support as the others were already being supported by the behaviour policy. In this LA, audit procedures had been extended to some non-BIP schools, its usefulness having been demonstrated very clearly.

Relevant here was the extensive use of collaboration among all school staff and the pupils. Pupils' perspectives were valued and they were involved in the entire process.

The audits, in some cases, provided evidence to challenge headteachers about school practices, led to the restructuring of classroom systems to vertical grouping, the introduction of pastoral prefects to provide 'good' role models and the development of a new *Code of Conduct* being taken to the school council. Other examples included rescheduling of the school day by reducing the lunch hour, changes to lunch time supervision arrangements, the establishment of a time out room, and the rewriting of the school's behaviour policy. The audits raised awareness within schools of the greater need for consistency. They were also used to develop training both within schools and across the LA. The most common difficulties occurred with headteachers, some of whom were very resistant to change even when they were presented with evidence indicating that it was necessary.

Behaviour and Education Support Teams (BESTs) and whole-school policies

Behaviour and Education Support Teams (BESTs) are multi-agency teams which aim to promote emotional well-being, positive mental health, positive behaviour and school attendance among children and young people, and to help in the identification and support of those with, or at risk of developing emotional and behavioural problems, through the provision of multi-agency support in target schools and to individual families (DfES 2003b). BESTs work in partnership with a cluster of primary schools and one or two secondary schools: this may include Pupil Referral Units or schools for pupils with emotional, behavioural and social difficulties. BESTs offer support at three broad levels:

1. The whole school including developing school strategies, curriculum input and consultancy work with individual school staff.
2. Group support for children and their parents (for example nurture groups, transition groups, parenting groups) according to local need.
3. Intensive support for individual children and families on a case-management basis (for example counselling, family therapy).

This chapter focuses on the work of BESTs within the whole-school context. Later chapters provide other examples of their work (see Chapters 4, 6, 7 and 9).

An important strand of the work of BEST coordinators was working alongside school staff to develop internal procedures and policies. In one secondary school this meant reviewing the processes that the school used in relation to target setting and supporting students within the school. In another primary school the involvement of the BEST coordinator and the action plan that arose from the behaviour audit meant that the school focused more closely on behaviour. A particular strength of this work was the establishment of effective systems for monitoring behaviour through computer databases.

In one secondary school internal systems and strategies were improved so that referrals to the BEST were more effective, previously some referrals had been rejected as the school had not previously undertaken sufficient work with the child. The SENCO revised the monitoring of School Action and School Action Plus so that a more coordinated system was in place and that the referrals to BEST focused on the additionality that the BEST could offer. In another secondary school, where there was concern about girls' self-harming, the BEST coordinator, who was also the LBP, put together guidelines for staff pointing out what to look for and what action to take.

In many instances the focus on behaviour at school level shifted from being concerned with bad behaviour to valuing good behaviour. Schools were encouraged and facilitated in reviewing their behaviour systems and were actively involved in making appropriate referrals to the BEST. This additional level of support was welcomed and also meant that staff could focus on teaching and learning, while being aware that the individual needs of pupils were being met:

> In terms of BIP, good behaviour is now part of the whole school. Children want to behave well, because they see that good behaviour is valued, rather than bad behaviour getting them noticed, which was the case in the past. This positive aspect of improving behaviour has been the most important.
>
> (*Headteacher*)

> The BEST coordinator has been in regularly and met with the LBP to work on and develop a number of things. These have included planning meetings where children were identified who were at risk, putting in place key workers and helping the LBP think about interventions for the at risk pupils. The school has worked on its whole behaviour system and INSET has been given to all teachers and the support staff.
>
> (*Headteacher*)

From the school's perspective there is a recognition that there is another place to turn to. There are an enormous number of referrals. What has been important is that few of these have been felt to be inappropriate. There have been changes in the way staff manage behaviour and recognition that some pupils need additional support, that the staff, themselves, cannot provide.

(*Acting BEST Coordinator*)

Lead Behaviour Professionals

Recently, schools have been encouraged to appoint senior members of staff to take responsibility for behaviour improvement (Steer Report 2006). Clearly defined senior and pastoral roles within schools contribute to improving behaviour (Ofsted 2002). In Scotland, as part of the Staged Intervention (FFI) scheme a member of staff is trained as a behaviour coordinator to provide support for colleagues in managing behaviour in the classroom more effectively. Emphasis is placed on promoting peer support among school staff (Wilkin et al. 2006). In the Primary Behaviour and Attendance Pilot the teacher coach's responsibilities included facilitating the school behaviour and attendance audit and school self-review, providing coaching to teaching staff, and running training and staff development activities (Hallam et al. 2006). As part of the BIP, primary and secondary schools appointed Lead Behaviour Professionals (LBPs).

LBPs were appointed to undertake a key role in the school in relation to policy and practice concerned with pupil behaviour. The managerial role of the LBP was seen as important to the success of the BIP. The specific activities undertaken by the LBP depended to some extent on the phase of school, primary or secondary, and whether the LBP had other competing roles in the school or as part of a BEST. The role of the LBP was viewed positively by schools and BIP coordinators. Meetings with LBPs were described as 'excellent' and there were favourable comments about the local training and the way in which LBPs had 'developed links with each other'. In many schools LBPs adapted their role from an existing one, but in some cases they were new appointments.

The impact of having someone in the school with overall responsibility for behaviour was considerable. Having clear behaviour policies and structures for referring pupils provided clear guidance for teachers. In some schools, pupils were more aware of how they could access help and some pupils felt able to approach the LBP and ask for support. There was no stigma attached to this. Overall, the behaviour audits and the recruitment of LBPs raised the status of pastoral support and behaviour management in schools.

In the primary sector LBPs were sometimes headteachers, learning mentors, Learning Support Assistants or members of the BEST. Generally, it was considered better for the headteacher not to be the LBP as the role required considerable time, which headteachers did not have available. Although the role was taken on by a broader range of individuals than in secondary schools, it was key in facilitating the development of whole-school policies and consistency in the way in which schools dealt with behaviour issues (Hallam et al. 2005). Box 3.2 provides an example.

Box 3.2   The role of the Lead Behaviour Professional

Example of the LBP role in a primary school

In primary schools, staff in the school rather than staff external to it undertook much of the implementation of the BIP. For example, in one school, as a result of the appointment of the LBP a whole-school approach was adopted alongside support for individuals. The impact was reported to be dramatic. Training was provided for all staff including teaching assistants, playground staff and Newly Qualified Teachers (NQTs), and involved establishing a code of behaviour and developing strategies to help those having problems. The code was based on mutual respect. During Key Stage 1 the children were taught how to behave, including the teacher using a digital camera to take photographs of models of good behaviour, which were then displayed to the children. Improving behaviour in the playground was a major part of the initiative and involved Year 5 and 6 pupils in peer negotiation training. Children also learned about making choices and accepting responsibility for their own behaviour. All of the staff adopted the same code of behaviour and better communication developed between those working in the playground and classroom. Parents were informed of the code as there was a perceived need to involve them more. Much of this work was initiated by the LBP and implemented as a result of the LBP being able to engage the Senior Management Team (SMT). NQTs and teachers new to the school were made aware of a school's behaviour code on their arrival in the school. The major impact was that staff were consistent. Pupils knew what was acceptable and unacceptable behaviour across the school. As a result staff felt that the school had become more relaxed. They attributed this to the role, influence and training provided by the LBP.

At secondary school, it was important that the LBP was a member of the senior management team (Hallam et al. 2005) to enable him/her to challenge and influence whole-school practice. The role of the LBP was crucial in raising the profile of behaviour and attendance issues in the school. Box 3.3 provides examples.

Box 3.3 Examples of the work of Lead Behaviour Professionals

Case studies illustrating the work of LBPs

In one LA where there were no primary LBPs, the LBP was also the BEST manager and worked in primary schools as well as in the secondary school where he was based. The LBP focused on whole-school issues, analysing data, looking at collaboration and working on developing first-day cover for pupils excluded from primary schools. Brokering played a substantial part of his role. He attended the school's Social Inclusion Board, a forum for dissemination of any matters which were related to helping to retain pupils in school, and used this forum to influence policy in the school and to establish clearly what was meant by inclusion. He influenced the way in which the school developed its support systems questioning previous practice and changing the way that the school integrated its systems for the benefit and inclusion of challenging pupils, whereas previously the response was to exclude.

The implementation of BIP and the introduction of the BEST led to data being used more often and more systematically. Staff who worked closely with the LBP indicated that his energy and drive were important to the success of the role. He had been responsible for establishing, in collaboration with the Youth Service, an off-site centre which provided both first-day cover for exclusion and alternative curricula and, together with the Head of ICT and the Deputy Head, was successful in putting in a bid to gain a bank of computers for the centre through an urban regeneration fund. In the primary schools, he undertook classroom observation of pupils and used his brokering skills with the educational psychologists in order to introduce training into the schools. He was instrumental in managing the work of the BESTs, for instance, the Child and Adolescent Mental Health Services (CAMHS) workers' provision of Webster-Stratton training for parents. In addition the LBP had an LA role in analysing data and providing the information to area meetings which included non-BIP schools. He continued to teach a small number of lessons in the secondary school and closely monitored the timetables of the BEST team. Considerable emphasis was put on transition with pupil screening assessing self-esteem and identifying difficulties early. The LBP also undertook transition interviews in primary schools.

In another LA, the LBP visited other LAs prior to providing training for school staff. He used comparisons of exclusion figures with other schools in discussions with schools in his LA which 'made people think'. An extended day for excluded pupils (3 pm – 6 pm) was introduced which served to change staff attitudes to exclusion. 'Behaviour for Learning' (based on Assertive Discipline) was introduced to deal with the 'niggling bad behaviour in class' as a result of the LBP's visit to schools in another LA. The LBP role was viewed as managerial and interventionist and one in which the use of data (e.g. relating to persistent offenders) was crucial. It was hoped that as a result of early intervention by BEST in primary schools a stage could be reached where pupils would not be referred in the secondary school.

Despite the success of LBPs there were some difficulties. Overload was common and constituted a major obstacle to the successful implementation of BIP initiatives. For instance, in one school, the LBP was the BEST coordinator for a cluster of schools, Assistant Deputy Head in charge of inclusion and for most of the summer term took on the role of SENCO because of staff absence. The SMT in the school was unresponsive to requests for a reduction in responsibilities to enable sufficient time to be given to the role of LBP. In some of the schools there was a reluctance to appoint an LBP as it was believed that some staff would pass on all responsibility for behaviour in the school to that individual.

Transition between primary and secondary schools as part of a whole-school approach

The transfer from primary to secondary school occurs at different ages in different countries. In New Zealand the majority of students change schools on two occasions: once between Years 6 and 7 and then again between Years 8 and 9. In some countries, such as the USA, children can be held back a year if they have not made sufficient progress. Research into transition has often focused on achievement since the international literature demonstrates that there is often a decline in achievement following it (NCES 1995; Collins and Harrison 1998; Galton et al. 1999; Isakson and Jarvis 1999; Ofsted 2002). This same dip occurs regardless of the age of transition and it appears that students who make two transitions experience the transition drop twice (Felner et al. 1981; Alspaugh 1998).

So what is problematic about transitions? On a practical level there are many changes. For instance, between primary and secondary school changes include the move from a small to a larger school; from having one teacher for most subjects to having different teachers for different subjects, usually in a different room, with different seating arrangements, a wide range of teaching styles, different expectations about homework; and the introduction of new ways of learning and independent study (Ofsted 2002). Few schools take sufficient account of these changes (Ofsted 2002). Pupils need to be able to adjust to their new environment. The rate of adjustment varies according to a range of factors and for some pupils is stressful. Recently, there has been an increase in transition programmes to support all pupils (Smith 2006). For disaffected students, those at risk of exclusion, or with social, emotional and behavioural difficulties, transition can be particularly difficult (Osler et al. 2001). In some countries, particular groups of students never make the transition into secondary schools. For instance, aboriginal students in Australia are at particular risk (Gray and Beresford 2001) and Traveller children in the UK (Derrington and Kendall 2004). In response, many countries have established support programmes for pupils at risk during the transition period. These are discussed in Chapter 9.

Also problematic is the disjunction between the curriculum in different educational phases and the lack of harmonization of teaching approaches (Galton et al. 1999, 2000; Ofsted 2002). In England it was hoped that the implementation of the National Curriculum would alleviate these problems but this has not happened (Galton et al. 1999). In Victoria, Australia, concerns about student disengagement after transition led to organizational changes including reducing the number of teachers that students had contact with by blocking subjects together, and developing collaborative teams of teachers with special pastoral responsibility for groups of students. In other parts of Australia, schools were structured for gradual transition from one class with one teacher to a number of classes with several teachers who were specialist subject teachers in the senior secondary school (Bezzina 1988). While curriculum continuity is important, insufficient attention has been paid to some of the social aspects of transition (McGee et al. 2003).

From the pupil perspective, anxiety about transition seems to focus on five main areas:

1. The size and more complex organization of the new school.
2. New forms of discipline and authority.
3. New work demands.
4. Fear of being bullied.
5. Fear of losing one's friends (Measor and Woods 1984).

So what have schools done to facilitate more effective transition for students? In the UK, transition programmes have become more common and induction programmes more user-friendly (Galton et al. 1999; Ofsted 2002). Schools run induction days, special visits related to sport or drama, and summer literacy and/or numeracy programmes (Galton et al. 1999). In New Zealand prior visits, orientation programmes and peer-support programmes are common (Education Review Office 1994). Similarly in the USA, peer-mentoring programmes and buddying systems are popular and arrangements have been made for pupils to shadow a pupil in their new school for a day so that they gain some understanding of what the high school day is like. Effective programmes address a range of issues: curriculum, including the academic rigour of courses; facilities, including the location of classrooms; safety and discipline, including rules and discipline code; and provision of accurate information about organization and logistics (Mac Iver 1990).

Difficulties remain though. Zeedyk and colleagues (2003) suggested that attention needs to be paid to expanding the number and duration of visits between schools; allowing students to spend a day with secondary school students; inviting secondary school students and teachers to speak at feeder schools; and providing peer mentoring. In England, primary schools recognize that good transfer arrangements are important; however, this is often low on their list of priorities. Little attention is given to arranging additional familiarization days for pupils with Special Educational Needs (SEN) and little provision is made for meeting the needs of pupils identified as Gifted and Talented. Few secondary schools identify transition as a specific activity that needs to be part of their action plan to improve provision, there is variability in the information received from primary schools, curricular targets set in primary schools are not utilized by secondary schools, and very few primary schools are aware of how the information they pass on is being used by secondary schools (Ofsted 2002).

A particular focus of the work of BESTs, as part of the BIP, was the development of transition strategies to support all pupils, with a separate strand to support those at risk of exclusion. One LA developed an initiative that addressed many of the concerns highlighted by Ofsted above. A designated Transition Worker with responsibility for overseeing the transition programme was appointed to the BEST, a former secondary school teacher. Once Key Stage 2 Standard Attainment Tests (SATs) were over, a transition programme was offered to all Year 6 pupils. Together with support from the BEST Home School Liaison Worker (HSLW) every child progressing to secondary school received a visit and took part in the programme.

At the time of the research pupils came into the secondary school from 53 primary schools. Within this there was a core of eight to ten primary schools which provided larger numbers of pupils. The Transition Worker and the HSLW collected data from the pupils about themselves, from the Year 6 teacher, support teachers and the SENCO, if appropriate. This information was collated for appropriate members of secondary staff. The outcome of this was that on the first day in Year 7, English as an Additional Language (EAL), SEN, and Gifted and Talented systems were in place for those pupils requiring them, form teachers had some background information about their pupils, and Heads of Year knew which pupils were at risk and why. Where pupils had a learning mentor in the primary school a one-to-one handover with a learning mentor in the secondary school was arranged. The Transition Worker went into Year 7 registration periods during the first six weeks of the autumn term to ensure that all pupils were supported.

The open-door policy of the BEST meant that pupils could talk to any of the team if they were experiencing difficulties. Teachers reported that when Year 7 arrived they were comfortable within the school, settled in quickly and did not experience difficulties that went unnoticed during the first six weeks. A transition booklet was produced, a passport to secondary schools, which all Year 6 pupils had the opportunity to complete. It addressed practical issues about reading timetables, provided scenarios for pupils to discuss including consideration of how they might feel about leaving friends and their first day at secondary school.

The same LA implemented a project focused on junior citizenship that involved the Transition Worker, the learning mentor, two teachers and Year 11 pupils. The Year 11 pupils visited the primary schools and worked with staff on the junior citizenship project with Year 6 pupils. This provided the Year 6 pupils with positive adolescent role models who behaved well towards them. Another project involved Year 7 pupils returning to the primary school so that links were established in both directions. The Year 7 pupils listened to Year 3 children reading and modelled good behaviour. This broke down barriers between the primary and secondary schools and provided Year 6 pupils with the opportunity to see that young people in the secondary school were 'upright young citizens' who supported learning in the primary school.

The teachers in the primary schools involved in these initiatives placed a high value on the transition work:

> Most definitely the Year 6 pupils who had this experience last year and went on to the secondary school have really benefited. The school had a really in-depth knowledge of the different needs of the Year 6 pupils who were going to attend the school. They knew about special needs, issues with child protection and personal information. Normally when you send off the 60 files to the secondary schools you are aware that they don't really read them and are not aware of the needs of the children. They met with class teachers and spoke one-to-one with them, they met with the pupils and spoke one-to-one with them, they met with me, they had the pupils going over there for lessons, they did some sessions in our school. They certainly have gained knowledge of each individual pupil, which is fantastic. I have never seen anything like this before.
>
> (*Headteacher*)

Headteachers were confident that the Year 6 pupils had been successfully inducted into secondary school life. The transition work enabled pupils to explore what they needed to know about the secondary school.

Endnote

Improving Behaviour in school is a complex issue. Schools can make a difference if a proactive approach is taken that considers factors operating at the level of the organization, the class and the individual. Important is that all those involved in the school community have ownership of school policies and implement them consistently.

Chapter summary

- Improving behaviour in school requires consideration of issues at the level of the school, the classroom and the individual.
- A focus on promoting good behaviour is more effective than reacting to poor behaviour.
- Critical factors in developing effective whole-school polices include:
  — strong commitment of the senior management team;
  — adopting a whole-school approach to any initiatives put in place so that pupils and staff (teaching and non-teaching) are involved in developing school policy: ownership is important;
  — ensuring that all staff are familiar with the school behaviour policy;
  — ensuring that new staff have an induction period which includes introducing the school behaviour policy;
  — establishing coherent approaches across the school in relation to behaviour and rewards;
  — implementing policies consistently and equitably;
  — making use of the data from behaviour audits;
  — reviewing behaviour policies on a regular basis;
  — clearly allocating key responsibilities and roles within the school and giving senior members of staff responsibility for behaviour; and
  — implementing whole-school approaches to transition.

Further reading

Hallam, S., Castle, F. and Rogers, L. with Creech, A., Rhamie, J. and Kokotsaki, D. (2005) *Research and Evaluation of the Behaviour Improvement Programme. Research Report 702.* London: DfES.

Hallam, S., Shaw, J. and Rhamie, J. (2006) *Evaluation of the Primary Behaviour and Attendance Pilot. Research Report 717.* London: DfES.

Ofsted (2006) *Improving Behaviour*. London: HMSO.

Turner, C. (2003) How effective and inclusive is the school's behaviour policy? *Emotional and Behavioural Difficulties*, 8(1): 7–18.

References

Alspaugh, J.W. (1998) Achievement loss associated with the transition to middle school and high school. *Journal of Educational Research*, 92(1): 20–5.

American Federation of Teachers (2003) *Setting the Stage for Strong Standards: Elements of a Safe and Orderly School*. Washington, DC: American Federation of Teachers.

Bezzina, M. (1988) Meeting the needs of children in transition: A middle school program for preservice teacher education. *South Pacific Journal of Teacher Education*, 16(1): 101–8.

Collins, J. and Harrison, B.T. (1998) Claiming and reclaiming education: The experiences of multilingual school students in transition from primary to secondary school. *Unicorn*, 24(1): 16–29.

De Jong, T.A. (2004) *Best Practice in Addressing Student Behaviour Issues in Australia*. Report submitted to the Ministerial Council on Education, Employment, Training and Youth Affairs' (MCEETYA). Perth, Western Australia.

Department for Education and Skills (DfES) (2003a) *Advice on Whole-school Behaviour and Attendance Policy*. London: HMSO.

Department for Education and Skills (DfES) (2003b) *Good Practice Guidance for Behaviour and Education Support Teams*. London: DfES.

Department for Education and Skills (DfES) (2004) *Working Together: Giving Children and Young People a Say. Pamphlet 134/2004*. London: DfES.

Derrington, C. and Kendall, S. (2004) *Gypsy Traveller Students in Secondary Schools: Culture, Identity and Achievement*. Stoke-on-Trent: Trentham Books.

Education Review Office (1994) *Form 1 to 4: Issues for Students: Transition, Curriculum, Assessment and Discipline*. National education evaluation reports, 5. Wellington: New Zealand Education Review Office.

Elton Report (1989), Committee of Enquiry into Discipline in Schools. *Discipline in Schools*. Department of Education and Science. London: HMSO.

Felner, R.D., Primavera, D. and Cauce, A.M. (1981) The impact of school transitions: A focus for preventive efforts. *American Journal of Community Psychology*, 9(4): 449–59.

Galton, M., Gray, J. and Ruddock, J. (1999) *The Impact of School Transitions and Transfers on Pupil Progress and Attainment DfEE. Research Report 131.* London: The Stationery Office.

Galton, M., Morrison, I. and Pell, T. (2000) Transfer and transition in English schools: Reviewing the evidence. *International Journal of Educational Research,* 33: 341–63.

Gray, J. and Beresford, Q. (2001). *Alienation from School among Aboriginal Students.* Perth: Institute for the Service Professionals.

Great Britain Statutes (1997) *Education Act 1997* Chapter 44 (Part 2). London: HMSO.

Hallam, S., Castle, F. and Rogers, L. with Creech, A., Rhamie, J. and Kokotsaki, D. (2005) *Research and Evaluation of the Behaviour Improvement Programme. Research Report 702.* London: DfES.

Hallam, S., Shaw, J. and Rhamie, J. (2006) *Evaluation of the Primary Behaviour and Attendance Pilot. Research Report 717.* London: DfES.

HM Inspectorate of Education (HMIE) (2005) *A Climate for Learning.* Livingston: HMIE.

Isakson, K. and Jarvis, P. (1999) The adjustment of adolescents during the transition into high school: A short-term longitudinal study. *Journal of Youth and Adolescence,* 28(1): 1–26.

Kerr, D., Ireland, E., Lopes, J., Craig, R. and Clever, E. (2004) *Citizenship Education Longitudinal Study: Second Annual Report: First Longitudinal Study.* London: DfES/NFER.

Luiselli, J.K., Putnam, R.F., Handler, M.W. and Feinberg, A.B. (2005) Whole-school positive behaviour support: Effects on student discipline problems and academic performance. *Educational Psychology,* 25(2–3):183–98.

Macbeath, J., Demetriou, H., Rudduck, J. and Myers, K. (2003) *Consulting Pupils: A Toolkit for Teachers.* Cambridge: Pearson.

McGee, C., Ward, R., Gibbons, J. and Harlow, A. (2003) *Transition to Secondary School: A Literature Review.* Wellington: Ministry of Education.

Mac Iver, D.J. (1990). Meeting the needs of young adolescents: Advisory groups, interdisciplinary teaching teams and school transition programs. *Phi Delta Kappan,* 71: 458–64.

Measor, L. and Woods, P. (1984) *Changing Schools: Pupil Perspectives on Transfer to a Comprehensive.* Milton Keynes: Open University Press.

Ministerial Advisory Committee for Educational Renewal (MACER) (2005) *Smart Schools, Smart Behaviour: Advice to the Minister on Behaviour Management in Queensland Schools*. Queensland Government.

National Center for Education Statistics (NCES) (1995) *Digest of Education Statistics*. Washington, DC: US Government Printing Office.

Ofsted (2001) *Improving Attendance and Behaviour in Secondary Schools*. London: HMSO.

Ofsted (2002) *Changing Schools: An Evaluation of the Effectiveness of Transfer Arrangements at Age 11*. London: HMSO.

Ofsted (2003) *National Curriculum Citizenship: Planning and Implementation*. London: Ofsted.

Ofsted (2006) *Improving Behaviour*. London: HMSO.

Osler, A. (2000) Children's rights, responsibilities and understandings of school discipline. *Research Papers in Education*, 15(1): 49–67.

Osler, A., Watling, R. and Busher, H. (2001) *Reasons for Exclusion from School. Research Report 244*. London: DfEE.

Pearce, N. and Hallgarten, J. (eds) (2000) *Tomorrow's Citizens*. London: Institute for Public Policy Research.

Reed, J. (2005) *Toward Zero Exclusion: An Action Plan for Schools and Policy Makers*. London: Institute for Public Policy Research and Centre for British Teachers.

Rowe, D. (2006) Taking responsibility: School behaviour policies in England, moral development and implications for citizenship education. *Journal of Moral Education*, 35(4): 519–31.

Smith, J.S. (2006) *Research Summary: Transition from Middle School to High School*. Westerville, OH: National Middle School Association.

Steer Report (2006) *Learning Behaviour: The Report of the Practitioners' Group on School Behaviour and Discipline*. London: DfES.

Stephens, P., Kyriacou, C. and Tønnessen, F.E. (2005) Student teachers' views of pupil misbehaviour in classrooms: A Norwegian and an English setting compared, *Scandinavian Journal of Educational Research*. 49(2): 203–16.

Turner, C. (2003) How effective and inclusive is the school's behaviour policy? *Emotional and Behavioural Difficulties*, 8(1): 7–18.

Watkins, C. and Wagner, P. (2000) *Improving School Behaviour*. London: Paul Chapman.

Wilkin, A., Moor. H., Murfield, J., Kinder, K. and Johnson, F. (2006) *Behaviour in Scottish Schools*. Edinburgh: Scottish Executive Social Research.

Zeedyk, M.S., Gallacher, J., Henderson, M., Hope, G., Husband, B. and Lindsay, K. (2003) Negotiating the transition from primary to secondary school: Perceptions of pupils, parents and teachers. *School Psychology International*, 24(1): 67–79.

4 Behaviour in and around school

This chapter explores issues concerning pupil behaviour in and around school and the way that all school staff can play a part in improving behaviour, at break and lunch times, in the playground and through the wider school community. The work of extended schools, Behaviour and Educational Support Teams (BESTs) and Police in Schools will be considered and research evaluating the role of a range of Local Authority initiatives.

Introduction

In Chapter 2 the causes of poor behaviour and attendance at school were outlined in relation to the interactions between factors operating at the level of society, communities, families, schools and individuals. The development of extended schools and multi-agency teams, including police in schools, reflects the recognition that education systems in contemporary society will fail to meet the needs of their pupils unless they acknowledge these complex relationships (Dryfoos 1993; Coltoff et al. 1997). In the USA, the underlying principle of extended schools was founded on the recognition that for many pupils issues relating to education could only be addressed once a range of welfare and health services were in place. In England there has been growing recognition that schools themselves cannot solve the problems associated with social exclusion and multiple disadvantage (Tett 2000).

This chapter focuses on three initiatives which have as their aim improving behaviour in and around school, in part through engaging with the wider community: Extended and Full Service Extended Schools; the involvement of multi-agency teams in improving behaviour in the playground; and Safer School Partnerships and the police. All value multi-agency working, stress the importance of developing partnerships within the school and the community, and support the aims of the *Every Child Matters* agenda (DfES 2003a).

Extended schools

Historically, schools have often been involved with their local communities and initiatives. The Village College approach of the 1920s in the UK and the community school movement in Michigan in the 1930s could be seen as forerunners of the more strategic interventions of today.

The concept of the Full Service School first emerged in the USA during the early 1980s with the aim to provide integrated school-based health and social services as a means of supporting individuals and families in combating educational underachievement in disadvantaged areas. During the 1980s and 1990s the Full Service School concept became firmly established in relation to educational and social reform movements in the USA with the anticipation that they could respond to the reality of contemporary problems (Coltoff et al. 1997). Dryfoos (1994) suggested that Full Service Schools were 'one stop, collaborative institutions' that integrated education, medical, social and/or human services that were beneficial to meeting the needs of children and youth and their families on school grounds or in locations which were easily accessible. A variety of delivery models are in place, ranging from small-scale extensions to the traditional remit of schools to fully integrated systems. Beginning in California in 1991, Healthy Start legislation and grants enabled schools and their partners to create child- and family-centred services near or at school sites. Early evidence suggested that student behaviour, performance and school climate improved in Healthy Start Schools. Children and families gained access to a broad range of services and families' unmet needs for basic goods and services were reduced by half (Dryfoos 2000). Other initiatives included Beacons, originating in New York in 1991 whereby school-based community centres were developed that offered a wide range of recreation and social services, cultural and educational enrichment and vocational activities for young people, and involved families and the community. Evidence suggested that the Beacons helped prevent drug use and fighting and that they encouraged motivation for school work and developed leadership skills (Dryfoos 2000).

In Scotland the New Community Schools Initiative (NCS) was established in 1998 with three phases of development between 1998 and 2003 (Illsely and Redford 2005). The strategy for rolling out the NCS approach across Scotland began in 2002 and the Scottish Executive set a target of all public-funded schools in Scotland becoming Integrated Community Schools

(ICS) by 2007. The ICS were expected to follow the development of integrated provision within the NCS projects but also to expand and integrate the range of services offered. ICS evolved from the Full Service School model that originated in the USA. The aim was to improve educational attainment and health, and promote social inclusion among all members of the community. The key aspect of this initiative was the development of multi-agency collaboration whereby professionals from education, health, social work, community services, the police and the voluntary sector were encouraged to work together to deliver improved services to children and families. In relation to the multi-agency objective the initiative had some success (Sammons et al. 2003). Central to the philosophy of the initiative was the notion of working *with* rather than *on* parents and children through the collaborative effort of different agencies and groups of professionals. The NCS projects had eight essential characteristics: meeting the needs of all pupils, integrated provision, engagement with families, engagement with the wider community, integrated management, measurable outcomes, commitment and leadership, and multidisciplinary staff development (Scottish Office 1998).

In England, government funding to support schools to develop extended services was first available in 2002–03 when 25 Local Authorities (LAs) were asked to develop extended school pathfinder projects. By 2005–06 all LAs received funding to support the development of extended schools in line with the government's vision. The National Remodelling Team (NRT) was appointed in 2005 to support LAs and schools in taking forward this agenda and by November 2005, 4400 schools had indicated their willingness to work on developing extended services. In the first year (school year 2003–04) of the Full Service Extended Schools initiative (FSES) 61 projects were funded. All of these were in Behaviour Improvement Programme areas.

The government has defined a set of core services that extended schools should be able to offer by 2010. As an interim target, it is intended that half of all primary schools and a third of all secondary schools will have these in place by 2008. The aim is for extended schools to provide a range of services and activities, often beyond the school day, that help meet the needs of children (including those with disabilities or Special Educational Needs (SEN)), their families and the wider community. Crucial is that all parties are involved in planning so that schools develop the package of services which best meet the needs of their community. It is expected that there will be variation between schools.

The core comprises:

- childcare and a varied menu of activities for children and young people between the hours of 8 am and 6 pm, all year round;
- a varied menu of activities including study support, homework clubs, music tuition, dance and drama, arts and crafts, special

interest clubs, visits to museums and galleries, learning a foreign language, volunteering, business and enterprise activities;

- parenting support, including information sessions at key transition points, family learning and parenting programmes;
- ensuring swift referral from schools to a wider range of specialized support services for pupils such as speech therapy, Child and Adolescent Mental Health Services, family support services, intensive behaviour support and, for young people, sexual health services. It is intended that some of these may be delivered on school sites; and
- widespread community use of the school's facilities including ICT, sports and arts facilities, including adult learning (DfES 2005).

All of these initiatives are aimed at the creation of integrated child and family services based near points of need in local communities. The 'full service' addition to extended schools derives, in part, from the children's services proposals outlined in *Every Child Matters* (DfES 2003a), the Children Act (2004) and *Every Child Matters: Next Steps* (DfES 2004) whereby a closer integration of the work of education and social services departments and health services in the interests of children is advocated. The intention, for the future, is that children's trusts will commission schools to deliver integrated children's services, co-located on the school site thus widening the services that they offer.

The Department for Education and Skills's (DfES) specification sets out eight strands of activity in which Full Service Extended Schools (FSESs) should become involved: childcare, health and social care, lifelong learning, family learning, parenting support, study support, sports and arts, and ICT. Evaluation of the first year of extended schools found considerable diversity in how FSESs had interpreted the guidance, reflected in the particular activities engaged in by different schools, the range of partnerships they had established, and the underlying rationales that they had begun to construct. Although all FSES are similar, no two were identical (Cummings et al. 2005). Where FSES had achieved high levels of multi-agency working there were positive benefits in the coordination of approaches to vulnerable children and their families, improved information sharing procedures, appropriate targeting of services and enhanced access to services for children and families. Most saw the provision of childcare as an important benefit having an impact on children's learning, supporting more positive relationships between schools and families, and providing support for parents. Overall, the evidence suggests that FSESs can have significant positive effects on children, adults and families (Cummings et al. 2006).

At the time of the evaluation of the Behaviour Improvement Programme (BIP) most extended schools were in the early stages of development. The examples that follow demonstrate how the various strands were grouped within different school contexts, and the range of activities and agencies involved. In one LA, one of the four BIP secondary schools was designated as a FSES and had approached 20 different agencies with a view to them being based in the school, the aim being for the local population to see the school as a focus and for families to have easy access to the agencies. The FSES, a sports college, was intended to function as a community centre and was open for 48 weeks of the year, with possible access for seven days a week and extended hours. It was regarded as a model of good practice for the other BIP schools in terms of the management of the multi-agency approach.

In another LA where the FSES coordinator was also the Behaviour and Education Support Team (BEST) coordinator, a variety of services including health, occupational therapy, housing and police were to be based in the extended school with additional links with the retired community, Positive Activities for Young People, and activities previously run through Connexions. There were also activities for pupils during the school holidays and in-service training for staff. In another LA, the aim of the extended school was to be the focus for all the cluster schools and to develop links with the primary schools. Extra-curricular activities included after-school music activities, a physical education club, art, healthy living activities, a parent-and-child reading club, a wildlife club, and taster sessions with Adult Education in relation to healthy eating. Another extended school provided the base for the transfer mentor who was responsible for supporting primary pupils moving to the secondary school including arranging events in the summer holidays.

Overall, the FSESs offer considerable potential for the future (USA: Dryfoos 2000; Scotland: Sammons et al. 2003; England: Cummings et al. 2005, 2006). Particularly important for their success is the involvement of multi-agency working and improved access to specialist resources. However, some difficulties remain. Based on a review of the international literature, Wilkin and colleagues (2003) highlighted issues relating to the ownership of the infrastructure and site, governance, funding, training, differences in aims, cultures and procedures, and increased workload or overload of staff. In the UK, difficulties remain in relation to establishing effective partnerships with other agencies and organizations: lack of clarity and commitment between partners, competing priorities and professional barriers in bringing staff together from different agencies, and sustainability. In rural communities transport can be problematic and there remain difficulties relating to the development of comprehensive childcare. Cummings and colleagues (2006) suggest that FSESs need to clarify what they hope to achieve and how they expect to achieve it, how their work relates to that of other child, family and community agencies, and how their aims relate to the issues faced by the local community.

Initiatives to improve playground behaviour at break and lunchtime

Events during breaks and lunchtimes have a substantial impact on what happens in the classroom. Promoting positive activities and behaviour at these times requires the involvement of all school staff. A case study drawn from the evaluation of the Primary Behaviour and Attendance Pilot illustrates this (Hallam et al. 2006). The Social and Emotional Aspects of Learning element of the pilot (SEAL) sought to develop children's social, emotional and behaviour skills. Its implementation involved all school staff and pupils. Following participation in the programme support staff had a better understanding of anger and the way that the emotions can override logical thought and determine behaviour, tended to shout at the children less, and understood that children needed to calm down, have time out to talk to an adult about the incident, and work through why it happened and what the consequences of their actions would be. Schools reported that changes in lunchtime behaviour had a major impact on school life (see Box 4.1 for an example).

Box 4.1 Improving behaviour in the playground

Case Study: the impact of improved playground behaviour on the classroom

There has been an impact on the Deputy, particularly at lunchtime, where she is not needed as much by lunchtime staff because of the blue sky behaviour chart. It has given the dinner ladies a lot of help and support. The coach has worked with them. The pastoral side of the Deputy Head's role has improved, with all staff being able to go through the progression better before it reaches the Deputy or the Head. Other people have been able to intervene along the way. My class is much calmer. It has not reduced my workload but stress level is better as children are able to talk through before things reach crisis point. Children know that they will have time to talk. After lunch a lot of time was spent dealing with issues from the playground. Things have improved so that it is now possible to begin teaching and learning far sooner in the afternoon.

(Teacher)

The Elton Report (1989) acknowledged the importance of lunchtime as a feature of school life, while recognizing that it also represented the biggest single behaviour-related challenge facing staff and recommended that lunch-time supervisors be trained in behaviour management. Problems that arise during lunchtimes often spill over into lessons and waste teacher time in settling children and sorting out the problems before teaching can begin (Blatchford and Sharp 1994). A recent national survey in Scotland found that primary school staff felt that indiscipline was most problematic in the playground, whereas for secondary teachers the classroom was perceived as most difficult (Wilkin et al. 2003).

Inadequate playgrounds can contribute to poor behaviour and disorder (Steer Report 2006) but other important factors include relationships and control within the school, supervision and equipment. The quality of supervision in the playground and who provides it are crucial. In England and Wales most supervision is carried out by lunchtime supervisors. In Scotland classroom assistants are often responsible for primary playground supervision, whereas in Australia supervision is provided by teachers, al-though not all look upon this task favourably. It is only recently that training for supervision has been provided for support staff.

Drawing on research from the USA and the UK, Pellegrini and Blatch-ford (2002) argue that break and lunchtimes are crucial to academic achieve-ment, developing peer relationships and promoting general school adjust-ment. They suggest that most children learn social skills by interacting with their peers in meaningful social situations including those occurring at breaks and lunchtimes. As playground experiences offer opportunities for enhancing social skills, the trend towards decreasing lunch and break time and the abolition of the afternoon break is surprising (Blatchford and Sumpner 1998). This is not confined to schools in England but has been reported in Australia (Evans 1989) and the USA (Pellegrini 1995). Some school districts, for instance, in Atlanta, New York and Chicago, have built schools without playgrounds (Johnson 1998). The main reasons cited by teachers for reducing break times are the need for increased teaching time, and the perceived behavioural problems of pupils.

Children spend up to a quarter of their school day in the playground. Making good use of play times can help tackle the inactivity, boredom and poor behaviour that can intimidate children and affect lessons and impact significantly on school life. In England, in addition to the work of BESTs, improving behaviour in the playground has been linked with other initia-tives concerned with engagement in sporting activities. For instance, since 2000, as part of Physical Education and School Sport (PESS) QCA has been working with schools to improve the quality of PESS and explore the contribution it might make. While the main focus has been to increase the percentage of 5–16-year-olds who spend a minimum of two hours each week engaged in sport, one element has been to use breaks and lunchtimes to provide skill and health enhancing activities. The involvement of pupils in purposeful lunchtime activities has had a positive impact on behaviour and afternoon lessons are perceived as being more productive with less disruption (QCA 2006).

The following sections outline useful strategies for improving and maintaining behaviour in the playground. It is important that children are involved in consultation about new systems or new playground designs.

The development of effective reward systems and strategies

Effective reward systems are as important outside the classroom as inside. Pupils need to see that good behaviour is rewarded. Strategies and rewards need to be applied consistently by all school staff (Steer Report 2006). As part of the Primary Behaviour and Attendance Pilot, one primary school initiated a Humpty Wall:

> The infants have the Humpty Wall. Children have to be good through lunchtime and if they are seen being good they will get a little slip, which is stuck on the Humpty Wall. They also have the top table at lunchtime where a chosen group of children sit at a table, which is covered with a tablecloth, and they have plastic wine goblets and there is a vase of flowers on the table. The dinner hall is so much calmer. They can actually speak to each other.
>
> *(Infant lunchtime supervisor)*

Buddying systems

Break times can be particularly problematic for rejected children who are unable to join playground games or who are disliked by their friends (Evans 1989). Relevant then are interventions which provide additional support for children who might otherwise have no one to play with. In one primary school in the Primary Behaviour and Attendance Pilot, a system of buddying was put in place whereby a buddy stop was created in the playground. Usually, this was manned by two Year 6 children: *'If anyone feels unhappy or they have not got a friend they can go to the buddy stop and they can either talk to the Year 6s or the Year 6s will find them someone to play with'* (*Infant lunchtime supervisor*).

Zoning the playground

The Steer Report (2006) suggested that all schools should zone play areas separating quiet and boisterous activities. New playground markings and the development of different play zones can encourage more active play during break and lunchtimes in primary schools (Ofsted 2005). In the USA, the Peaceful Playground Program aims to introduce children and staff to the many types of activity that can take place in playgrounds and field areas. Important here is the redesign of the playground space so that effective areas are created for different games. Within the UK, much work has been undertaken on redesigning school playgrounds. In 2000, the DfES funded 13 pilot projects to transform uninspiring urban primary school playgrounds. Schools used the Zoneparc model developed in partnership with the Youth Sport Trust and Nike. Since then a further 600 primary schools have become involved with the project and in 2006, an additional £2 million from the Department for Culture, Media and Sport was put forward to benefit more schools. The programme forms part of the national Physical Education, School Sport and Club Links (PESSCL) strategy. The key features of Zoneparc include:

- zoning the playground into three coloured activity areas;
- introducing and managing innovative play equipment;
- training pupils and lunchtime supervisors to guide activities; and
- providing activity resources.

Giving children responsibilities

In the BIP, in one school, the BEST interviewed, selected, and trained Year 6 pupils to be the Playground Squad. Pupils attended a club to learn how to de-escalate situations in the playground. Squad members reported enjoying helping other children and promoting a positive social environment. As part of the Primary Behaviour and Attendance Pilot children were also given particular responsibilities:

> The children have been given clear guidelines at playtime. They have been given responsibilities such as toilet duty, litter duty, giving them a chance to contribute to their playground environment. They feel that they are responsible and are listened to by the adults. Their views are just as important.
>
> (*Lunchtime supervisor*)

Primary schools following the Zoneparc model are also encouraged to give pupils playground responsibilities. Children are drawn from Years 5 and 6 and act as play leaders. They wear distinctive clothing so that they can be easily identified. Responsibilities include organizing the loan and return of equipment, supporting other children in taking part in different activities regardless of their ability, and working with lunchtime supervisors to keep the activities working and enjoyable. Research undertaken by the Institute of Youth Sport suggests that these responsibilities improve citizenship and leadership skills.

Training for playground supervisors

The importance of effective supervision of playtime has been acknowledged and it is now accepted that training and support are needed. Problematic are the demands and complexity of the role and the pervasive problem of lack of status (Sharp 1994; PlayLink 1999). In Scotland, following the recommendations of the McCrone Report (Scottish Executive 2001) teachers were discharged from non-teaching-based break time duties. Subsequently, LAs were recommended to include play-related training in the staff development of classroom assistants and playground supervisors. The training included raising awareness of the importance of play, the value of risk, and best practice for adults in facilitating play, in addition to addressing safety issues (McKendrick 2005).

The key elements for developing good practice include:

- appropriate training for lunchtime supervisors;
- involvement of the school council and staff;
- building on pupils' experiences of the games that they know and/or play;
- remarking and zoning of the playground to support the games to be played;
- adoption of a system for recording playground incidents that involves pupils, lunchtime supervisors, teachers and the Senior Management Team (SMT);
- systems for rewarding positive behaviour so that good behaviour is seen to be valued;
- consistency of approach in the way behaviour is dealt with in the playground and the classroom; and
- a whole-school approach.

Box 4.2 provides an extended case study illustrating aspects of good practice in seeking to improve and maintain playground behaviour.

Box 4.2   Changing playground behaviour

Extended case study: whole-school change arising from a different approach to playground behaviour

Prior to the intervention the current Headteacher had observed that pupils' behaviour was poor in the playground and throughout the building. This had a negative impact on behaviour in the classroom and learning as pupils were going into the classroom angry and aggressive over incidents in the playground. Two senior lunchtime supervisors were appointed and received training so that they were sufficiently skilled to deal with problems. Some existing supervisors lacked the assertiveness to deal with difficult behaviour in the playground. The Head worked with the school council and teachers to consider how they might improve behaviour. The BIP Primary Consultant introduced a project to develop playground games. Initially, how the pupils used the playground, what they did in different parts of it and what games they knew and/or played was established. Information was also received from the school council and the lunchtime supervisors. Time was spent teaching some of the children games and also learning games from them that could be taught to others. INSET was provided for lunchtime supervisors on how to play some of the games and also to provide an opportunity for them to develop their ideas. The schools purchased equipment to support the initiative and some lunchtime supervisors made equipment including board games that could be played outside in the summer months.

The markings on the playground were redone to support the children's games and help them play cooperatively in small groups. This was achieved through the BIP Primary Consultant working with the site manager. This had an impact on behaviour.

The Head also introduced a system of recording incidents where pupils behaved badly. The lunchtime supervisor dealt with the incident but recorded the details on a slip which was logged both by the SMT and the class teacher. If pupils were persistently given slips the parents were informed and called into school. This was a real deterrent to poor behaviour.

At the same time, a raffle system was introduced to support positive behaviour. If children implemented the playground rules and were seen to be doing so the lunchtime supervisors awarded them a raffle ticket. These were placed into a classroom draw, which took place each Friday. The raffle tickets allocated at lunchtime were a different colour to those allocated for good behaviour within the classroom. The teachers valued this, as good playtime behaviour supported concentrated afternoon learning as the children began afternoon school calm, happy and focused:

> In terms of BIP, good behaviour is now part of the whole school. Children want to behave well, because they see that good behaviour is valued, rather than bad behaviour getting them noticed, which was the case in the past. This positive aspect of improving behaviour has been the most important.

> The staff are much happier. The playground activities have impacted on their teaching, since they are not spending the afternoon sorting out the problems that occurred in the playground. Now that the lunchtime supervisors deal with the problems effectively, it has taken a load away from the teachers, which has impacted on the quality of teaching and also on the morale of the teachers. The teachers were being ground down with numerous incidents. Some of the incidents they didn't know how to deal with since the pupils were bringing in lunchtime incidents and the teacher had not been there. That the supervisors have taken control of the lunchtime has relieved a lot of pressure from the teaching staff. There is real consistency in following positive behaviour within the classroom and the playground. This is fundamental to the success of the initiative.
>
> (*Headteacher*)

Safer School Partnerships and police in schools

The Safer School Partnership (SSP) in England had its origins in the USA. The COPS in Schools (CIS) grant programme in the USA was designed to help law enforcement agencies to hire additional school resource officers to engage in community policing in and around primary schools. Emphasis was placed on developing collaborative partnerships with the school community. The National School Safety Centre, funded since 1984 as a resource and training centre, provided training for the COPS in Schools programme. In England, the Safer School Partnerships was piloted by Thames Valley Police in Banbury using restorative principles and by the Metropolitan Police in Southwark, supported by the Roehampton Institute, before being adopted by the DfES in 2002 as a response to the Street Crime Initiative. Prior to this initiative there had been little involvement of police in schools (Bowles et al. 2005).

The main aims of SSP are to:

- reduce victimization, criminality and antisocial behaviour within the school and its community;
- work with schools on 'whole-school' approaches to behaviour and discipline;
- identify and work with children and young people at risk of becoming victims or offenders;
- ensure the full-time education of young offenders;

- support vulnerable children and young people through periods of transition, such as the move from primary to secondary school; and
- create a safer environment for children to learn in (Bowles et al. 2005).

The different SSP projects adopt various forms depending on funding, the views of the school, and the local policing policy strategy in respect of schools. The common underlying theme though is of building closer relationships between police and schools. Current models include:

- a fully operational police officer based full-time in a school, working closely with a member of the school's senior management team, project worker and administrator;
- police officers seconded to BESTs and working with this multi-agency partnership in a secondary school and its feeder primary schools;
- police officers, both full-time and part-time, providing reactive support to a cluster of schools in a SSP-style of policing; and
- police officers or police community support officers (PCSOs) based with the neighbourhood policing team, working part-time in a problem solving and educational role (DfES 2006).

Over half of BIP Phase 1 LAs implemented strategies which involved police working in schools. In many schools there was initial reluctance to have a police officer on site. In some cases there had been bad publicity relating to the scheme and in other cases a lack of appropriate planning. In some schools there were concerns that the initiative might criminalize pupils' behaviour. These difficulties were transitory. As the programme developed there was evidence that the initiative was overwhelmingly successful. The police were described as 'highly regarded' and 'flexible in approach and attitudes'. Schools were reported as being positive 'despite early anxiety'. However, some LAs experienced difficulties with recruiting police officers to work in schools.

There was wide variation in the way the police worked in schools including:

- Police who, during the course of their beat, were required to call into schools on that beat and report back to their inspector. Their role was largely seen as a 'policing' one.
- Police who were in school on a regular basis, whom pupils recognized and who recognized pupils if they were out of school, thus deterring truancy. These officers were often involved in citizenship lessons.

- Police who had a physical base in a school and whose roles included being available to offer advice or support on a 'drop-in' basis for staff and students, working with the BEST, attending BEST meetings and training, and attending reintegration meetings. They also undertook 'policing' activities.
- Police who worked as active members of the BEST team with specific groups of pupils, for instance, on anger management, or with colleagues, for instance, Child and Adolescent Mental Health Service (CAMHS) workers developing emotional literacy in pupils or working on a whole-class basis in primary schools with an Education Welfare Officer and a learning mentor (Hallam et al. 2005).

There was also variation in the role of the police officers in BESTs. In one LA, the police officer was involved in a wide range of negotiations, home visits and other activities. The BIP manager was keen to break down barriers between police and community, and between police and other professionals, in preparation for *Every Child Matters*. Her vision was to shift perceptions among other professionals towards a position where police would be perceived as equal. One police officer worked in each BEST, and his or her 'beat' consisted of the group of schools served by the BEST. The BEST was in some cases led by a police officer. Where this was not the case the police officer was line managed by the BEST leader. This strategy for connecting to the police force was regarded as a major strength, and was groundbreaking in the LA. Overall the contribution made by the police was welcomed. Over time they were able to overcome the negative attitudes of pupils. For instance, in one school the minibus and some computers were stolen. The following day a group of pupils informed the police officer about the whereabouts of the minibus which was then recovered. This represented a major change in pupil behaviour.

The police also implemented restorative justice procedures in schools. While this originated within the criminal justice system such programmes are now employed in many countries, for instance, Australia, the USA, New Zealand and Europe in a variety of settings, although to a limited extent. Programmes operating in schools have been developed, particularly to deal with incidents of bullying (Strang 2001). In Australia, restorative justice in the school setting began in 1994 in southern Queensland. A series of trials were set up where one person in each school was trained in restorative techniques for dealing with disputes and conflict including assaults, property offences, truancy and drug offences, as well as bullying and harassment (Strang 2001).

In the school context, the aim of restorative justice is to enable pupils to acknowledge and apologize for the damage or harm their actions have caused and to help the victims of those actions come to terms with their experience. As part of the process conferences are held in which pupils and 'victims' meet together to discuss what happened. These conferences are time-consuming and require trained staff to run them (Bowles et al. 2005). In England and Wales, Youth Offending Teams were given the responsibility for implementing restorative justice practices in schools. In approximately one-third of the areas police officers were involved in running conferences (Bitel 2004). Early evaluation indicated that the process was successful in that many schools reported:

- a reduction in pupils that reported missing school due to bullying;
- an increased perception that the school was safe;
- a reduction in levels of bullying;
- a reduction in persistent levels of victimization, such as hitting and kicking, verbal threats and spreading rumours;
- dramatic increases in the perception that the school was doing a good job in preventing bullying;
- a reduction in the perception that bullying was a serious problem in the school; and
- a reduction in the perception that telling a member of staff about bullying was 'grassing' (Bitel 2004).

Within BIP police in schools made use of restorative justice techniques. In one secondary school, a girl had been excluded for 10 days for bullying and subsequently went through a restorative justice process with the police officer. Following this the victims felt safer, and the girl and her parents had had the opportunity to confront and explore some of the issues. Without the BIP the Deputy Head felt that it was most likely that she would have been excluded. Box 4.3 provides a further example.

Box 4.3   Dealing with bullying

Case study: restorative justice intervention involving police in schools and BEST

Joanne, a Year 9 pupil reported that she was being bullied and as a result started truanting:

The BEST Educational Social Worker (ESW) got in touch with my mother to find out why I wasn't attending school and she explained what was happening. At the time it was very stressful for my mother who commented, 'Normally my daughter is very bubbly and to watch her turn into this depressed child who didn't go out and just stayed at home was very difficult.'

The involvement of the BEST led to a process of restorative justice being put in place. Joanne received counseling support, had help from the police officer and support from the Pastoral Manager in school:

I talked to some of the bullies yesterday with the police officer and Pastoral Manager. It went better than I thought it would. On Monday I'm starting back fresh at school. I've got a logbook and I'm going to write down any problems that I have in lessons and when they occur. I'll be able to take this to the police officer, or Base 25 or the Pastoral Manager. I'm nervous about coming back to school because of everything that has happened. If I hadn't had that help I would have stopped coming to school. Now I know that the help is there all the time. I can speak to the police officer any time or even ring her at the station outside school hours. I just want to get my head down now since I've got SATs next term. I want to get good qualifications.

Despite the many positive outcomes of the Police in Schools initiative there were some difficulties. For instance, in one cluster a policeman resigned as he felt isolated, had no base in school, and experienced resistance from the headteacher. He felt that he had failed, although staff in the school indicated that he was beginning to have an impact. There were also tensions in some schools about the line management of the police officer. In some schools, headteachers wanted control (Hallam et al. 2005).

In some LAs in Phase 2 of BIP, the Police in Schools initiative was not directly linked to the BIP. In one LA the extended schools project strengthened links with the police, and a new pilot scheme Bullied Partnership was developed which focused on rehabilitation processes and encouraged communication between police and other agencies, for instance, reported anti-social behaviour might result in drug abuse specialists being involved.

The SSP makes a positive contribution to schools and their communities in particular through:

- speedier responses to behaviour problems;
- more activities for pupils;
- increased engagement with the local community;
- improved attitudes and social climate in schools with a greater emphasis on mutual respect and inclusion; and
- greater familiarity with the police for parents, pupils and staff facilitating the establishment of trust in the police (Bowles et al. 2005; Hallam et al. 2005).

The programme also integrates with the wider preventative agenda including the Children Act (2004), *Every Child Matters* (DFES 2003a), the Respect Action Plan (Home Office 2006), and Neighbourhood Policing and Extended Schools.

Endnote

Although the initiatives described in this chapter are quite different in their approach, there is an underlying commonality in their importance in relation to the *Every Child Matters* agenda. All of the initiatives adopt a multi-agency approach that involves the wider school community. For the future, it will be important that LAs put in place opportunities to extend the work of FSES building on the introduction and development of Primary Care Trusts and Children's Trusts.

Chapter summary

Multi-agency working is key to improving behaviour in and around school.

In seeking to improve and maintain behaviour in and around schools those involved need to:

- make sufficient time for effective collaboration across all agencies, teachers and support staff involved in interventions – this includes clarifying roles and responsibilities, setting up systems for communication;
- recognize that pupil experiences outside the classroom have an impact on teaching and learning and behaviour inside the classroom;
- involve pupils in improving all aspects of behaviour in and around the school;
- encourage an integrated approach to the school behaviour policy;
- ensure that pupils have a clear awareness of understanding consequences and celebration in relation to their behaviour in and around school;
- provide opportunities for support staff to increase their understanding of emotional and behavioural difficulties;
- provide effective training and support for all school staff, including lunchtime supervisors;
- share good practice with colleagues in school and across clusters of schools; and
- encourage community involvement.

Further reading

Blatchford, P. and Sharp, S. (eds) (1994) *Break Time and the School: Understanding and Changing Playground Behaviour*. London: Routledge.

Department for Education and Skills (DfES) (2006) *Mainstreaming Safer School Partnerships*. Produced by the Department for Education and Skills, supported by the Home Office, Association of Chief Police Officers (ACPO) and Youth Justice Board (YJB). London: The Stationery Office.

Wilkin, A., White, R. and Kinder, K. (2003) *Towards Extended Schools: A Literature Review. Research Report 432*. London: DfES.

References

Bitel, M. (2004) *National Evaluation of the Restorative Justice in School Programme* (Summary). London: Youth Justice Board for England and Wales.

Blatchford, P. and Sharp, S. (eds) (1994) *Break Time and the School: Understanding and Changing Playground Behaviour*. London: Routledge.

Blatchford, P. and Sumpner, C. (1998) What do we know about break time? Results from a national survey of break time and lunchtime in primary and secondary schools. *British Educational Research Journal*, 24(1): 79–94.

Bowles, R., Reyes, M.G. and Pradiptyo, R. (2005) *Monitoring and Evaluating the Safer School Partnerships Programme*. London: Youth Justice Board for England and Wales.

Coltoff, P., Kaplan, M., Warren, C. and Stack, K. (1997) *Building a Community School*. New York: Children's Aid Society.

Cummings, C., Dyson, A., Papps, I., Pearson, D., Raff, C. and Todd, L. (2005) *Evaluation of the Full Service Extended Schools Project: First Year Report. Research Report 680*. London: DfES.

Cummings, C., Dyson, A., Papps, I., Pearson, D., Raff, C. and Todd, L. (2006) *Evaluation of the Full Service Extended Schools Initiative, Second Year: Thematic Papers. Research Report 795*. London: DfES.

Department for Education and Skills (DfES) (2003a) *Every Child Matters*. London: The Stationery Office.

Department for Education and Skills (DfES) (2003b) *Full Service Extended Schools: Requirements and Specifications*. London: DfES.

Department for Education and Skills (DfES) (2004) *Every Child Matters: Next Steps*. London: The Stationery Office.

Department for Education and Skills (DfES) (2005) *Extended Schools: Access to Opportunities and Services for All*. London: DfES.

Department for Education and Skills (DfES) (2006) *Mainstreaming Safer School Partnerships*. Produced by the Department for Education and Skills, supported by the Home Office, Association of Chief Police Officers (ACPO) and Youth Justice Board (YJB). London: The Stationery Office.

Dryfoos, J. (1993) Full-Service Schools: what are they and how to get to be one? *NASSP Bulletin*, 77(557): 29–35.

Dryfoos, J. (1994) *Full-Service Schools: A Revolution in Health and Social Services for Children, Youth and Families*. San Francisco, CA: Jossey-Bass.

Dryfoos, J. (2000) *Evaluation of Community Schools: Findings to Date*. Washington, DC: Coalition for Community Schools.

Elton Report (1989) Committee of Enquiry into Discipline in Schools *Discipline in Schools*. Department of Education and Science. Great Britain: HMSO.

Evans, J. (1989) *Children at Play: Life in the School Playground*. Melbourne: Deaken University Press.

Evans, J. (1996) Children's Attitudes to Recess and the Changes Taking Place in Australian Primary Schools. *Research in Education*, 56: 49–63, Manchester University Press, London.

Hallam, S., Castle, F. and Rogers, L. with Creech, A., Rhamie, J. and Kokotsaki, D. (2005) *Research and Evaluation of the Behaviour Improvement Programme. Research Report 702*. London: DfES.

Hallam, S., Shaw, J. and Rhamie, J. (2006) *Evaluation of the Primary Behaviour and Attendance Pilot. Research Report 717*. London: DfES.

Home Office (2006) *Respect Action Plan*. London: The Stationery Office.

Illsely, P. and Redford, M. (2005) 'Drop in for coffee': Working with parents in North Perth New Community Schools. *Support for Learning*, 20(4): 162–6.

Johnson, D. (1998) Many schools putting an end to child's play. *New York Times*, April.

McKendrick, J.H. (2005) *School Grounds in Scotland: Research Report*. Edinburgh: Scottish Poverty Information Unit.

Ofsted (2005) *The Annual Report of Her Majesty's Chief Inspector of Schools 2004/05*. London: The Stationery Office.

Pellegrini, A. (1995) *School Recess and Playground Behavior*. Albany, NY: State University of New York Press.

Pellegrini, A. and Blatchford, P. (2002) Time for a break: The developmental and educational significance of break time in school. *The Psychologist*, 15(2): 60–2.

PlayLink (1999) *Play at School*. London: PlayLink.

QCA (2006) *PE and Sport: Changing Schools for the Better*. London: The Stationery Office.

Sammons, P., Power, S., Elliot, K., Robertson, P., Campbell, C. and Whitty, G. (2003) *Evaluation of New Community Schools Programme*. Edinburgh: Scottish Executive Education Department.

Scottish Executive (2001) *A Teaching Profession for the 21st Century: Agreement Reached Following Recommendations Made in the McCrone Report*. Edinburgh: Scottish Executive.

Scottish Office (1998) *New Community Schools Prospectus*. Edinburgh: HMSO.

Sharp, S. (1994) Training schemes for lunchtime supervisors in the United Kingdom: An overview, in P. Blatchford and S. Sharp (eds) *Breaktime and the School: Understanding and Changing Playground Behaviour*. London: Routledge.

Steer Report (2006) *Learning Behaviour: The Report of the Practitioners' Group on School Behaviour and Discipline*. London: DfES.

Strang, H. (2001) *Restorative Justice Programs in Australia*. Report to the Criminology Research Council. Canberra: Australian Institute of Criminology.

Tett, L. (2000) Working in partnership? Limits and possibilities for youth workers and school teachers. *Youth and Policy*, 68: 58–71.

Wilkin, A., White, R. and Kinder, K. (2003) *Towards Extended Schools: A Literature Review. Research Report 432*. London: DfES.

5   Home–school relationships

In recent years there has been a greater emphasis on developing closer links between the home and the school. This chapter explores which elements of parental involvement in their child's education are important in influencing attainment and behaviour and how these can be promoted. It also considers the way that home–school links workers and learning mentors have been used to provide additional support to those children and their families experiencing particular difficulties with behaviour and attendance at school.

Introduction

Parents across the globe regardless of their economic, social or cultural position share the desire that their children will excel in school and acquire academic credentials. Particularly in the developing countries, parents perceive schooling as a means for their children to acquire knowledge and skills to better their socio-economic status (Hiatt-Michael 2005). Diversity in parental engagement in education between countries reflects cultural beliefs, the social structure of families, economic influences and political pressures, the major influence on parental educational involvement being the power relationship between parents and official schooling. Some situations are fully family controlled (e.g. home schooling), others school controlled.

In recent years in the developed world there has been an increased recognition of the importance of parents in supporting their children's education. For instance, in the UK, in *Excellence in Schools* (DfEE 1997) the government encouraged parents to meet teachers, establish relationships with schools, keep informed about their child's progress, discuss problems, help out at school, and become school governors. However, there is evidence that these may not be the most effective ways in which parents can maximize their children's educational success.

How and why parents support their child's education

Parental involvement has been defined in a number of different ways. In the USA, Singh and colleagues (1995) identified four components: parental aspirations; parent–child communication about school; home structure (degree of insistence on homework completion); and parental participation in school-related activities. Of these parental aspirations had the most powerful influence on achievement. Parental involvement in the form of parent–child discussion had a moderate effect, involvement in school activities no effect, while home structure had a small negative association. Home discussion has been found to be the most important element in parental involvement in relation to children's attainment (Sui-Chu and Willms 1996), behaviour, attendance and dropout (McNeal 2001). Interest in the child and positive conversational interactions have a positive effect on children's behaviour and achievement even when the influence of background factors, such as social class or family size, have been factored out (e.g. Sui-Chu and Willms 1996; Sacker et al. 2002).

In young children, Melhuish and colleagues (2001) concluded that a high quality home learning environment was associated with greater conformity and cooperation, peer sociability and confidence, lower antisocial and worried or upset behaviour, and greater cognitive development. The home learning environment was a more important influence than socio-economic status (SES). Where parents and professional educators share the same aims the child's progress is further enhanced (Siraj-Blatchford et al. 2002). The types of activities that contribute to a positive home learning environment for pre-schoolers include reading, library visits, playing with letters, numbers and shapes, painting and drawing, parental teaching of letters and nursery rhymes, and singing (Sylva et al. 1999).

Although the effects of parental involvement diminish as the child gets older, high levels of parental expectation, consistent encouragement, and actions to enhance learning opportunities in the home are all positively associated with adolescent students' high aspirations and college enrolment regardless of socio-economic status or ethnic background (Sacker et al. 2002). Parental values and aspirations are exhibited continuously through parental enthusiasms and positive parenting styles and internalized by pupils impacting on learning, motivation, self-esteem and personal educational aspirations (Lynch 2002). Overall, parental involvement in the form of 'at-home good parenting' has a significant positive effect on children's achievement and adjustment even when a wide range of other factors are taken into account (Desforges and Abouchaar 2003).

Working-class parents face a number of barriers in exchanges with teachers and other school staff (e.g. Vincent 2001). They have less social capital than middle-class parents and may place less value on education. As schools accept involvement on their own middle-class terms this places working-class parents at a disadvantage. Parents' evenings tend to create frustration and confusion and, in some cases, mutual fear between parents and teachers. Many parents perceive teachers as superior and distant, perceptions which are reinforced by teachers' ways of behaving, teachers engaging with parents only on their own terms (Power and Clark 2000).

The way that parents perceive their role in their child's education is also important (Hoover-Dempsey et al. 2001). Most parents believe that they have equal responsibility with the school for their child's education but a very small minority believe that the responsibility lies wholly with the school (Williams et al. 2002). Parents tend to regard the extent of their involvement in relation to their own limitations, particularly the time that they have available. Lone parents feel particularly disadvantaged in this respect (Anning 2000). Parental education level, maternal depression, and single parent status also impact on general parental involvement in education (Kohl et al. 2000), other contributory factors being problems with drugs, alcohol, overcrowding and debt (Britt 1998).

The level of parental involvement declines with the child's age (Izzo et al. 1999). Parents typically feel more involved with their child's education and more able to help with homework in primary than secondary schools (Williams et al. 2002). The nature of parental involvement behaviours also changes. For younger children direct help with school-relevant skills is useful, while for older students activities which promote independence and autonomy are more important. Confidence in helping is higher for parents of younger children, men, those of higher socio-economic status, and those in full-time education aged 21 or older. Lack of confidence relates to lack of understanding, changes in teaching methods, and lack of knowledge of particular subjects (Moons and Ivins 2004).

Cultural differences in parental involvement

Comparative studies conducted in Hong Kong, South Korea, Taiwan and Singapore have shown that Asian parents invest time and resources at home to support their children's learning rather than in developing activities within the school (e.g. Lam et al. 2002), although there is a high level of cooperation between parents and teachers (Jeynes 2005). This may account for the relatively smaller impact of socio-economic status on attainment in Asian societies than in the USA (Ho 2005). Of particular importance are having high expectations and parental involvement at the pre-school level (Jeynes 2005) where children are expected to learn social skills (Stevenson and Stigler 1992), the emphasis being on moral rather than cognitive development (Wray 1999).

In virtually every East Asian nation parental involvement is valued, with teacher–parent partnerships seen as crucial to effective education (Benjamin 1997). In several Asian nations the teacher visits the homes of students before the school year begins, the purpose being to form a partnership and support parental involvement in the child's schooling. Asian educators view parents as team players rather than as adversaries (Stevenson and Stigler 1992), the home being viewed as a second school. Asian parents not only provide an effective learning environment at home but also supplement the material that schools teach by sending pupils to after school learning institutes (Okamura-Bichard 1985). These provide a means for parents to continue to help when children progress to the higher grades. Parental involvement has an impact regardless of ethnicity, although ethnic minority parents may express their support and involvement with their children's education in different ways the impact being mediated by parenting style (Zellman and Waterman 1998).

The role of children in mediating parental involvement

Children can play active or passive roles in mediating home–school relations. Most examples of children encouraging parental involvement are in the home, and relate to enjoying their parents' company. Children are generally reluctant to encourage their parents into school. Children adopting a passive stance feel that responsibility lies largely with their parents to get involved according to their tastes or resources. Some children, particularly boys and children of lower socio-economic status, actively discourage or obstruct involvement, particularly as they get older and increasingly view themselves as autonomous with a right to privacy (Deslandes and Cloutier 2002).

Enhancing parental involvement in practice: international perspectives

Internationally, there have been many attempts to increase parental involvement in education. The OECD suggests that the degree of parental participation can be enhanced through:

- statutory advisory and decision-making bodies;
- evaluation of schools;
- voluntary associations;
- voluntary involvement in after-school activities;
- voluntary involvement in classroom activities; and
- improved communications with school.

Despite increased activity in recent years, schools seem to have relatively little influence on the extent of parental involvement in their child's education or the learning climate in the home (Sui-Chu and Willms 1996). In part, this may be because communication between parents and schools is frequently school directed with little genuine interaction. Teachers need training in working with parents, particularly in developing positive attitudes towards low socio-economic status parents and those from minority ethnic groups (Bridgemohan et al. 2005).

In the USA, parental involvement programmes have featured in federal, state and local education policies (Epstein 1991). Parent involvement was one of the targeted areas in the No Child Left Behind Act of 2001. However, there is relatively little evidence that most programmes have improved student achievement, changed parents' behaviour, or that of pupils or teachers (Mattingly et al. 2002). Where effective, collaboration between parents and school:

- is active rather than reactive;
- engages all parents;
- is sensitive to the wide-ranging circumstances of all students and families;
- recognizes and values the contribution that parents have to make to the educational process;
- engenders parental empowerment; and
- gives all parents a voice that must be heard.

To achieve these ends takes time and requires planning and ongoing evaluation (Raffaele and Knoff 1999).

The largest parental involvement programme in the USA, the National Network of Partnership Schools (Sanders and Epstein 2000), comprises more than 1000 schools across 14 states. It provides training and technical support, a website, newsletters and a handbook based on extensive research and development over many years. An evaluation of the impact of engaging parents on indiscipline showed that schools that improved the quality of partnership activity from one year to the next reported lower levels of students involved in disciplinary action (Sheldon and Epstein 2001). Similar effects were found for attendance (Epstein and Sheldon 2000). Three partnership activities seemed to be particularly effective in increasing daily attendance rates and reducing chronic absenteeism: rewarding attendance, providing parents with a contact person at school to call as needed and communicating school expectations to all parents.

Enhancing parental involvement in practice: the UK perspective

The UK government has promoted parental involvement through the enhancement of parent governor roles, involvement in inspection processes, the provision of annual reports and prospectuses, the requirement for home/school agreements, and provision for increasing information about the curriculum, school performance and a range of other matters. While there is much activity in schools little is directed at where it would have the most impact, enhancing the home learning environment (Desforges and Abouchaar 2003).

Ofsted (2002), reporting on the achievement of Black Caribbean pupils, concluded that relatively successful schools had close links with parents based on shared values and expectations of behaviour, attitudes and habits of work. Schools listened to parents' concerns, were open with them, and worked with them on resolving differences. Parents' understanding of their children's progress was founded on rigorous discussion, honest reporting, and swift contact when information needed to be shared. Ofsted (1999a, 1999b, 2000a, 2001a, 2001b, 2001c) have identified a range of elements that contribute to good practice in the pursuit of parental involvement:

- a commitment of time and resources;
- posts of special responsibility dedicated to parental involvement;
- programmes of meetings to explain the curriculum and school practices, and to consider the progress of individual pupils and celebrate their success;
- the provision of courses for parents on curriculum-relevant topics;
- the provision of transport to school to meet parents' needs;
- constructive listening;
- a commitment to raising educational standards;
- effective and frequent communication;
- consultations which are flexible, relevant and planned to maximize response rates or attendance;
- the provision of community rooms and facilities;
- the provision of opportunities for school-based adult learning;
- support for parents wanting to re-enter education;
- induction programmes;
- parent evenings focusing on literacy, ICT and numeracy;
- parenting programmes; and
- invited guest speakers for parents.

A number of UK projects have had some success in engaging parents in their child's education with a subsequent impact on a range of outcomes including school ethos, raised aspirations, bullying and improved attainment (e.g. Bastiani 1999). Some programmes have focused on particular areas, for instance, literacy and maths (e.g. Hannon and Nutbrown 2001); Special Educational Needs (e.g. Vernon 1999) and raising parental aspirations (Hardie and Alcorn 2000).

Projects where parents and children work together

There have been a number of programmes in adult and community education which have attempted to bring different family members together to work on a common theme. Most widely known are the literacy and numeracy schemes set up by the Adult Literacy and Basic Skills Unit (ALBSU) which comprised accredited basic skills instruction for parents, early literacy development for young children, and joint parent/child sessions on supporting pre-reading, early reading and reading skills. Completion of the programme was associated with statistically significant advances in achievement in reading and writing for parents and children and these were sustained nine months later. The percentage of children with very low levels of achievement fell and parents gained in confidence and competence in helping their child (Brooks et al. 1996). These gains were sustained two years later. The children involved in the project were rated by teachers as superior to their peers in classroom behaviour and the support received from their families, and equal to their peers in other academic and motivational respects (Brooks et al. 1997). Initial literacy schemes for ethnic minority families also indicated positive outcomes (Brooks et al. 1999).

Similarly, Family Learning programmes, targeted at areas of economic deprivation, promoted greater understanding of child development and children's learning in parents; improved skills in literacy, numeracy, and parenting and confidence in school contacts; and enhanced progression to Further Education, further training or a better job. Children demonstrated accelerated development in early oracy and literacy, positive attitudes and behaviour, and increased confidence. However, Ofsted (2000b) reported that the teaching was better when parents and children were taught separately.

Parent councils

A recent UK government proposal has initiated the setting up of parent councils. These have developed differently in particular contexts and variously involved:

- holding whole-class parents' meetings;

- regular meetings between parent representatives and the class teacher;
- enhanced communication (telephone tree, online discussion group, newsletters, text messaging, email, telephone calls);
- establishment of parent forums (e.g. African Caribbean boys, Special Educational Needs);
- social events for parents and staff;
- use of translators;
- outreach work (home visits, community centres);
- provision of a community room;
- formation of a parents' council; and
- workshops for parents (helping with homework, parenting, literacy, numeracy, English language classes, drugs, bullying).

Across all of the participating schools the Setting up Councils project demonstrated:

- an improvement in the information sent to parents;
- an increase in the number and range of opportunities for parents to communicate with schools;
- development and improvement of the areas for parents on school websites;
- an increase in the number of consultative meetings held involving parents; and
- an increase in the range of parents involved in school life.

For success the commitment of the headteacher was crucial, as was the involvement of staff, team working, clarity of roles and responsibilities, allowing time for ideas to develop and be implemented, early success to gain commitment, and support for parents (Carnie 2006).

In general, successful meetings of parents require that:

- groups and meetings are inclusive and that all parents have the opportunity to be involved;
- parent groups feed back to the governing body (parent governors are an important link);
- meetings are held at parent-friendly times to meet the needs of different groups (this may mean varying the time of meetings);
- different cultural needs and language requirements are taken into account;
- there is an opportunity for some meetings to be held in small groups with a relaxed environment; and
- parents have the opportunity to meet on their own without staff if they wish.

Barriers to involvement include too frequent meetings, long agendas, and no time for discussion.

Home-school agreements

In 1999, Home-School Agreements (HSAs) were statutorily introduced in the UK. By 2003, most schools had introduced them and most parents had signed them. Reasons given for not signing included antipathy towards HSAs, fear, apathy and difficulties with literacy and English. The majority of schools thought that their introduction had had a positive impact on the communication of school expectations and responsibilities, and some thought that there had been a positive impact on parent–teacher liaison, parents supporting learning at home, pupil behaviour and homework. Pupil involvement in signing the HSA was associated with a more positive impact. However, some schools saw no benefits to the agreements and perceived them as a burden (Coldwell et al. 2003).

Learning mentors

The evaluation of the Behaviour Improvement Programme (BIP) (Hallam et al. 2005) indicated a key role for learning mentors which included some liaison between home and school, particularly in primary schools in relation to attendance and poor behaviour. The learning mentors made home visits and some set up groups for parents, for instance, in one school a breakfast club was established to support children whose parents worked early in the morning. The learning mentors were able to relate to parents and pupils, provide an avenue for parents to approach the school more informally than was previously possible, provide pupils with someone to talk to at playtime or lunchtime, liaise with lunchtime assistants, identify possible playground incidents, and challenge and support the school in relation to behaviour issues.

Initiatives under the auspices of the Behaviour and Education Support Teams

In addition to the parenting programmes reported in Chapter 6, the Behaviour and Education Support Teams (BESTs) worked more generally with parents. In one secondary school parent events called Time 4u and those focusing on bullying were made possible because BEST arranged a 'crèche' for children. The sessions were designed to be non-threatening, with the provision of coffee, the opportunity for informal introductions, and the establishment of simple rules such as no use of mobile phones, no swearing and a commitment to confidentiality. Some Year 10 boys contributed to the parents' sessions giving their perspective on being teenagers and advice on how parents might deal with their teenage children. Planned were asking existing parents to help with an induction for new Year 6 parents and for sessions to become more parent-led.

In one primary school Child and Adolescent Mental Health Services (CAMHS) workers from the BEST established a weekly clinic for parents when they could meet with the CAMHS workers individually and were able to access information and services which would previously not have been easily accessible. In another Local Authority (LA), the New Deal Parent Partnership Project operating in an area of extreme deprivation provided food and clothing and worked alongside BIP providing parenting courses, support for behaviour and attendance, drop-ins for parents, and encouragement for parents going back to work. Parent-partnership workers attended BIP training, and supported home visits with the learning mentors. This improved relationships with parents and their involvement with the school. The outreach workers lived in the community and so had easier contact with and access to parents.

A school principal's personal account of how to engage parents

Davis (1995), an American school principal with extensive experience of working in multicultural schools described a range of strategies which he used to actively involve parents in their children's education. Each week the school nominated two children from each class for Student of the Week or Reader of the Week, awards being presented in Friday assembly. Where parents were unable to attend the ceremony they were contacted personally by phone, if necessary at the weekend. In this way he spoke to each family at least once a year regarding an award also using the opportunity to pass on teachers' positive comments. Parental satisfaction surveys were conducted every two years. The questions were open and parents could raise whatever issues they wished. Photocopies of responses were made available to staff and parents. Complaints were followed-up by a phone call and compliments passed on to teachers. A report was compiled explaining what had been done in response to the survey, and if necessary why some things could not be changed.

In each school Davis took time to get to know the local population and the culture. He travelled to their countries, read about them, brought in experts to brief staff, learned basic phrases in each language, ate the food, travelled, and took photographs of the various countries which he hung in his office. He learned about the socio-economic status of the area served by the school, parents' levels of education, their religions, political views, plans for the future, and their expectations of the school. In dealing with parents he considered what parents needed to know and how best to communicate it. Parents were sent messages by voice mail, which was particularly useful in emergencies. Parents who offered active support to the school were mentioned in the school bulletin, and sent handwritten thank you notes. He involved himself in community events locally, helped raise funds for a variety of causes, and wrote notes to parents about any good activity or idea that their children were involved with. Students were persuaded to make pledges about attendance and homework which their parents countersigned. High standards of behaviour were expected and he personally spoke regularly to each individual student. He worked hard at creating good relationships with the local press, invited celebrities and politicians to the school, and organized community events at weekends when parents would be able to attend. He consistently maintained close links with people within the community so that he was always well informed. These efforts paid off in ensuring parental commitment and support.

Endnote

The most valuable contributions that parents can make to their children's education is through at-home learning, discussion, support, and the sharing of values and aspirations. Current initiatives aimed at engaging parents generally do not address these issues. While it is important that there is good communication between schools and parents, active participation by parents in school activities is overvalued. Supporting parents in creating more supportive and engaging learning environments at home would be more productive as would ensuring positive home–school relationships, offering support, and taking parents' concerns seriously.

Chapter summary

- The extent of parental involvement in their child's education depends on: social class; mother's level of education; material deprivation in the family; maternal psychosocial health; single parent status; the child's level of attainment; the child's feelings about parental involvement; and the ethnic culture of the family.
- The extent of involvement decreases as children get older.
- Some parents do not see involvement in their child's education as part of their role, others lack confidence about undertaking the role, some are deterred by their memories of school.

- Parental involvement can include:
  - home-based provision of a secure, intellectually stimulating, learning environment;
  - support for the development of a positive self-concept;
  - high aspirations and values;
  - contact with the school and teachers to learn about rules, procedures, the curriculum, homework and assessment;
  - visits to school to discuss progress and issues arising;
  - participation in school events;
  - working in the school; and
  - taking part in school governance and management.
- It is the at-home relationships, discussions and modelling of aspirations which play the major part in the impact on school outcomes.
- Engaging parents in education requires time, effort and commitment from schools.

Further reading

Davis, B. (1995) *How to Involve Parents in a Multicultural School*. Alexandria, VA: Association for Supervision and Curriculum Development.

Desforges, C. and Abouchaar, A. (2003) *The Impact of Parental Involvement, Parental Support and Family Education on Pupil Achievement and Adjustment: A Literature Review*. London: DfES.

References

Anning, A. (2000) *New Deals and Old Dilemmas: Lone Parents of Young Children Balancing Work and Parenthood*. Paper presented at the British Educational Research Association Annual Conference, Cardiff.

Bastiani, J. (1999) *Share: An Evaluation of the First Two Years*. Coventry: CEDC.

Benjamin, G. (1997) *Japanese Lessons*. New York: NYU Press.

Bridgemohan, R., van Wyk, N. and van Staden, C. (2005) Home–school communication in the early childhood development phase. *Education*, 126(1): 60–77.

Britt, D.W. (1998) Beyond elaborating the obvious: Context-dependent parental-involvement scenarios in a pre-school program. *Applied Behavioural Science Review*, 6(2): 179–98.

Brooks, G., Gorman, T., Harman, J., Hutchinson, D. and Wilkin, A. (1996) *Family Literacy Works*. London: Basic Skills Agency.

Brooks, G., Gorman, T., Harman, J. et al. (1997) *Family Literacy Lasts*. London: Basic Skills Agency.

Brooks, G., Harman, J., Hutchinson, D., Kendall, S. and Wilkin, A. (1999) *Family Literacy for New Groups*. London: Basic Skills Agency.

Carnie, F. (2006) *Setting up Parent Councils: Case Studies*. Bristol: Human Scale Education.

Coldwell, M., Stephenson, K., Fathallah-Caillau, I. and Coldron, J. (2003) *Evaluation of Home School Agreements. Research Report 455*. London: DfES.

Davis, B. (1995) *How to Involve Parents in a Multicultural School*. Alexandria, VA: Association for Supervision and Curriculum Development.

Desforges, C. and Abouchaar, A. (2003) *The Impact of Parental Involvement, Parental Support and Family Education on Pupil Achievement and Adjustment: A Literature Review*. London: DfES.

Deslandes, R. and Cloutier, A. (2002) Adolescents perception of parental involvement in schooling. *School Psychology International*, 23(2): 220–32.

Epstein, J.L. (1991) Paths to partnership: What can we learn from federal, state, district and school initiatives. *Phi Delta Kappan*, 72: 344–9.

Epstein, J. and Sheldon, S. (2000) *Improving Student Attendance: Effects of Family and Community Involvement*. Paper presented to the Annual Meeting of the American Sociological Society, Washington, DC.

Hallam, S., Castle, F., Rogers, L., Rhamie, J., Creech, A. and Kokotsaki, D. (2005) *Evaluation of the Behaviour Improvement Programme. Research Report 702*. London: DfES.

Hannon, P. and Nutbrown, C. (2001) *Outcomes for Children and Parents of an Early Literacy Education Parental Involvement programme*. Paper presented at the British Educational Research Association Annual Conference, Leeds.

Hardie, A. and Alcorn, M. (2000) Parents and the school working together to achieve success: One school's experience, in S. Wolfendale and J. Bastiani (eds) *The Contribution of Parents to School Effectiveness*, pp. 102–15. London: David Fulton.

Hiatt-Michael, D.B. (ed.) (2005) *Promising Practices for Family Involvement in Schooling Across the Continents*. Greenwich, CT: Information Age Publishing.

Ho, S.C. (2005) The contribution of family involvement and investment on students' literacy performance: A comparative study of the United States and three Asian Societies Utilizing PISA, in D.B. Hiatt-Michael (ed.) *Promising Practices for Family Involvement in Schooling Across the Continents*. Greenwich, CT: Information Age Publishing.

Ho, S.C. and Willms, J.D. (1996) The effect of parental involvement on the achievement of eighth grade students. *Sociology of Education*, 69(2): 126–41.

Hoover-Dempsey, K.V., Battiato, A.C., Walker, J.M., Reed, R.P., De Jong, J.M. and Jones, K.P. (2001) Parental involvement in homework. *Educational Psychologist*, 36(3): 195–209.

Izzo, C.V., Weissberg, R.P., Kasprow, W.J. and Fendrich, M. (1999) A longitudinal assessment of teacher perceptions of parent involvement in children's education and school performance. *American Journal of Community Psychology*, 27(6): 817–39.

Jeynes, W.H. (2005) Parental involvement in East Asian schools, in D.B. Hiatt-Michael (ed.) *Promising Practices for Family Involvement in Schooling across the Continents*. Greenwich, CT: Information Age Publishing.

Kohl, G.O., Lengua, L.J. and McMahon, R.J. (2000) Parent involvement in school: Conceptualizing multiple dimensions and their relations with family and demographic risk factors. *Journal of School Psychology*, 38(6): 501–23.

Lam, C.C., Ho, S.C. and Wong, N.Y. (2002) Parents' beliefs and practices in education in Confucian heritage cultures: The Hong Kong case. *Journal of South-East Asian Education*, 3(1): 99–114.

Lynch, J. (2002) Parents' self-efficacy beliefs, parents' gender, children's reader self-perceptions, reading achievement and gender. *Journal of Research in Reading*, 25(1): 54–67.

McNeal, R.B. (2001) Differential effects of parental involvement on cognitive and behavioural outcomes by socio-economic status. *Journal of Socio-Economics*, 30: 171–9.

Mattingly, D.J., Prislin, R., McKenzie, T.L., Rodriguez, J.L. and Kayzar, B. (2002) Evaluating evaluations: The case of parent involvement programmes. *Review of Educational Research*, 72(4): 549–76.

Melhuish, E.K., Sylva, C., Sammons, P., Siraj-Blatchford, I. and Taggart, B. (2001) *Social Behavioural and Cognitive Development at 3–4 Years in Relation to Family Background: The Effective Provision of Pre-school Education, EPPE project (Technical paper 7)*. London: Institute of Education.

Moons, N. and Ivins, C. (2004) *Parental Involvement in Children's Education. Research Report 589*. London: DfES.

Ofsted (1999a) *Homework: Learning from Practice*. London: Ofsted.

Ofsted (1999b) *Raising the Attainment of Ethnic Pupils.* London: Ofsted.

Ofsted (2000a) *Improving City Schools.* London: Ofsted.

Ofsted (2000b) *Family Learning: A Survey of Current Practice.* London: Ofsted.

Ofsted (2001a) *Improving Attendance and Behaviour in Secondary Schools.* London: Ofsted.

Ofsted (2001b) *Providing for Gifted and Talented Children.* London: Ofsted.

Ofsted (2001c) *Managing Support for the Attainment of Pupils from Minority Ethnic Groups.* London: Ofsted.

Ofsted (2002) *Achievement of Black Caribbean Pupils: Good Practice in Secondary Schools.* London: Ofsted.

Okamura-Bichard, F. (1985) Mother tongue maintenance and second language learning: A case of Japanese children. *Language Learning*, 35(1): 63–89.

Power, S. and Clark, A. (2000) The right to know: parents, school reports and parents' evenings. *Research Papers in Education*, 15(1): 25–48.

Raffaele, L.M. and Knoff, H.M. (1999) Improving home–school collaboration and disadvantaged families: Organizational principles, perspectives and approaches. *School Psychology Review*, 28(3): 448–66.

Sacker, A., Schoon, I. and Bartley, M. (2002) Social inequality in educational achievement and psychological adjustment throughout childhood: Magnitude and mechanisms. *Social Science and Medicine*, 55: 863–80.

Sanders, M.G. and Epstein, J.L. (2000) The national network of partnership schools: How research influences educational practice. *Journal of Education for Students Placed at Risk*, 5(1 and 2): 61–76.

Sheldon, S. and Epstein, J. (2001) *Improving Student Behaviour and Discipline with Family and Community Involvement.* Baltimore, MD: Johns Hopkins University, Centre for Research on the Education of Students Placed at Risk.

Singh, K., Bickley, P.G., Trivette, P., Keith, P.B. and Anderson, E. (1995) The effects of four components of parental involvement on eighth grade student achievement. *School Psychology Review*, 24(2): 299–317.

Siraj-Blatchford, I., Sylva, K., Muttock, S., Gilden, R. and Bell, D. (2002) *Researching Effective Pedagogy in the Early Years. Research Report RR356.* London: Institute of Education, University of London.

Stevenson, H.W. and Stigler, J.W. (1992) *The Learning Gap.* New York: Summit Books.

Sui-Chu, E.H. and Willms, J.D. (1996) Effects of parental involvement on eighth grade achievement. *Sociology of Education*, 69(2): 126–41.

Sylva, K., Melhuish, E., Sammons, P. and Siraj-Blatchford, I. (1999) *The Effective Provision of Pre-school Education (EPPE) Project: Technical Paper 2: Characteristics of the EPPE Project Sample at Entry to the Study.* London: Institute of Education, University of London.

Vernon, J. (1999) *Parent Partnership and Special Educational Needs: Perspectives on Developing Good Practice. Research Report 162.* London: DfEE.

Vincent, C. (2001) Social class and parental agency. *Journal of Education Policy*, 16(4): 347–64.

Williams, B., Williams, J. and Ullman, A. (2002) *Parental Involvement in Education. Research Report 332.* London: DfES.

Wray, H. (1999) *Japanese and American Education: Attitudes and Practices.* Westport, CT: Bergin and Garvey.

Zellman, G.L. and Waterman, J.M. (1998) Understanding the impact of parental school involvement on children's educational outcomes. *Journal of Educational Research*, 91(6): 370–80.

6 Supporting parents through the use of parenting programmes

This chapter considers the ways that parents can be supported through the use of parenting programmes. It outlines the importance of parenting in relation to behaviour; discusses the importance of culture in determining the aims of parents; describes the nature of different parenting programmes; indicates what evaluations have shown about their success; and considers current issues relating to families and education in the UK and practices which are being developed to address them.

Introduction

Families play a crucial role in contributing to individual well-being and the wider society. For individuals they can provide a sense of belonging; offer meaning and direction; support the development of personal and social identity; provide economic support, nurturance and education; and support the development of social values. They can also protect, support and care for vulnerable members (Patterson 2002). They are key to ensuring the healthy physical, social, emotional and cognitive development of children.

Positive proactive parenting is associated with high child self-esteem and social and academic competence, and protects against antisocial behaviour and substance abuse (Cohen et al. 1994). Harsh inconsistent discipline, little positive involvement with the child, and poor monitoring and supervision are associated with a range of poor outcomes including delinquency, criminality, violence and substance abuse (Patterson et al. 1993). A small number of dysfunctional parenting practices have been shown to account for as much as 30 to 40 per cent of antisocial behaviour in children and adolescents (Barlow 1999; Gibbs et al. 2003). A high proportion of emotional and behavioural problems in childhood persist into adolescence and adulthood (Rutter 1996; Stewart-Brown et al. 2002).

Parenting is challenging. There are many uncontrollable elements in life which can impact on parents including unemployment, ill health, death, divorce or separation, difficult relationships and children's difficulties at school. Despite the recognition of the importance of parenting and the difficulties that parents can face in bringing up children, in most societies parents receive no training for the role, although there is now considerable evidence that social support for families and children is linked to both physical and mental health (Limber and Hashima 2002). Parenting programmes aim to increase the level of social support available to families. This may be through providing advice, education, emotional support, enhancing the quality of relationships or providing practical support.

What constitutes 'successful' parenting?

There is no consensus about what constitutes 'normal' or 'successful' parenting. Practices tend to be judged on 'outcomes' – whether children are well adjusted and meet society's expectations. This is reflected in the aspirations which most parents hold for their children. They want them to be 'normal' and well adjusted (Grimshaw and McGuire 1998). Parents seem to share three primary goals in relation to parenting irrespective of race, culture or class: the child's physical, social and emotional well-being; providing the child with the economic competencies necessary for survival in adulthood; and transmitting the values of their cultures (Levine 1977). While these aspirations seem to be common to all societies, the nature of parenting is influenced by cultural values (National Research Council Institute of Medicine 2000), for instance, European and American cultures place value on independence, achievement, competition, personal empowerment and individuality while African-American and Asian cultures place greater value on interdependence (Gross 1996). As a result they attach more importance to socializing children to be cooperative, obedient, able to share and to respect authority without question. These different cultural values preclude the possibility of defining what would constitute 'optimal' parenting worldwide. However, the evidence suggests that whatever values parents hold, for healthy psychological development, responsive and sensitive parenting is needed that is neither over- or under-stimulating (Carlson and Harwood 2003).

Parenting styles

In western cultures, a range of different parenting styles has been identified. An early categorization was developed by Adler (1963). His typology is set out in Table 6.1. Baumrind (1971) developed a simpler formulation where parents are viewed as adopting positions along two axes: demanding/ undemanding and responsive/unresponsive. Parents who are demanding and responsive are described as authoritative, while demanding and unresponsive parents are described as authoritarian. Undemanding and responsive parents are described as permissive while undemanding and unresponsive are described as uninvolved/neglecting. The relationships between these styles and outcomes for children have been explored in a range of cultural settings. These are set out in Table 6.2. Permissive and authoritarian parenting can have negative effects (McClun and Merrell 1998). Overall, four attributes of parental behaviour seem to be particularly important in contributing to antisocial behaviour in children: lack of positive regard, lack of warmth, inconsistent and harsh discipline, and poor monitoring and supervision. Displaying a supportive presence, giving clear instructions, and limit setting predict the presence of fewer behaviour problems (Denham et al. 2000).

Table 6.1 Early typology of parenting styles

Parenting styles	Descriptor
Democratic	Sense of connection with others, assertive and cooperative, values others as well as self, giving and sharing
Perfectionist	Nothing is ever quite good enough, may feel superior to other but is always striving to do better, never content, prone to depression
Neglecting	Sense of emptiness, tendency to be manipulative and superficial in relationships, taking rather than giving, slightly aloof, impulsive
Rejecting	Expects rejection and provokes it, feels worthless, is suspicious, hostile, aggressive, oversensitive to criticism, can be masochistic and self-destructive
Punitive	Harsh, narrow focus on retributive justice, self-righteous, sense of lack of connection, hatred
Overindulgent	Lack of initiative, apathetic, indecisive, lacking in application, poor communicator
Oversubmissive	Thoughtless, impulsive, impatient, inconsiderate, short-tempered, narcissistic

Overcoercive	Preoccupied with status issues and ritualistic formulae for relating to others
Overresponsible	Workaholic, unable to relax and be, not good at sharing responsibility, or allowing others to contribute effectively
Hypochondriacal	Difficulties exaggerated, seeking support and sympathy constantly, very restricted social life
Sexually arousing	Preoccupation with sensuality/sexuality and lack of engagement in emotional closeness, devalues friendship

Source: Adler (1963).

Recently, interest has focused on the styles adopted by parents to satisfy different cultural values. For instance, the emphasis on interdependence in African-American and Asian cultures has led some to conclude that those belonging to these groups tend to combine high levels of control and forceful discipline, adopting an authoritarian parenting style (Carlson and Harwood 2003). The stress on interdependence in Japan means that Japanese babies share beds with parents, grandparents or siblings until they are 15 years of age while European/American parents put in place independent sleeping arrangements in the first few days or weeks of an infant's life (Gross 1996). Some authors, however, suggest that in practice there are few cultural differences. Honig and Chung (1989) studied Korean, Indian, Swedish, French and American parental practices and found more similarities than differences in parental styles. Categorization of parenting styles in ethnic terms seems to be an oversimplification.

While some have argued that physical punishment is a feature of black parenting (Myers et al. 1992), studies of intergroup differences between African-Americans have shown that it is less educated mothers who are more restrictive, while older and better educated mothers are less likely to use physical punishment (Kelley et al. 1993). Socio-economic status is important. Abusive and neglectful parenting practices are more frequently found in families receiving welfare benefits (Brown et al. 1998), while encouragement and support are more common in families which are economically advantaged (Hart and Ridley 1995). Overall, economic and social factors influence parenting including educational status, social network support, marital status, poverty, unemployment, dissatisfaction with work, and lack of information about child development (Belsky and Vondra 1989).

Parents from minority ethnic communities are faced with the additional parental responsibility of preserving and transmitting aspects of their own value system and helping their child succeed within a dominant culture which may not support their success. As we have seen in earlier chapters, in many countries children from minority ethnic groups have a disproportionately high risk of a range of poor outcomes including early behaviour problems, school failure and delinquency.

Table 6.2 Relationships between parenting styles and outcomes for children

Parenting styles	Outcomes for children
Authoritative (demanding and responsive): they are rational, democratic, warm, affectionate, firm, have child-centred expectations and they respect children's rights.	High self-esteem, self-control, confident, responsible, mature, popular, happy, fulfil academic potential
Authoritarian (demanding and unresponsive): they are autocratic, non-negotiable, cold, rejecting, inflexible, have adult-focused expectations. Children have no rights or voice.	Anxious, withdrawn, can be hostile, conforming, fairly successful academically
Permissive (undemanding and responsive): laissez-faire, dictated to by child, often immature, easy-going, overly tolerant, disorganized, children make all decisions.	Impulsive, disobedient, inconsiderate, poor self-control, lack of persistence so underperform academically
Uninvolved/neglecting (undemanding and unresponsive): minimal interaction, preoccupied, can be detached, no clear expectations. Children's needs not noticed.	Relationship problems, anxiety, moodiness, sometimes acting out, aggressive, lack concentration, problems with learning.

At-risk families

Some families are more likely to experience difficulties than others. Currently, there are no reliable ways to identify families where children are likely to develop antisocial behaviour at a sufficiently early stage to provide additional support (Barrett 2000; Loeber et al. 2003), although some factors are known to increase the likelihood of difficulties, for instance, family breakdown or where a family has not been formed, (e.g. single teenage parents). Adverse social circumstances, such as poverty, unemployment, illness, poor access to health care, education or housing, crime, alcohol or drug abuse and violence are all risk factors but even where families are at risk there can be protective or compensatory factors which can buffer the negative effects of stress and may strengthen families when they face difficulties (Patterson 2002).

Some families are resilient. Such families are more stable and cohesive, cope with stress and change by being flexible, have clearly agreed routines and communicate well (McCubbin and McCubbin 1988). A study of families in 27 different countries identified six qualities which contributed to family strength: commitment to the family; appreciation of and affection for each other; positive interactions and good communication; enjoyment of each other's company; a sense of spiritual well-being and shared values; and experience of and confidence in being able to manage difficulties (Stinnett and DeFrain 1985). Despite this, there are no agreed optimal ways in which families should function.

Some families experience high levels of unresolved conflicts which lead to children experiencing high levels of stress. Where families are high in conflict and hostility stress response systems become sensitized and over-reactive and are no longer controlled by rational threat appraisal processes and are therefore unresponsive to real environmental threat. In these circumstances family members become unable to read social cues accurately and are also prone to poor emotional self-regulation. The lack of a nurturing emotional environment leads to a lack of understanding of emotions (Repetti et al. 2002).

When parents have problems managing their children's behaviour they are frequently unclear in the way they have communicated their expectations, and inconsistent in setting and enforcing rules and monitoring and supervising their children's behaviour (Patterson 1982). Parents sometimes reinforce children's negative behaviour by paying more attention when children misbehave and then responding with threats of punishment which they do not carry through (Patterson et al. 1992). A meta-analysis of British, American and Scandinavian studies (Loeber and Stouthamer-Loeber 1986) supported this, showing a link between harsh and inconsistent parental discipline, parent–child and inter-parental conflict, family disruption (to a lesser degree) and a cold emotional atmosphere with later delinquent behaviour.

While prediction based on risk factors remains inadequate, there have nevertheless been attempts to develop strategies which will reduce risk factor impact. In the USA there has been a range of programmes including the Strengthening Families Project and the Strengthening Multi-ethnic Families Programme. In Australia, the Australian Stronger Families and Communities Strategy has supported the development of resilience in families (Emerson 2000). This is underpinned by eight principles:

1. Working together in partnership.
2. Encouraging a preventive and early intervention approach.
3. Supporting people through life transitions.
4. Developing better integrated and coordinated services.
5. Developing local solutions to local problems.

6. Building capacity (maximizing personal and collective resources of individual and communities).
7. Using the evidence that early interventions are effective and looking to the future.
8. Making investment count by ensuring that the basis is sound and its outcome monitored.

Programmes like the Elmira Prenatal/Early Infancy Project (PEIP) and the Perry pre-school project have shown cost savings in the long term in relation to welfare, health, education and criminal justice for high-risk families and when the broader benefits to society are taken into account for low-risk families as well (Karoly et al. 1998). At the moment comparable long-term UK data are not in place. However, programmes such as Sure Start and SPOKES, which has a parenting programme for reducing disruptive behaviour within a parent-led literacy programme for primary school children (Scott and Sylva 2003), have the potential to deliver such benefits.

The need for parenting programmes

Not everyone believes that parenting programmes are necessary or desirable, some seeing them as a means of social control. However, most parents experience some difficulties with their children at some time and about a fifth consider these difficulties to be severe (McGaw and Lewis 2002). Patterson and colleagues (2002) reported from a survey of parents of children aged 3–8 years in three medical practices that 20 per cent were experiencing problems with their children's behaviour. In the region of 20 per cent had attended a parenting programme and 58 per cent expressed an interest in attending such a programme in the future. The National Family and Parenting Institute (2001) suggested that most parents saw parenting skills as needing to be learnt and wanted more information about where to find support. This suggests that many parents would be amenable to attending some form of educational programme relating to parenting. In the UK, there is currently no universal training for parenthood. While parents receive support before and immediately after birth in how to care physically for their newborn child, and regular health checks are made in the first years, subsequent to this parents have to draw on other sources for advice and guidance.

In recent years, the UK government has acknowledged the importance of parenting and the role of the family, partly as a means of reducing antisocial behaviour but also because parents value parenting education and support it because it improves their emotional well-being and their relationships with their children (Barlow and Stewart-Brown 2001; Patterson et al.

2002). Parents also see it as a means to improve their influence on the behaviour of their children, this being the most common reason that parents report for attending parenting programmes (Webster-Stratton and Spitzer 1996).

Different theoretical approaches to working with families

Parenting programmes are embedded in psychological theory drawn from a range of therapeutic approaches, including behaviourist, cognitive-behavioural, humanistic, psychoanalytic and multisystemic. Behavioural approaches assume that inappropriate ways of behaving and interacting with others have been learned because they have been rewarded. Changing behaviour involves rewarding appropriate behaviour and ignoring inappropriate behaviour. Cognitive-behavioural approaches recognize that individual beliefs and expectations underlie and play a large part in maintaining behaviour so therapy aims to change the negative thoughts and feelings that accompany particular behaviours, replacing them with more positive ones. Humanistic approaches anticipate that the person best-positioned to work out solutions to problems is the person themselves, while psychodynamic theories focus on the inner meaning of experiences rather than the behaviour itself. Treatment tries to uncover unconscious meanings of attitudes and other patterns of response stemming from childhood experiences assuming that these influence subsequent parenting practices. Multisystemic theory is based on ecological and family systems approaches and involves collaboration between professionals and family with the focus on enabling families to become empowered to take responsibility for themselves. Treatment consists of evaluation of all influences within the family and its social setting which are related to the issues and which might prevent effective parenting (for a more detailed account see Barrett 2003).

Most parenting programmes are based on one of two main approaches: behavioural or improving relationships. The former seem to be more effective in changing children's behaviour while the latter seem to have more positive effects on the cohesive functioning of families (Barlow 1997). Practices in delivering parenting programmes in the UK, in relation to behavioural approaches, are largely derived from the work in the USA of Webster-Stratton with conduct-disordered young children and their families. Those based on improving relationships tend to be based on Bavolek's approach with dysfunctional families (Lloyd 1999). Behavioural approaches are relatively easy to teach and, where they are successful, tend to produce results quickly (Munger 1993). Their effectiveness depends on the same reward systems being put in place across social contexts, for instance, at home and at school. Rewards need to be tailored to the needs of each child individually. Parents also need to be educated to realize that the most effective rewards are based on social interactions, for instance, time spent engaging with their children and praise (Hallam et al. 2004).

Values in parenting education and issues relating to minority ethnic groups

No parenting programme can be value free. Each programme carries with it cultural values, although these are rarely made explicit. Recently there has been recognition of the potential problems this may create regarding gender, race and religious stereotyping (e.g. Smith 1996). Currently, programmes are more likely to recruit white parents, and minority ethnic parents who do volunteer to take part are more likely to drop out and often feel that parenting programmes are not for them (Barlow et al. 2004). As most programmes have been developed in the USA for white parents they are often less acceptable to other cultural groups (Catalano et al. 1993) and may not even be entirely appropriate for other white cultures.

Three approaches to developing parenting programmes for minority ethnic parents have been identified: 'translated' (translated into the target population's native language); adapted (modified to include some of the values and traditions of the target population); and 'culturally specific' (designed to specifically incorporate the values of the target population) (Cheng Gorman and Balter 1997). Culturally specific parenting programmes include the Effective Black Parenting Programme which is widely used in the USA (Rowland and Wampler 1983). One unit of this is entitled 'Pride in Blackness' and involves discussion on culture and history and ways in which parents can communicate positively about being black and dealing with racism. Evaluations of the programme have been mixed. Some have shown positive change in parents' attitudes and behaviours while others have not (Barrett 2003; Barlow et al. 2004; Moran et al. 2004).

There are few culturally specific parenting programmes in the UK, one exception being the Moyenda Black Families Project (Hylton 1997). Typically, minority ethnic parents are included in mixed programmes. Barlow and colleagues (2004) in a review concluded that both traditional and culturally sensitive parenting programmes have a role to play in supporting parents and in challenging parenting practices. Culturally specific programmes can take account of discrepant values, and offer opportunities for parents to consider specific problems that challenge them and understand their culture better and what has led to current practices and traumas. This can help them in moving on. Where minority ethnic parents attend traditional programmes, facilitators need to explain the values underpinning the programme, recognize diversity in family composition and the parenting role of others in addition to the child's birth parents, acknowledge and support diversity in child rearing attitudes and practices, make adaptations to their programmes to meet parents' needs, provide additional support to minority ethnic parents whose value systems are being challenged, and be aware of other programmes locally which may better meet needs. There is evidence that where individuals within programmes identify their own goals, diverse viewpoints can be respected. In relation to drug and alcohol abuse, programmes can be equally effective in producing change in minority ethnic and white populations (Botvin et al. 1995). The perceived trustworthiness of the service provider is an important element in the recruitment and retention of parents from some ethnic groups (Gross et al. 2001). The use of ethnic group workers and of individuals of social standing within the social networks of potential participants can enhance recruitment.

Are parenting programmes effective?

Evaluations of parenting programmes have largely relied on parental reports and there have been relatively few studies which have included independent observations of children's behaviour or the use of control groups (for overviews of the reviews see Barrett 2003; Barlow et al. 2004; Moran et al. 2004). Where evaluations have relied on parental self-report, satisfaction has tended to be very high. Qualitative research exploring parents' views of parenting programmes also shows favourable results (e.g. Webster-Stratton and Spitzer 1996; Barlow and Stewart-Brown 2001). Overall, the reviews indicate that parenting programmes can be effective in improving behaviour, although effective behaviour change at home does not always transfer to other environments including school (Firestone et al. 1980). After attending programmes some groups of parents still experience problems, typically related to single parent status, maternal depression, low socio-economic status, or a family history of alcoholism and drug abuse (Webster-Stratton and Hammond 1998). There is also an acknowledgement that particular community factors can be important (Bronfenbrenner 1979). Another factor is the high dropout rates, typically in the region of 30 per cent which affect programmes' efficacy (Forehand et al. 1983). Those parents dropping out are often those in most need. There has also been little evaluation of the impact on children's educational outcomes.

What are the characteristics of parenting programmes which make them effective?

As most parenting programmes adopt an eclectic mix of approaches for pragmatic and practical reasons it has proved difficult to compare the relative success of different types of programmes and identify those elements which might be important. However, the findings from the various reviews that have been undertaken suggest that programmes are most effective when they:

- have strong theoretical underpinnings and are clear about the mechanisms of change;
- have elements which focus on changing attitudes and cognitions;
- have elements which focus on the development of skills for managing behaviour;
- have concrete objectives in addition to overall aims;
- are clear about the needs of the particular groups or individuals participating in the programme;
- pay attention to recruiting and maintaining parents in the programme;
- have multiple referral routes;
- adopt a range of media for engaging parents including video, verbal and written materials;
- offer long-term support for parents with particular needs;
- provide opportunities for follow-up activities and longer term peer group support;
- are implemented by well trained staff with appropriate management and support; and
- ensure that transport and child care arrangements are in place to support attendance.

Overall, programmes that engage parents and children at home, in school and in the wider community, and meet the needs of parents for material, practical, informational and relational support seem to have the greatest and longest lasting effects. Group-based programmes are more cost effective than individual programmes and have the benefit of providing parents with peer support, although for some severely dysfunctional families individual programmes may be essential (Cunningham et al. 1995). The numerous reviews acknowledge that there is relatively little evidence regarding the long-term impact of parenting programmes.

Reaching the most needy parents

While many parents are well satisfied by the services that they receive through parenting programmes (Barlow and Stewart-Brown 2001; Ghate and Ramella 2002), a significant proportion of parents drop out or their problems are not ameliorated. They tend to be parents with multiple overlapping difficulties, such as poverty, poor housing, social isolation, marital conflict, and poor health, and whose children have emotional and behavioural problems at the most severe end of the spectrum (e.g. Forehand and Kotchik 2002). There are programmes which can address multiple difficulties, for example, the Triple P Programme or Multisystemic Treatment (Henggeler et al. 1998). They are intensive and can tackle adversity across a range of multiple areas but they are expensive to run. Other factors in ensuring the engagement of parents who may have the greatest need include the sex of the parent (Ghate et al. 2000). To attract fathers specially designed activities are required. Parent training may be enhanced when both parents attend (Coplin and Houts 1991).

Other ways of offering support to parents

Telephone support can be a useful means of assisting parents. For instance, in the UK, Parentline Plus offers anonymous non-stigmatizing support to callers who often have significant needs that are not met by other provision. The most common problems raised with Parentline Plus in relation to children are challenging behaviour, educational problems and mental health issues (Boddy et al. 2005). Another approach is the use of newsletters producing research-based information about parenting in an accessible and user-friendly way. These can be effective in providing information and support for the majority of parents, although there can be difficulties relating to the literacy of some parents, English as an additional language, social class differences, and reaching out to fathers as well as mothers (Shepherd and Roker 2005).

Provision of educationally focused parenting programmes in the UK

In the UK, the Children's Act (1989) defined parental responsibilities in relation to ensuring their children's moral, physical, and emotional well-being and obliged Local Authorities (LAs) to support parents with such services as might be required. Subsequently, the Antisocial Behaviour Act (2003) enabled schools and LAs to arrange parenting contracts which involve the parent agreeing to carry out specific actions to improve their child's attendance or behaviour in return for the LA or school providing or arranging support, typically a parenting programme. These requirements have meant that LAs have a duty to ensure that sufficient and appropriate parenting programmes are available.

A recent survey indicated that there were very few parenting programmes which focused specifically on children's behaviour and attendance at school (Hallam et al. 2004). In addition, the systems in place for coordinating and providing parenting programmes in LAs were fragile. Provision was generally inadequate to meet need and often operated in an uncoordinated way because of a lack of organization at local level. Links between LAs and providers were on the whole not well established and in many cases communication was limited, although there were some examples of good practice where LAs either acted to coordinate the activity of the various voluntary bodies, offered support, or were developing their own parenting programmes. The key features of five case study examples of good practice are set out in Table 6.3 (full details are available in Hallam et al. 2004).

Table 6.3 Key features of LAs with well established systems of parenting programmes

	Key features
Case study 1: LA acting as coordinator for programmes run by other providers	• Wide range of providers including those from the voluntary sector; • Programmes offered in a variety of venues; • Programmes based on a range of different approaches; • LA provides support and training; • LA provides financial support to voluntary sector coordinator; • LA provides one programme to ensure availability of places for statutory referrals; • Referrals dealt with by providers.
Case study 2: programmes provided by Sure Start and Parentline Plus	• Focused group of programmes catering for parents of children of different ages; • Programmes provided by Sure Start and Parentline Plus; • Promotion of programmes through outreach in the community, local advertising, mail shots and other means; • Programmes held at central venue; • Limited number of places available.
Case study 3: school-based programmes for children and parents based on a nationally run programme	• School-based programmes for parents and children to run concurrently; • Programmes run within a nationally coordinated framework; • Programmes based in schools and the community.

Case study 4: LA developed courses run in schools by LA staff	• Programmes developed by LA staff; • Programmes embedded within an educational context; • Links built in between education and social services; • Parent helpline for all parents; • Open access to all parents; • Programmes provided for parents of children of different ages; • School staff encouraged to train as facilitators.
Case study 5: LA developed courses run in schools with schools continuing the support after the classes have been completed	• Course developed by LA staff; • Open access for parents; • Programme linked to the behavioural procedures adopted in schools; • Parents encouraged to continue meeting in a support group after the programme was completed; • Provision to be supported by the school in the long term.

Most programmes were eclectic in nature, although increasingly LAs were developing their own parenting programmes with a focus on the child's educational outcomes rather than more generalized outcomes relating to family functioning. This provision was sometimes, although not always, school based. Some programmes included parallel group work for children. This was particularly appropriate as children's behaviour was affected by circumstances at school over which the parents had no control. While most programme providers sought feedback from parents about the programme, few assessed the impact on the behaviour of the child. It was clear that more systematic evaluation, particularly in relation to the impact on the child's behaviour at home and in educational settings was required. Where inclusion in a parenting programme was the result of action taken by the Education Welfare Service, the impact on the child's attendance was monitored. Evidence from this suggested that there could be a positive impact, although improvement was not always seen immediately. Required attendance at the parenting programme enabled other agencies to be involved, and supported parents in identifying why there were problems and developing strategies to address them. The impact was greater if the children were still at primary school. Engendering change in older children was more difficult. Even where attendance did not improve there were other benefits, for instance, in relation to parent–child communication. Where school and home worked together the impact could be substantial:

> When I started the course Jenny (aged 12) was bordering on being excluded from school. She was violent or abusive, kicking doors and

screaming and shouting and constantly swearing. The swearing has decreased. The school has noticed a difference. Before Christmas they brought in the Educational Psychologist but two months into the course she has changed. She was not affectionate before the course but is now. She was truanting but by putting into practice the positive reinforcement at school and at home there has been a great improvement.

(*Mother*)

Examples of education-focused programmes

Typical of school-based work was the Stepping Stones Programme, an eight-week group-based parenting support programme with prior home visits. The Behaviour and Education Support Team (BEST) established programmes in specific schools, although parents of children from other schools attended with the venue being rotated. The programme was developed from existing programmes including, 'What Can a Parent Do', 'Systematic Training for Effective Parenting' (STEP), 'Living with Teenagers' and the 'Webster-Stratton' course. All facilitators were Webster-Stratton trained. The programme emphasized child development and age-appropriate behaviour, managing behaviour, the use of praise and encouragement, consequences, boundary setting and life after children. The programme reduced punitive behaviour in parents and taught them how to diffuse situations. Parents were provided with information about further courses and follow-up sessions were arranged. A parent helpline was offered on a weekly basis for any parent in the LA to ring for advice.

In the same LA, a programme called Family Workshops was developed with an education focus for the parents of primary school children. It ran for six sessions, each lasting two hours. Group meetings took place in schools during school hours. The programme was written within the LA and drew on material from the Webster-Stratton and Familywise programmes. All the sessions involved practical exercises, problem solving and discussion, including a focus on life as a parent, acknowledging the difficulties of the role. Parents worked in small groups and pairs, and Familywise cartoons were used as a stimulus for discussion, since many parents had difficulties with literacy. The programme considered how to deal with stressful situations and manage difficult behaviour, developed skills and strategies, and focused on listening and communication, developing awareness of emotions, rewarding positive behaviour, and setting rules and boundaries. The providers offered a top-up session in the term following the programme and encouraged schools to set this up. The workshops were open access and schools encouraged parents to attend whether their children had difficulties or not. Parents attended because they thought that it would be interesting, to increase their social networks because their children had specific difficulties, such as ADHD, Asperger's syndrome, and because of concerns about their child's attitudes, back chatting, shouting, slamming doors, fighting with siblings and attention seeking. For many, discovering that other parents had difficulties with their children was a huge relief. A parent helpline ran within the LA and parents were given information about other options and courses, and holiday play schemes. Some parents went on to the Stepping Stones programme which was for parents who had teenage children. An early years programme was being developed, the aim being that there would be provision for parents at each stage of their child's development (early years, primary and secondary). The LA encouraged staff in schools to train as facilitators so that schools could offer the programme themselves. Evaluation of the programme revealed that parents were calmer, more organized in terms of routines, more positive in their parenting style, and that relationships with their child had improved. There were positive changes in the children's behaviour.

In some LAs there was recognition that there might be benefits from running courses for pupils and parents in parallel. In one LA, such programmes were run by the Education Welfare Service. The parents' course was called ESCAPE while the pupil's programme was called Parallel Lines. This aimed to enable children to develop an understanding of the role of parents and their concerns. A common vocabulary was used with parents and pupils and the programmes shared the same themes. The LA reported considerable benefits.

Parenting programmes for the parents of disaffected adolescents

The most extensive evaluation of a parenting programme for adolescents was undertaken by the Policy Research Bureau for the Youth Justice Board (Ghate and Ramella 2002) and focused on the effect of parenting programmes on reducing reoffending among children and young people who had been convicted of a crime. The work with parents addressed issues related to dealing with conflict and challenging behaviour; learning to constructively supervise and monitor young people's activities; setting and maintaining boundaries; communication and negotiation skills; and family conflict in general. Many programmes offered a mix of group work and individually tailored one-to-one work. Parents, mainly single mothers, reported very high levels of need including debt and housing problems, health difficulties and problems with personal relationships. Most said that they particularly wanted help in managing difficult behaviour in their children all of whom were prolific offenders.

Parents who completed programmes reported improved communication with their child; improved supervision and monitoring; reduction in conflict and better approaches to dealing with it when it occurred; better relationships; giving more praise and approval; being less critical and losing their temper less; feeling better able to influence behaviour; and feeling better able to cope with parenting in general. Exit ratings were very positive. There was also evidence of positive change in the young people. Reconviction rates reduced by nearly one-third, offending dropped to 56 per cent and the average number of offences was reduced by half. While the parenting programme alone may not have been responsible for these changes, it is likely to have made a contribution. An important additional positive outcome was the benefit to parental relationships with younger children.

Running programmes in schools

Where parenting programmes operate in schools, this is usually at primary level. Such programmes are welcomed by school staff and parents and schools are supportive, although lack of space is sometimes an issue. These programmes tend to have low dropout rates, parents seem to be more willing to engage with their children's activities at school, and home–school relations improve. Parents visit school more often and sometimes take on voluntary or paid work. Particularly positive features are the facilitation of consistent approaches to dealing with behaviour at home and school, and the ease of monitoring the impact on the child (Hallam et al. 2004).

The factors supporting the success of parenting programmes in educational contexts are similar to those for more general programmes with the addition of a focus on working with the child and the need for coordination between school and home. These are particularly important as attendance and behaviour at school will not improve through parents attending a parenting programme if the problems are school-based, for instance, bullying, an inappropriate curriculum, or difficulties in relationships with teachers. An approach which improves parenting skills alongside developing skills in the child is therefore more effective.

School-based provision at primary level enhances home–school communication and supports parents in responding in a more measured way when there are issues relating to their child's behaviour facilitating progress in addressing problems. Crèche facilities and suitable accommodation are necessary for classes to take place. Success also requires the support of school staff. Teachers and parents need to work together to ensure consistency and schools need to monitor change in the child's behaviour. Having a key staff member with responsibility for parenting issues and providing training for school staff in developing relationships with parents are also important.

Where programmes are held in local schools and made available for all parents, not only those experiencing difficulties, the stigma attached to attendance reduces and parents are more likely to attend. Once a programme is set up it can be continued by the school providing that training is made available to facilitators. These might be parents who have previously attended the course or a range of school staff, for instance, teachers, Learning Support Assistants, learning mentors, Home-School Liaison Officers and school nurses. Such an approach enables programmes to be made available locally for all parents, and cater for the parents of children of different ages.

Chapter summary

- Local Authorities need to ensure that a range of parenting programmes are available to meet the needs of parents of children of different ages, and parents with a range of concerns.
- Where programmes are available for all parents they are likely to be less stigmatizing and enhance the quality of parenting across the whole community.
- Each parenting programme needs to ensure that attention is paid to:
    - differences in parents' personal and cultural contexts;
    - providing a non-stigmatizing and welcoming climate;
    - ensuring that parents in receipt of compulsory orders have a home visit prior to attending a group-based programme;
    - providing childcare facilities;
    - providing transport arrangements if the location is not convenient;
    - ensuring that programmes are timed to meet the needs of those attending;
    - ensuring appropriate publicity for programmes;
    - rewarding attendance and following up non-attendance rigorously;
    - providing opportunities for the establishment of follow-up classes;
    - providing facilitators who have credibility and can establish trust;
    - staff training;
    - making sessions fun and adopting a range of teaching approaches which engage parents with different backgrounds and educational levels and draw on their own experiences;
    - the provision of appropriate support materials;
    - rigorously evaluating outcomes and acting on feedback; and
    - developing good links with other agencies.
- Setting up programmes in primary schools has advantages where problems are related to educational outcomes and can provide the basis for universal provision.

Further reading

Barlow, J., Shaw, R. and Stewart-Brown, S. in conjunction with REU (2004) *Parenting Programmes and Minority Ethnic Families*. London: National Children's Bureau.

Barrett, H. (2003) *Parenting Programmes for Families at Risk: A Source Book*. London: National Family and Parenting Institute.

Hallam, S., Rogers, L. and Shaw, J. (2004) *Improving Children's Behaviour and Attendance through the Use of Parenting Programmes: An Examination of Good Practice. Research Report 585*. London: DfES.

Moran, P., Ghate, D. and van der Merwe, A. (2004) *What Works in Parenting Support? A Review of the International Evidence. Research Report 574*. London: DfES.

References

Adler, A. (1963) *The Problem Child*. New York: Capricorn Books.

Barlow, J. (1997) *Systematic Review of the Effectiveness of Parent training Programmes in Improving Behaviour Problems in Children aged 3–10 years*. Oxford: Health Services Research Unit, Department of Public Health.

Barlow, J. (1999) What works in parenting programmes, in E. Lloyd (ed.) *Parenting Matters: What Works in Parenting Education?*, pp. 64–84. London: Barnados.

Barlow, J. and Stewart-Brown, S. (2001) Understanding parent programmes: Parents' views. *Primary Health Care Research and Development*, 2: 117–30.

Barlow, J. Shaw, R. and Stewart-Brown, S. in conjunction with REU (2004) *Parenting Programmes and Minority Ethnic Families*. London: National Children's Bureau.

Barrett, H. (2000) The politics and chemistry of early intervention. *Emotional and Behavioural Difficulties*, 5(2): 3–9.

Barrett, H. (2003) *Parenting Programmes for Families at Risk: A Source Book*. London: National Family and Parenting Institute.

Baumrind, D. (1971) Current patterns of parental authority. *Developmental Psychology Monograph*, 4: 1–103.

Belsky, J. and Vondra, J. (1989) Lessons from child abuse: The determinants of parenting, in D. Cicchetti and V. Carlson (eds) *Child Maltreatment: Theory and Research on the Causes and Consequences of Child Abuse and Neglect*, pp. 153–202. Cambridge: Cambridge University Press.

Boddy, J., Smith, M. and Simon, A. (2005) Telephone support for parenting: An evaluation of Parentline Plus. *Children & Society*, 19: 278–91.

Botvin, G.J., Schinke, S.P., Epstein, J.A., Diaz, T. and Botvin, E.M. (1995) Effectiveness of culturally focused and generic skills training approaches to alcohol and drug abuse prevention among minority adolescents: Two year follow-up results. *Psychology of Additive Behaviours*, 9: 183–94.

Bronfenbrenner, U. (1979) *The Ecology of Human Development*. Cambridge, MA: Harvard University Press.

Brown, J., Cohen, P., Johnson, J.G. and Salzinger, S. (1998) A longitudinal analysis of risk factors for child maltreatment: Findings of a 17 year prospective study of officially recorded and self-reported child abuse and neglect. *Child Abuse and Neglect*, 22: 1065–78.

Carlson, V.J. and Harwood, R.L. (2003) Attachment, culture and caregiving system: The cultural patterning of everyday experience among Anglo and Puerto Rican mother–infant. *Infant Mental Health Journal*, 24: 53–73.

Catalano, R.F., Hawkins, J.D., Krenz, C. et al. (1993) Using research to guide culturally appropriate drug abuse prevention. *Journal of Consulting and Clinical Psychology*, 61: 804–11.

Cheng Gorman, J. and Balter, L. (1997) Culturally sensitive parent education: A critical review of quantitative research. *Review of Educational Research*, 67: 339–69.

Cohen, D., Richardson, J. and Labree, L. (1994) Parenting behaviours and the onset of smoking and alcohol use: a longitudinal study. *Pediatrics*, 20: 368–75.

Coplin, J. and Houts, A. (1991) Father involvement in parent training for oppositional child behaviour: Progress or stagnation? *Child and Family Behaviour Therapy*, 13: 29–51.

Cunningham, C.E., Bremner, R. and Boyle, M. (1995) Large group community-based parenting programmes for families of pre-schoolers at risk from disruptive behaviour disorders: Utilization, cost-effectiveness and outcome. *Journal of Child Psychology and Psychiatry and Allied Disciplines*, 36: 1141–59.

Denham, S.A., Workman, E., Cole, P.M., Weissbrod, C., Kendziora, K.T. and Zahn-Waxler, C. (2000) Prediction of externalizing behaviour problems from early to middle childhood: The role of parent socialization and emotion expression. *Development and Psychopathology*, 12: 23–45.

Emerson, L. (2000) Stronger families and community strategy. *Family Matters*, 57: 66–71.

Firestone, P., Kelly, M.J. and Fike, S. (1980) Are fathers necessary in parent education groups? *Journal of Clinical Child Psychology*, 9(1): 44–7.

Forehand, R. and Kotchik, B. (2002) Behavioural Parent Training: Current Challenges and Potential Solutions. *Journal of Child and Family Studies*, 11: 377–84.

Forehand, R., Middlebrook, J., Rogers, T. and Steffe, M. (1983) Dropping out of parent training. *Behavioural Research Therapy*, 21(6): 663–8.

Ghate, D. and Ramella, M. (2002) *Positive Parenting: The National Evaluation of the Youth Justice Board's Parenting Programme*. Policy Research Bureau London: Youth Justice Board for England & Wales.

Ghate, D., Shaw, C. and Hazel, N. (2000) *Fathers and Family Centres: Engaging Fathers in Preventative Services*. York: Joseph Rowntree Foundation/York Publishing Services.

Gibbs, J., Underdown, A. and Liabo, K. *Group-based parenting programmes can reduce behaviour problems of children aged 3–10. What Works for Children group*. Evidence Nugget April 2003.

Grimshaw, R. and McGuire, C. (1998) *Evaluating Parenting Programmes: A Study of Stakeholders' Views*. London: National Children's Bureau and Joseph Rowntree Foundation.

Gross, D. (1996) What is a good parent? *American Journal of Maternal Child Nursing*, 21: 172–82.

Gross, D., Julion, W. and Fogg, L. (2001) What motivates participation and dropout among low-income urban families of color in a prevention intervention? *Family Relations: Interdisciplinary Journal of Applied Family Studies*, 50: 246–54.

Hallam, S., Rogers, L. and Shaw, J. (2004) *Improving Children's Behaviour and Attendance through the Use of Parenting Programmes: An Examination of Good Practice. Research Report 585*. London: DfES.

Hart, B. and Ridley, T.R. (1995) *Meaningful Difference in Children's Everyday Lives*. Baltimore, MD: PH Brookes.

Henggeler, S.W., Schoenwald, S.K., Borduin, C.M., Rowland, M.D. and Cunningham, P.B. (1998) *Multisystemic Treatment of Antisocial Behaviour in Children and Adolescents*. New York: Guildford.

Honig, A. and Chung, M. (1989) Child rearing practices of urban poor mothers of infants and three-year-olds in five cultures. *Early Child Development and Care*, 50(1): 75–97.

Hylton, C. (1997) *Family Survival Strategies: Moyenda Black Families Talking: An Exploring Parenthood Project.* York: Joseph Rowntree Foundation.

Karoly, L. A., Greenwood, P. W., Everington, S. S., Hoube, J., Killburn, M. R., Rydell, C. P., Sanders, M. and Chiesa, J. (1998) *Investing in our children. What we know an don't know about the costs and benefits of our early childhood interventions.* http://www.rand.org/publications/MR/MR898 [2 August 2004].

Kelley, M.I., Sanchez-Hucles, J. and Walker, R.R. (1993) Correlates of disciplinary practices in working to middle-class African-American mothers. *Merrill-Palmer Quarterly*, 39: 252–64.

Levine, R. (1977) Child rearing as cultural adaptation, in P.H. Leiderman et al. (eds) *Culture and Infancy: Variations in Human Experience*, pp. 15–27. New York: Academic Press.

Limber, S.P. and Hashima, P.Y. (2002) The social context: What comes naturally in child protection, in G.B. Melton, R.A. Thompson et al. (eds) *Toward a Child-centred, Neighbourhood-based Child Protection System: A Report of the Consortium on Children, Families, and the Law*, pp. 41–66. Westport, CT: Praeger.

Lloyd, E. (ed.) (1999) *Parenting Matters: What Works in Parenting Education?* Ilford: Barnado's.

Loeber, R. and Stouthamer-Loeber, M. (1986) Family factors as correlates and predictors of juvenile conduct problems and delinquency, in M. Tonry and N. Morris (eds) *Crime and Justice: An Annual Review of Research, Vol 1.*, pp. 729–49. Chicago, IL: University of Chicago Press.

Loeber, R., Green, S.M. and Lahey, B.B. (2003) Risk factors for adult antisocial personality, in D.P. Farrington and J.W. Coid (eds) *Early Prevention of Adult Antisocial Behaviour*, pp. 79–108. Cambridge: Cambridge University Press.

McClun, L.A. and Merrell, K.W. (1998) Relationship of perceived parenting styles, locus of control orientation, and self-concept among junior-school age students. *Psychology in the Schools*, 35: 81–90.

McCubbin, H.I. and McCubbin, M.A. (1988) Typologies of resilient families: Emerging roles of social class and ethnicity. *Family Relations*, 37: 247–54.

McGaw, S. and Lewis, C. (2002) Should parenting be taught? *The Psychologist*, 15(10): 510–2.

Moran, P., Ghate, D. and van der Merwe, A. (2004) *What Works in Parenting Support? A Review of the International Evidence. Research Report 574.* London: DfES.

Munger, R.L. (1993) *Changing Children's Behaviour Quickly.* Lanham, MD: Madison Books.

Myers, H.F., Alvy, K.T., Arrington, A. et al. (1992) The impact of a parent training program on inner city African-American families. *Journal of Community Psychology,* 20: 132–47.

National Family and Parenting Institute (2001) Listening to parents: a National Family and Parenting Institute survey conducted by MORI. London: National Family and Parenting Institute.

National Research Council Institute of Medicine (2000) *From Neurons to Neighbourhoods: The Science of Early Childhood Development.* Washington, DC: National Academy Press.

Patterson, G. R. (1982) *Coercive Family Process* Eugene, OR: Castalia.

Patterson, J.M. (2002) Integrating family resilience and family stress theory. *Journal of Marriage and the Family,* 64(2): 349–60.

Patterson, G.R., Chamberlain, P. and Reid, J.B. (1992) A comparative evaluation of a parent-training program. *Behaviour Therapy,* 13: 638–50.

Patterson, G., Dishion, T. and Chamberlain, P. (1993) Outcomes and methodological issues relating to treatment of effective psychotherapy, in T.R. Giles (ed.) *Handbook of Effective Psychotherapy,* pp. 43–88. New York: Plenum.

Patterson, T., Mockford, C., Barlow, J., Pyper, C. and Stewart-Brown, S. (2002) Need and demand for parenting programmes in general practice. *Archives of Disease in Childhood,* 87: 468–71.

Repetti, R.L., Taylor, S.E. and Seeman, T.E. (2002) Risky families: Family social environments and the mental and physical health of offspring. *Psychological Bulletin,* 28(2): 330–66.

Rowland, S.B. and Wampler, K.S. (1983) Black and White Mothers' preferences for parenting programs. *Family Relations,* 32: 323–30.

Rutter, M. (1996) Connections between child and adult psychopathology. *European Journal of Child and Adolescent Psychology,* 5: 4–7.

Scott, S. and Sylva, K. (2003) *The SPOKES Project: Supporting Parents on Kids' Education: A Preventative Trial to Improve Disadvantaged Children's Life Chances by Boosting Their Social Functioning and Reading Skills.* London: Department of Health.

Shepherd, J. and Roker, D. (2005) The parenting of young people: Using newsletters to provide information and support. *Children & Society*, 19: 264–77.

Smith, C. (1996) *Developing Parenting Programes*. London: National Children's Bureau.

Stewart-Brown, S., Patterson, J., Shaw, R. and Morgan, L. (2002) *The Roots of Social Capital: A Systematic Review of Longitudinal Studies Linking Relationships in the Home in Childhood with Mental and Social Health in Later Life*. Oxford: Health Services Research Unit, University of Oxford.

Stinnett, N. and DeFrain, J. (1985) *Secrets of Strong Families*. Boston, MA: Little Brown.

Webster-Stratton, C. and Hammond, M. (1998) Conduct problems and level of social competence in Head Start children: Prevalence, pervasiveness and associated risk factors. *Clinical Child and Family Psychology Review*, 1: 101–24.

Webster-Stratton, C. and Spitzer, A. (1996) Parenting a young child with conduct problems: New insights using qualitative methods. *Advances in Clinical Children Psychology*, 18: 1–62.

7   Behaviour in the classroom

This chapter considers how teachers can maintain and improve behaviour in the classroom. It draws on existing literature relating to classroom management and also considers the support that can be offered to teachers through the use of curriculum materials to enhance pupils' social, emotional and learning skills, and the work of teacher coaches and Behaviour and Education Support Teams.

Introduction

Classrooms are complex, busy places with teachers regularly involved in over 1000 interactions a day. They are also public places since the behaviours of teachers and pupils are visible to all those in the class. Classroom events are multidimensional with participants having different goals, interests, purposes and experiences which are simultaneous. Teachers have to learn to monitor multiple situations at one time. Lastly, classroom events are unpredictable (Doyle, 1980, 1986, 1989, 1990). While disruptive incidents can be generated by external and internal factors, routines that are developed effectively within the classroom can reduce ambiguity and add to a sense of predictability. Teachers need highly developed skills to manage events.

Teachers make a difference to the behaviour of pupils (Rutter et al. 1979; Mortimore et al. 1988; Elton Report 1989; Brown and McIntyre 1993; Smith and Laslett 1993). Sparing use of praise and a lack of emphasis on individual responsibility and social competence can lead to disruptive and aggressive behaviour in the classroom, and poor academic performance. Effective classroom management can reduce disruptive behaviour and enhance social and academic achievement. Teachers' key skills are important in creating and managing learning activities whereby they establish an 'activity system' which includes attention to goals, tasks, social structure, timing and pacing, and resources. These need to be planned and managed to support good behaviour (Doyle 1990). Where teachers are pressured to take increased responsibility for standards of attainment they tend to become more controlling and the development of learner autonomy is reduced with potentially negative effects on behaviour (Ryan et al. 1985).

Teachers' perspectives on behaviour in the classroom

Although there are variations in levels of disruption in the classroom there is consensus about the most common forms of misbehaviour. Stephens and colleagues (2005) found that teachers in Norway generally encountered similar but fewer discipline problems than teachers in England with the most frequently cited problems including talking out of turn, work avoidance, hindering other pupils and lack of punctuality. Evidence from school inspections in England supports this, with Ofsted (2005a) reporting that the most common forms of misbehaviour are incessant chatter, calling out and inattention. All these irritate staff and disrupt learning. These misbehaviours were identified almost 20 years ago by the Elton Report (1989).

In Australia, 68 per cent of secondary school teachers' time is reported to be taken up with controlling the behaviour of students and there are reported to be four to six troublesome children in each class (Little 2005). The most frequent and disruptive problems as identified by teachers are minor in nature, for instances, small breaches of rules. Although these behaviours are not particularly serious it is their high frequency that makes them stressful. In England, Houghton and colleagues (1988) indicated that over half the teachers studied believed that they spent too much time on order or control. Interestingly in an Australian study, Infantino and Little (2005) found that more than 50 per cent of students responded that teachers spent too much time on order and control. Pupils, like their teachers, are frustrated by disruptions caused by poor behaviour.

There is a lack of agreement about what constitutes challenging behaviour in schools (Ofsted 2005b). Although equitable comparison is difficult, figures for challenging behaviour in the USA, Canada and the UK are similar, with estimates suggesting that about 5 per cent of pupils have serious behavioural problems. While incidents involving firearms and other weapons capture media attention, these extreme acts are not commonplace. Challenging behaviour is mostly associated with boys aged 8 to 9 and 12 to 15, with Special Educational Needs (SEN), and from low-income families. Germany has a low incidence of challenging behaviour in schools, also involving boys aged 11 to 15, usually from low-income families among whose adult members antisocial behaviour is common; many of the pupils concerned have repeated a year of schooling. Figures for Scandinavian schools are substantially higher: the proportion of pupils with challenging behaviour is 11 per cent. This higher level might be explained by differences in perceptions of what constitutes challenging behaviour (Ofsted 2005b).

The role of teachers

At an international level there is variability in the perceived role of the teacher in the classroom that is linked to differences in the organization and structure of education. For instance, in France, teachers are national government servants with a job for life. There is tough competition to enter the profession and a high standard of academic achievement is expected of teachers. Traditionally, teachers working in France have taken charge of the academic progress of their pupils but not their personal and social development (Kitching 2001). In Britain, teacher shortages or difficulties in recruitment and retention have become the norm and teachers are expected to be far more than specialists in their chosen discipline.

These differences impact on pupil–teacher interaction. In Norway, for instance, teachers and pupils are usually on first-name terms and both are casually dressed. The setting is informal and school is perceived to be a place to undertake many activities – to surf the web, see friends, chat to the teacher, and attend classes where adults and young people are seen as equal even if their roles are different (Stephens et al. 2005). Being a teacher places emphasis on being a member of a caring profession rather than a strict disciplinarian. Minor behaviour issues, such as talking out of turn are sometimes tolerated in Norwegian classrooms since there is a more humanistic approach to discipline. By contrast, in England, there is a greater emphasis on discipline and control which engenders a more formal environment. Pupils address teachers formally, usually using their surnames and 'Miss' and 'Sir' and generally there is a dress code for pupils which is strictly enforced, and guidance for staff on what to wear. The dictum 'No smiling before Christmas in this class' (Kyriacou 2002) is illustrative of the UK approach.

A comparative study exploring classroom discipline in Australia, China and Israel found that although there were no significant differences in perceived levels of classroom misbehaviour, discipline techniques varied (Lewis et al. 2005). The teachers sampled in China were more inclusive and supportive of pupils' voices and less punitive and aggressive than those in Australia and Israel. Lewis and colleagues (2005) suggested that cultural differences might offer an explanation for the findings. In China teachers are held in very high esteem and hence students tend to comply with what teachers say out of respect. Although the levels of disruptive behaviour were similar in all three countries, the nature of the misbehaviour in Chinese classrooms may have been less extreme. Australian classrooms were perceived as having the least discussion and recognition of pupils' views, but the most punishment.

Martin and colleagues (1999) in a survey found that almost 20 per cent of teachers lacked confidence in their ability to manage disruptive classroom behaviour. In a review of research in 15 European countries, Maijer (2001) found that teachers in many schools found children with behaviour problems difficult to deal with. In Greece, two methods of controlling behaviour were reported, pressing the children or ignoring the disturbing behaviour. Neither was reported as being effective. Problems occurred due to lack of supportive services and teachers' lack of understanding of behaviour modification techniques. Similar concerns about problem behaviour and lack of support were in evidence in Iceland (Maijer 2001).

How can behaviour in the classroom be improved and maintained?

Minor problems such as talking out of turn, hindering other students, and distractibility can be altered by positive behavioural techniques and appropriate management strategies (Houghton et al. 1988; Merrett and Houghton 1989; Little et al. 2002; Little 2005). Positive management strategies rather than the use of disapproval have been shown to increase on-task behaviour. Reactive approaches to behaviour make matters worse. Important is what teachers do before misbehaviour occurs rather than the action that they take in response to problems. Consistency in using positive strategies is crucial as is the involvement of students in classroom decision-making. In well-disciplined schools teachers handle most of the routine discipline problems themselves (Watkins and Wagner 2000).

Given the consensus about problematic behaviour in the classroom it is not surprising that some intervention and prevention programmes have been used worldwide. Canter's Assertive Discipline programme is an example of this. Developed in the late 1970s for schools in the USA, this programme is now used in Australia, New Zealand, Canada and the UK (Nicholls and Houghton 1995). Indeed, guidance from the DfEE in *Excellence for All Children* (1997) suggested that the introduction of Assertive Discipline could help schools to establish settings where children were encouraged to behave well and where there were clear guidelines for behaviour. Although the programme is usually implemented at the whole-school level, the specific focus is on classroom behaviour management. The programme draws upon behavioural psychology and comprises one six-hour in-service course which teaches participants to develop a plan for classroom discipline. This involves consideration of establishing classroom rules, the enforcement of negative consequences when rules are broken and the use of positive consequences. While this 'one size fits all' approach might seem attractive to schools, the research evidence is inconclusive about the long-term effectiveness of the programme (see, for instance, Emmer and Aussiker 1989 in the USA and Nicholls and Houghton 1995 in the UK). Watkins and Wagner (2000) caution against the use of the Assertive Discipline programme as a 'cure all', given the wide variations in school communities and suggest that it is not useful when used as the sole intervention or in an automatic manner; when it implies that compliance brings improvement and hence encourages teachers to focus on being disciplinarians; and when it diverts attention from other aspects of school life, such as the curriculum, that also have an influence on behaviour in the classroom. As Munn and colleagues (1992) suggest, it is futile for schools to look for universal answers given that each has its own history, culture and circumstances.

In addition to brought-in programmes, teachers gain additional support for managing classroom behaviour from other sources. In Australia, research carried out by Arbuckle and Little (2004) showed that among almost 100 teachers 77 per cent sometimes or frequently used staff meetings as supports, 71 per cent attended in-service or professional development sessions and 56 per cent used journal articles or books. Interestingly, 24 per cent of the teachers requested information on behaviour support from the researchers, even though this was not a formal part of the survey. Requests included information related to student motivation and on-task behaviour, maximizing the learning benefits of disruptive students, bullying and practical solutions to disruptive classroom behaviour. More support was clearly required.

Types of interventions

As with the parenting programmes discussed in Chapter 6, most interventions to improve and maintain behaviour in the classroom operate within a psychological framework. There are four main approaches: behavioural, cognitive-behavioural, eco-systemic and psychodynamic (Visser 2000). Each of these advocates different types of interventions for improving and maintaining good behaviour.

Behavioural perspectives

Interventions adopting a behavioural perspective are associated with principles of reward, reinforcement and punishment as demonstrated in Canter's Assertive Discipline programme. A further example from Australia is the use of written teacher advice, termed TIP sheets, which have been found to be effective in primary settings for managing disruptive behaviours (Little et al. 2002). Teachers identify one behaviour that is problematic with a child in their classroom and receive support from a consultant in considering what strategies should be put in place to deal with it. The TIP sheets involve the routine and systematic use of preventative strategies, such as establishing rules and reactive strategies, and praise and reprimands within the classroom. Other examples of behavioural approaches include the use of time-out, behaviour contracts, token economies and targeted punishment. While behavioural strategies are seen to be effective in some circumstances, problematic is that they tend to situate disruptive behaviour as a characteristic of the student, the poor classroom management skills of the teacher, or a combination of both (Kaplan et al. 2002). Although behavioural approaches have had considerable success, particularly with young children, there has been an increasing recognition that cognitive and affective factors contribute to pupil behaviour (Powell and Tod 2004).

Cognitive-behavioural interventions

Cognitive-behavioural interventions focus on the ways in which behaviour problems are influenced by and associated with students' patterns of thoughts, beliefs, attitudes and attributions (Ayers et al. 2000). Interventions seek to change or modify these and the students' perceived self-efficacy leading to changes in behaviour. Problem solving techniques fall into this category, for example, Rogers's *Behaviour Recovery* (1994). Here, the teacher and the student work together to identify and clarify the problem and target behaviours to be changed. Alternative ways of coping with the problem are considered and steps outlined to achieve the appropriate behaviour. The possible consequences of behaving in certain ways are also discussed. Many anger management interventions are structured from this perspective. A typical programme for adolescents includes providing information about the cognitive and behavioural components of anger; teaching cognitive and behavioural techniques to manage anger; and facilitating the application of the newly acquired skills (Humphrey and Brooks 2006). Circle Time, which is featured later in the chapter, also adopts a key feature of cognitive-behavioural therapy, the creation of meaningful links between the thoughts, feelings and behaviours that shape our experience (Canney and Byrne 2006).

Eco-systemic approaches

Recently, greater emphasis has been placed on the need for preventative approaches that take a more holistic view of the school environment. The eco-systemic approach stresses that human development cannot be viewed in isolation but must be seen within the wider context of an individual's interactive relationships in social and cultural contexts (Bronfenbrenner 1979).

The eco-systemic approach to solving chronic problem behaviour in schools was first developed in the USA by Molnar and Lindquist (1989), but the approach has generated considerable interest in the UK (see Cooper 1993; Cooper et al. 1994; Tyler and Jones 1998, 2002). It is based on systems analysis (see Chapter 1), suggesting that situations develop within embedded contexts which all influence each other. Thus the problem is not identified within the individual in isolation nor within the environment but rather within the social ecosystem in which the behaviour occurs (Tyler 1998). From this perspective, important are the interactions that take place between teachers and students in the classroom and how these are interpreted, since interactions that are perceived as negative result in cycles of inappropriate behaviour developing.

Problem behaviours can arise from negative interactions whereby students have negative perceptions of their teachers' actions, of other students' behaviours, of teachers' perceptions and of parents' perceptions (Ayers et al. 2000). For instance, a teacher might view a child who keeps leaving their chair as disruptive and continue to reprimand him/her. However, different, more positive, interpretations can be attributed to this behaviour, for instance, the student is having difficulty with the work and as a coping strategy leaves his/her chair in order to prevent themselves failing at the task. Here, the teacher is likely to adopt a different strategy, acknowledging the students' learning difficulties and offering support. Tyler (1998) suggests that for all involved 'suspension of judgement' is required in order put aside assumptions and presuppositions and to consider alternative points of view.

From the eco-systemic perspective, whole-school and collaborative practices are crucial, prompting teachers to consider the wider picture in relation to the organization as a whole. Interventions are based on *paradoxical techniques* used to promote new interpretations. With regard to improving behaviour in the classroom, this requires teachers to use alternative explanations for problem behaviour. Although different techniques can be used, reframing has proved useful in the classroom research (Tyler and Jones 1998, 2002).

The psychodynamic perspective

The psychodynamic perspective suggests that problem behaviour has its source in the unconscious or subconscious thoughts of children. Interventions are complex and usually require long-term training; hence interventions in the fullest sense remain in the domain of trained specialists (Ayers et al. 2000). In Chapter 10 interventions for children with complex problems at risk of exclusion, including counselling, are considered.

Circle Time

In the UK many different initiatives and approaches have been developed for use within the classroom to improve behaviour, including Circle Time, Assertive Discipline, the use of positive praise, star charts and time-out. Circle Time deserves mention as it focuses on improving behaviour and relationships in schools and is widely practised in UK primary schools, usually as part of the pastoral programme or in relation to citizenship education. It is also popular in North America and Europe (Taylor 2003). Characteristically it involves regular timetabled sessions when teaching groups are given the opportunity to reflect on and share experiences, concerns, strengths and weaknesses, and to discuss, and arrive at solutions to issues of concern to the group. It is used to enhance group interaction and empathy, and to combat bullying by encouraging children to respect their peers and to view them positively. The emphasis is on strict adherence to a code of conduct that has been formulated by the group. This might include contributions being taken in turn, and no contributions being derided. Later in this chapter the use of Circle Time as a vehicle for the implementation of new curriculum materials to support Social and Emotional Aspects of Learning will be considered.

Classroom seating arrangements

Some interventions have considered the impact of different seating arrangements within the classroom on task engagement in primary classrooms (Hastings and Schwieso 1995). On-task behaviour is higher when pupils are seated in rows (rather than groups). Pupils who are least on task fare the worst when there are group seating arrangements. Seating in rows produces more homogeneous behaviour and less extreme off-task behaviour. Many pupils are given individual tasks to do while seated in groups, thus the seating arrangement does not match the nature of the task.

Whole-school approaches

As outlined in Chapter 4 the school context is important when considering how to improve and maintain behaviour since any strategies put in place need to take account of school history, culture and context. A single strategy for addressing behaviour will not be appropriate for all pupils so interventions need to be flexible. Strategies need to be matched to the needs of the students and of the teacher (Grossman 2005; Little 2005). The following sections provide illustrations from recent initiatives that had as a focus improving behaviour in the classroom. The first describes how a particular curriculum initiative was used to improve behaviour, the second explores the use of multi-agency teams to support staff in the classroom, and the third considers the role of teacher coaches.

Curriculum materials for improving children's social, emotional and learning skills

One strand of the Primary Behaviour and Attendance Pilot (PBAP) involved the implementation of curriculum materials to develop children's social, emotional and behaviour skills using the Social and Emotional Aspects of Learning programme (SEAL). Although much of the work was undertaken within the classroom, the whole-school approach was a particular strength since it ensured simultaneous engagement of all staff and children, encouraged whole-school dialogue about behaviour, attitudes and choices, and provided a structure for Personal, Social and Health Education (PSHE) (Hallam et al. 2006). The programme increased staff understanding of the importance of developing social, emotional and behavioural skills in children and the need to develop them through explicit teaching. It provided the staff with ways of introducing ideas:

> It's given me strategies to deal with things, behavioural and emotional issues. Stress levels have been helped in terms of the behaviour, giving you ideas to help deal with behaviours. Workload has slightly been increased because it is another thing to plan but it does not take long, because it is all there and you just pick out what you will use. Having the whole class focus helps to refer back to when there are issues. Behaviour issues were recorded in a book and that still happens now. What has changed is that I now also include the emotions of the child. I might include now, child was feeling very angry. I have got a fuller picture.
>
> (*Teacher*)

Understanding behaviour is important for managing it. The role of teachers is to teach. They are not counsellors but they need to manage pupils' behaviour and provide sufficient educational care and support to enable pupils to engage or re-engage in learning within the classroom (Visser 2000). The SEAL programme helped teachers to understand their pupils better:

It has helped me get to know the children more and therefore I might be more tolerant and understanding of their behaviours or idiosyncrasies. I think facilitating the programme and making it a pleasant experience for the children, but it is very difficult as a teacher to not hurry children up. It is creating the right atmosphere where children can give their answers. It has developed behaviour management skills in a different context through the normal class-room environment when I am directly teaching them and they are listening or they are working independently. Having confidence in dealing with a large group of children in managing their behaviour appropriately and reacting objectively rather than subjectively. I think the children are a lot better at dealing with things themselves. They seem to be able to resolve issues without having the teacher involved and what to do if you are being left out and how to deal with that or if you are being bullied. Also asking children how they feel if someone calls you a name. It is encouraging the children to step back and think they don't like it, so they will not do it to anyone else.

(Teacher)

A key aspect of the process was the involvement of the children in thinking about their behaviour. The programme also had an impact on the way that the teachers behaved as they became aware that they were role models for the children:

It has made me think very hard about how I talk to other people. We are extending the courtesy to the children of speaking in a positive way and guiding in a positive way and I think we should be doing it amongst the staff as well. We are all role models whether we like it or not.

(Teacher)

The programme had a major impact on staff confidence in dealing with behaviour issues in the classroom, all staff, not just those with academic teaching responsibilities. It enabled teachers to have a dialogue with pupils about behaviour and refer to the issues raised in the SEAL materials. Teachers were reported to be calmer in their approach:

They are calmer and more positive. More confident in being able to deal with these different situations, having the training, understand-ing the SEAL materials and the purpose of it. They are calmer in dealing with situations and incidents that may occur in children. It has raised the profile of teaching assistants and lunchtime supervi-sors. They know they are part of a team. Everybody feels part of a team and valued.

(Headteacher)

Teachers reported that they enjoyed working with their class on the materials and seeing the benefits. Relationships between teachers and pupils in the classroom were enhanced, problems were discussed and solved. Teachers listened to the children more and this created a friendlier atmosphere.

> On a personal level I really enjoy doing Circle Time with my class. I think it is really important that you and the children get time to reflect on things that are important to you as a class. It has helped my class deal with certain issues, name calling, bullying, fighting over the football in the playground. You can be proactive in the SEAL programme and there is always flexibility to react to certain issues that have come up in the class or playground. As a teacher I feel it has enhanced the emotional well being of my class, which makes them easier to teach. I can't imagine not doing Circle Time. What I have noticed, at the start of the year some children in my class were always passing and now they are growing in confidence and are able to contribute which is a big achievement for them. It gives everyone a chance to speak.
>
> (*Teacher*)

The specific characteristics of the SEAL programme which contributed to its success included:

- the adoption of problem solving approaches;
- the involvement of pupils to discuss behaviour and establish rules;
- teachers modelling behaviour to pupils;
- developing a shared understanding with pupils of the meaning of language and what constituted acceptable behaviour;
- staff training to support classroom implementation; and
- collaborative sharing and discussing of practice with all staff.

Behaviour and Education Support Teams

Much of the work of Behaviour and Education Support Teams (BESTs) is at the individual level (Hallam et al. 2005; Halsey et al. 2005) but they have also offered support in relation to improving behaviour in the classroom. Although the level of BEST involvement has varied between primary and secondary schools, there has been commonality in the perceived impact with four main areas identified:

1. Acquisition of skills and strategies for managing challenging behaviour and emotional difficulties.

2. Improved access to specialist support services.
3. Increased understanding of emotional and behavioural difficulties.
4. A general increase in the capacity to support pupils (Halsey et al. 2005).

BESTs offer group interventions in school, modelling of strategies in the classroom, and direct training sessions. A specific focus of many sessions is behaviour management. The work of BESTs is valued by schools as providing additional support, and offering the opportunity to engage in and develop a range of alternative strategies. The BESTs offered useful techniques which could be applied in classrooms resulting in increased staff confidence and schools being better able to cope with behavioural issues themselves, reducing the frequency with which they need to call on external support. BESTs also supplied additional specialist expertise for schools to draw on and extended contacts with other agencies that might offer support. This enabled pupils to access the support that they needed impacting on their behaviour in the classroom.

The presence of the BEST provided staff with a greater sense of security since they knew that additional support was available and led to some staff having a reduced workload, reduced stress and enabled teachers to focus on teaching as learning mentors dealt with home-related issues. One teacher spoke about a Year 3 girl who exhibited very challenging behaviour which she used to gain attention. Support from a counsellor and the BIP worker gave her more confidence, her work improved dramatically and she was able to gain attention through positive behaviour.

In one school the BEST Behaviour Support Teacher was valued for support provided for staff within the classroom and the strategies and advice offered. BEST involvement was not confined to individual teachers who had direct contact with members of the team, there was an impact on many staff within the school particularly in relation to the way that they perceived the problems that children may face. There was a greater awareness of 'why the children may be behaving badly rather than just seeing the behaviour' (LBP).

An important element of the work of the BESTs was that all school staff benefited. In one LA the BEST family therapist supported the learning mentors in developing their own practice, in addition to the cases that she undertook as part of her role. The learning mentors valued this support as it increased their understanding of theoretical issues, gave them new alternative strategies to use with pupils and provided them with supervision. In another LA the BEST Speech and Language Therapist developed a programme for Learning Support Assistants (LSAs) to use with pupils which included training to assess language. The LSAs were able to work with pupils in the periods between the therapy visits which was extremely beneficial. An example of BEST's work with support staff is provided in Box 7.1.

Box 7.1 Classroom support

Case study: BEST intervention for classroom support

Daniel's mother died during the last week of the summer holidays. This was a particularly traumatic experience for him, aged only 8. Throughout the year he received support from the learning mentor, who in turn was supervised by the BEST systemic family therapist. The learning mentor met with the family therapist weekly to discuss any difficulties arising, explore strategies that might be adopted, and get advice as how best to support Daniel as he worked through his bereavement. The form teacher provided feedback to the learning mentor weekly about how Daniel was in the class and this also informed the meeting that the learning mentor had with the family therapist:

> There has been a positive impact on the class as a whole. It means that the other children are able to work with him, not just play with him and then leave him. He used to sit on a table by himself but now he works with other children in a group. He needs constant praise all the time, even if it is just a look, just so that he feels reassured.
>
> *(Form Teacher)*

> I have learned an enormous number of things from the family therapist. It has changed the way I work.
>
> *(Learning Mentor)*

Important to the success of BESTs was that they worked closely with all school staff, offered a range of strategies for improving behaviour and tailored their activities to the needs of particular schools and children.

Teacher coaches

Improving behaviour in the classroom should be a collaborative process where teachers have the opportunity to review and discuss the approach they adopt in a detailed manner (Watkins and Wagner 2000). The notion of collaboration and development was pivotal to the role of teacher coaches in PBAP. The teacher coach's role was to provide an efficient and effective service to the targeted schools along with other professional colleagues including facilitating the school behaviour and attendance audit and school self-review, providing coaching for teaching staff, and running training and staff development activities. This section focuses on the role of the teacher coach in providing coaching to teaching staff.

Key criteria for the success of the teacher coach were:

- credibility and trust;
- providing a supportive model;
- having time for feedback;
- work with individual pupils and the whole class;
- considering alternatives;
- encouraging children to take responsibility for their own behaviour;
- strong support from senior management team; and
- the adoption of a whole school approach (Hallam et al. 2006).

Most staff raised the issue of credibility and trust. Coaches reported that the effectiveness of the intervention depended on the development of a long-term relationship. Time was needed to prepare the ground and ensure that schools understood the process and that the coaches understood the school, only then could the coaching have an impact in the classroom and on school management:

> Coaching is not a quick fix. All the schools and teachers have been open to it and in fact a lot of them have said it is lovely to be able to sit down with somebody and just to share and say how it is for them. I think they unburden themselves on to me because they know it is a confidential process. They know and trust that I will not be going back to the head teacher and revealing everything and they are telling me what is going wrong. It is not about being critical. They already know for themselves what is going wrong. It is about saying OK we recognize that there are problems, let's see if we can move forward together.
>
> (*Teacher Coach*)

It was crucial that there was sufficient time available for giving feedback. One school tried to organize coaching as a regular half to one day a week. The challenge was fitting the feedback sessions into the timetable. Initially supply cover was arranged but in the long term this proved too costly. As a result the teachers and the coach met either very early in the morning before school, at lunchtimes or after school. This required considerable commitment and sacrifice by the teacher coach and the teachers. Staff were prepared to give up their own time as they could see the benefits. In other schools, some staff were reluctant to leave the classroom for feedback as they did not wish to disrupt the flow of teaching. Sometimes the headteacher provided cover. Practices varied:

> Different schools have managed feedback in different ways. We have been quite strict that it has to be 45 minutes cover time and that it is not taken out of playtime. Some schools have employed someone to

cover for the day when we are coming in. Some schools have got teaching assistants they are happy to leave with a class. One school has reorganized their playtime to allow the feedback to happen.

(*Teacher Coach*)

The collegiate non-judgemental approach of the coaches enabled teachers to reflect on what was happening in their lessons with the coach, share their perceptions, and discuss how to move things forward: 'I like the way it is based on learning outcomes. It is giving the teacher the tools to unpack it and look at how they might progress in the future' (Primary Behaviour Consultant).

The teacher coach strand of the PBAP was viewed as very successful (Hallam et al. 2006). Coaching gave teachers greater confidence to admit that they had problems in the classroom, and within each school it encouraged teachers to adopt a more unified approach to positive behaviour management strategies leading to a calmer more positive ethos. It improved self-esteem, gave staff a sense that their work was appreciated, promoted consistency cross-phase, and consolidated good practice. The coaches had time to listen, reflect, discuss and develop a sense of worth in relation to each teacher's work. The teachers learned new strategies, for instance, in one Year 1 class, the teacher had difficulties with children fidgeting. The coach suggested getting the children to imagine they were sitting on golden eggs, they had to sit still or the eggs would be broken. A display of golden eggs was set up to act as a reminder.

The teacher coaches also focused on the behaviour of specific children to support the teacher where there were particular difficulties. The coaches were able to develop strategies based on close observation of the individual child reducing aggressive behaviour. Overall, academic attainment was enhanced as teachers were able to focus on teaching, not behaviour. The children's concentration and cooperation improved. The work of the teacher coach encouraged pupils to think about and take responsibility for their behaviour:

The children have been encouraged to consider the impact of their own behaviour. Children who have found it difficult to remain calm in situations are developing strategies. Calmer, focused children achieve more and leave playground problems behind outside. There is improved collaboration. Staff reflect on their behaviour strategies and have more confidence in the correct use of strategies. The pilot was a worthwhile event – teachers felt more positive and supported. There were more opportunities for discussion of behaviour strategies. They were very different to other observations and allowed a greater focus on behaviour.

(*Teacher*)

The process of engaging with the teacher coach was challenging for some teachers who recognized that there was room for improvement in the quality of their teaching:

> Teacher coaching has enabled me to recognize that although discipline in my class was good it was more containment. The coaching process has allowed me to develop the confidence to take risks with my teaching. I feel that my classroom is now a more dynamic learning environment with greater engagement from my pupils. We are all enjoying ourselves a lot more.
>
> *(Teacher)*

Rather than reacting to pupils' behaviour, teachers and support staff planned to manage it, and were more aware of the individual needs of children and how they might use teaching strategies to more effectively meet these needs.

Broad principles for developing good practice within the classroom

There is a plethora of books, strategies and programmes to support behaviour in the classroom, but the evidence reviewed here suggests that there are distinctive features that are essential to good practice. Particularly important is that schools do not look for singular interventions as a 'cure-all' but rather:

- make greater use of proactive rather than reactive strategies;
- ensure that pupils have a clear understanding of consequences and celebration;
- encourage all staff to think about the reasons underpinning behaviour in planning how to manage it;
- provide opportunities for all staff to increase their understanding of emotional and behavioural difficulties;
- encourage consistent implementation of school behaviour policy, rewards and sanctions;
- praise and reinforce good behaviour;
- ensure that staff model appropriate social and classroom behaviours;
- involve pupils in thinking about their behaviour;
- adopt problem solving approaches that involve all pupils and all staff;
- ensure that effective support is in place that encourages collaboration;
- be flexible so that interventions are matched to the needs of the pupils and the staff;
- allow sufficient time for staff development and reflection on practice;

- ensure that strategies involve all school staff, including lunchtime supervisors, LSAs and learning mentors, in the training and support offered;
- share good practice with colleagues in school and across clusters of schools;
- enlist the support of senior management team; and
- support effective collaboration across all agencies, teachers and support staff involved in interventions.

Teachers must also remember that having a well-behaved class does not necessarily lead to effective pupil learning. Poor behaviour needs to be managed as it almost always interferes with learning but the strategies adopted in the classroom need to enhance motivation to learn. This issue will be addressed in Chapter 11.

Endnote

Most problem behaviour within the classroom relates to low-level disruption that interferes with the process of learning and frustrates teachers and pupils alike. In developing strategies to improve and maintain behaviour in the classroom it is important to adopt a whole-school approach whereby teachers, support staff and multi-agency teams work collaboratively in sharing and discussing concerns and strategies for dealing with problem behaviour. Important, too, is the involvement of pupils in establishing acceptable conduct in the classroom, in thinking about their behaviour and being involved in problem solving approaches. To be effective in the long-term emphasis needs to be given to proactive rather than reactive approaches with children learning to take responsibility for their own behaviour. There are many different strategies which can be adopted in relation to maintaining and improving behaviour in the classroom, there is no simple 'quick fix' or 'off-the-shelf solution' that will solve all the problems. Strategies need to be matched to the needs of the pupils, the teachers and the school context.

Chapter summary

- Poor behaviour in the classroom is generally confined to low-level disruption.
- Whole-school approaches to improving behaviour in the classroom are effective as they support consistency in teacher behaviour.
- Rewarding positive behaviour is more effective than reacting to poor behaviour.

> • The strategies adopted need to be matched to the needs of the pupils, the teachers and the school context and promote learning in addition to managing behaviour.

Further reading

Ayres, H., Clarke, D. and Murray, M. (2000) *Perspectives on Behaviour: A Practical Guide to Effective Interventions for Teachers*. London: David Foulton.

Hallam, S., Rhamie, J. and Shaw, J. (2006) *Evaluation of the Primary Behaviour and Attendance Pilot. Research Report 717*. London: DfES.

Watkins, C. and Wagner, P. (2000) *Improving School Behaviour*. London: Paul Chapman.

References

Arbuckle, C. and Little, E. (2004) Teachers' perceptions and management of disruptive classroom behaviour during the middle years (years 5 to 9). *Australian Journal of Educational and Developmental Psychology*, 4: 59–70.

Ayres, H., Clarke, D. and Murray, A. (2000) *Perspectives on Behaviour: A Practical Guide for Effective Interventions for Teachers*. London: David Foulton.

Bronfenbrenner, U. (1979) *The Ecology of Human Development: Experiments by Nature and Design*. Cambridge, MA: Harvard University Press.

Brown, S. and McIntyre, K. (1993) *Making Sense of Teaching*. Buckingham: Open University Press.

Canney, C. and Byrne, A. (2006) Evaluation Circle Time as a support to social skills development: Reflections on a journey in school-based research. *British Journal of Special Education*, 33(1): 19–24.

Cooper, P. (1993) *Effective Schools for Disaffected Pupils: Integration and Segregation*. London: Routledge.

Cooper, P., Smith, C. and Upton, G. (1994) *Emotional and Behavioural Difficulties: Theory into Practice*. London: Routledge.

Department for Education and Employment (DfEE) (1997) *Excellence for All Children: Meeting Special Educational Needs*. London: Stationery Office.

Doyle, W. (1980) *Classroom Management*. West Lafayette, IN: Kappa Delta Pi.

Doyle, W. (1986) Academic work, in T.M. Tomlinson and H.J. Walberg (eds) *Academic Work and Educational Excellence: Raising Student Productivity*. Berkeley, CA: McCutchan.

Doyle, W. (1989) Classroom management techniques, in O.C. Moles (ed.) *Strategies to Reduce Student Misbehaviour*. Washington, DC: US Department of Education.

Doyle, W. (1990) Classroom knowledge as a foundation for teaching. *Teachers College Record*, 91(3): 347–60.

Elton Report (1989) Committee of Enquiry into Discipline in Schools. *Discipline in Schools*. Great Britain: HMSO.

Emmer, E.T. and Aussiker, A. (1989) School and classroom discipline programs: How well do they work? In O.C. Moles (ed.) *Strategies to Reduce Student Misbehaviour*. Washington, DC: US Department of Education.

Grossman, H. (2005) The case for individualizing behaviour management approaches in inclusive classrooms. *Emotional and Behavioural Difficulties*, 10(1): 17–32.

Hallam, S., Castle, F. and Rogers, L. with Creech, A., Rhamie, J. and Kokotsaki, D. (2005) *Research and Evaluation of the Behaviour Improvement Programme*. *Research Report 702*. London: DfES.

Hallam, S., Rhamie, J. and Shaw, J. (2006) *Evaluation of the Primary Behaviour and Attendance Pilot*. *Research Report 717*. London: DfES.

Halsey, K., Gulliver, C., Johnson, A., Martin, K. and Kinder, K. (2005) *Evaluation of Behaviour and Education Support Teams*. *Research Report 706*. Nottingham: NFER.

Hastings, N. and Schwieso, J. (1995) Tasks and tables: The effects of seating arrangements on task engagement in primary classrooms. *Educational Research*, 37(3): 279–91.

Houghton, S., Wheldall, K. and Merrett, F. (1988) Classroom behaviour problems which secondary school teachers say they find the most troublesome. *British Educational Research Journal*, 14: 297–312.

Humphrey, N. and Brooks, A.G. (2006) An evaluation of a short cognitive-behavioural anger management interventions for pupils at risk of exclusion. *Emotional and Behavioural Difficulties*, 11(1): 5–24.

Infantino, J. and Little, E. (2005) Students' perceptions of behaviour problems and the effectiveness of different disciplinary methods. *Educational Psychology*, 25(5): 491–508.

Kaplan, A., Gheen, M. and Midgley, C. (2002) Classroom goal structure and student disruptive behaviour. *British Journal of Educational Psychology*, 72: 191–211.

Kitching, R. (2001) *Violence, Truancy and School Exclusion in France and Britain: Report of a Seminar Held in London 28–29 March 2001*. London: Franco–British Council, Chameleon Press.

Kyriacou, C. (2002) A humanistic view of discipline, in B. Rogers (ed.) *Teacher Leadership and Behaviour Management*, pp. 40–52. London: Paul Chapman.

Lewis, R., Romi, S., Qui, X. and Katz, Y.J. (2005) Teachers' classroom discipline in Australia, China and Israel. *Teaching and Teacher Education*, 21: 729–41.

Little, E. (2005) Secondary school teachers' perceptions of problem behaviours. *Educational Psychology*, 25(4): 369–77.

Little, E., Hudson, A. and Wilks, R. (2002) The efficacy of written teacher advice (Tip Sheets) for managing classroom behaviour problems. *Educational Psychology*, 22(3): 251–66.

Maijer, C.J.W. (2001) *Inclusive Education and Effective Classroom Practices*. Middelfart: European Agency for Development in Special Needs Education.

Martin, A.J., Linfoot, K. and Stephenson, J. (1999) How teachers respond to concerns about misbehaviours in their classroom. *Psychology in the Schools*, 36: 347–58.

Merrett, F. and Houghton, S. (1989) Does it work with the older ones? A review of behavioural studies carried out in British secondary schools since 1981. *Educational Psychology*, 9(4): 287–310.

Molnar, A. and Lindquist, B. (1989) *Changing Problem Behaviour in Schools*. San Francisco, CA: Jossey-Bass.

Mortimore, P., Sammons, L. Stoll, L. and Ecob, R. (1988) *School Matters*. Wells: Open Books.

Munn, P., Johnstone, M. and Chalmers, V. (1992) *Effective Discipline in Secondary Schools and Classrooms*. London: Paul Chapman.

Nicholls, D. and Houghton, S. (1995) The effect of Canter's Assertive Discipline Program on teacher and student behaviour. *British Journal of Educational Psychology*, 65: 197–210.

Ofsted (2005a) *The Annual Report of Her Majesty's Chief Inspector of Schools 2003–04*. London: HMSO.

Ofsted (2005b) *Managing Challenging Behaviour in Schools*. London: HMSO.

Powell, S. and Tod, J. (2004) *A Systematic Review of How Theories Explain Learning Behaviour in School Contexts*. London: EPPI-Centre, Institute of Education.

Rogers, B. (1994) *Behaviour Recovery: A Whole-school Programme for Mainstream Schools*. Camberwell: ACER.

Rutter, M., Maughan, B., Mortimore, P. and Ouston, J. (1979) *Fifteen Thousand Hours*. London: Open Books.

Ryan, R.M., Connell, J.P. and Deci, E.L. (1985) A motivational analysis of self-determination and self-regulation in education, in C. Ames and R. Ames (eds) *Research on Motivation in Education Vol: 2 The Classroom Milieu*. San Diego, CA: Academic Press.

Smith, C. and Laslett, R. (1993) *Effective Classroom Management: A Teacher's Guide*. London: Routledge.

Stephens, P., Kyriacou, C. and Tønnessen, F.E. (2005) Student teachers' views of pupil misbehaviour in classrooms: A Norwegian and an English setting compared. *Scandinavian Journal of Educational Research*, 49(2): 203–16.

Taylor, M.J. (2003) *Going Round in Circles: Implementing and Learning from Circle Time*. Slough: NFER.

Tyler, K. (1998) A comparison of the No Blame approach to bullying and the eco-systemic approach to changing problem behaviour in schools. *Pastoral Care in Education*, 16(1): 26–32.

Tyler, K. and Jones, B.D. (1998) Using the eco-systemic approach to change chronic problem behaviour in primary schools. *Pastoral Care in Education*, 16(4): 11–20.

Tyler, K. and Jones, B.D. (2002) Teachers' responses to the eco-systemic approach to changing chronic problem behaviour in schools. *Pastoral Care in Education*, 16(4): 11–20.

Visser, J. (2000) *Managing Behaviour in Classrooms*. London: David Foulton.

Watkins, C. and Wagner, P. (2000) *Improving School Behaviour*. London: Paul Chapman.

8 Alternative curricula

This chapter considers the nature of the school curriculum and why many countries in the developed world offer alternative educational programmes. The role of the curriculum in influencing behaviour is discussed and consideration given to alternative curricular for disaffected pupils. Examples of good practice in alternative curriculum provision in the UK are explored.

Introduction

In the 21st century most schools follow a curriculum that is set at national, regional or state level. The degree of prescription varies from countries where requirements are laid out in detail, for instance, France, Japan, Korea and Singapore, to those in which frameworks are provided and schools develop individual curricula suitable for their students and context, for instance, England since Curriculum 2000, The Netherlands and Spain (Le Métais 2002). Where curriculum regulations are not statutory, teachers still tend to follow recommended guidelines, especially when illustrative material is provided (e.g. Scotland). In the USA the curriculum requirements in some states exert a huge influence over the textbook market (e.g. California).

In many European countries, although curriculum structures are diverse, there is some similarity in the way that a broad curriculum is offered up to the age of 16, with a limited number of optional subjects and some experience-oriented content (Nicaise et al. 2000). In Australia, Hungary, Italy, and Sweden students are required to follow a common curriculum throughout the compulsory stages of schooling (Le Métais 2002).

Despite the number of countries adopting a centralized curriculum there remains a lack of consensus about its value to pupils in relation to attainment. The Organization for Economic Co-operation and Development (OECD 2001), based on the PISA survey, reported no significant relationships between centralized curricula and high levels of student performance in reading, mathematics and scientific literacy. Concerns have also been expressed that centralized curricula might prevent schools from meeting the needs of individual students, and that current disaffection is largely the result of more standardization. There are also issues relating to the pressures that teachers are under to deliver standardized curricula which may impact negatively on other aspects of school life (Bridges 1994). In some countries, for instance, England, The Netherlands, Singapore and Spain, these concerns have led to a reduction in the extent of curricula prescription. In addition, many countries have developed and offer alternative curricula.

One of the main factors associated with school failure and pupils who dropout of education is the mismatch between the academic curriculum offered by the school and the interests and skills of the students (USA: Natriello et al. 1990; England: Cullen et al. 2000). In the USA students view school as boring and irrelevant (AYPF 2000), or as a grade game where they try to get by with as little effort as possible (Burkett 2002) with motivation declining as they progress through school (Eccles et al. 1984; Fredricks and Eccles 2002). Research among high school students in Brazil (Lannes et al. 2002) also highlights student dissatisfaction with the curriculum, most wishing to engage in activities not taught at school. In Australia concerns have been voiced about how the traditional school curriculum is unrelated to the lived experiences of many young people (Hattam 2004).

Similar problems are found in the UK. Pupils' enjoyment and motivation towards school decreases throughout Key Stages 3 and 4 (Keys and Fernandes 1993; Woolnough 1994; Harland et al. 2002). A particular concern relates to pupils in the last two years of compulsory school when they study for the General Certificate of Secondary Education (GCSE) (Ofsted 2003). Many students regard GCSEs as inappropriate or lacking relevance leading in some cases to disaffection, underachievement and truancy (Bayliss 1999; Cullen et al. 2000). There are concerns, too, that the curriculum is rigid and overloaded in terms of content and that pupils might benefit from a more equitable balance between the development of academic and social skills (Blyth and Milner 1994; Davie 1996; Smith 1996). Pupils report difficulties with the formality and prescription of the curriculum, the emphasis on literacy, and the continuous focus on assessment (Hilton 2006). The curriculum, especially at Key Stage 4, depresses students' interest and demotivates them (Morris 1996). Pupils are 'turned off' by their experience of secondary education (DfES 2003). Those pupils who are disengaged from education also fail to see the relevance of the curriculum in relation to their current or long-term interests and would like change in relation to the type of work they are expected to do (Kinder et al. 1996, 1997, 1999b; Rudduck et al. 1996). Although pupil disaffection from school is well documented, historically the introduction of the National Curriculum, its academic orientation, and the ongoing academic/vocational divide which downplays the value and expertise associated with vocational education have exacerbated the situation (Ball 1993; Hodgson and Spours 1997; Young 1998).

Webb and Vulliamy (2004) describe staff perceptions of the process of disaffection in a group of schools in North Yorkshire, where no appropriate vocationally-oriented curriculum could be offered to pupils who were unable to cope with GCSE courses. Disaffection was 'creeping in' during Year 8 as pupils began to struggle with the work, continued in Year 9 and reached a 'flashpoint' in Year 10 when the pupils returned to school after the summer break. Where the curriculum is perceived to be irrelevant, or is too difficult, behavioural difficulties can follow.

Alternative curriculum programmes, throughout the developed world, have been implemented predominantly in secondary schools in an attempt to encourage young people to remain in school and re-engage with their learning following evidence demonstrating links between disaffection and an overly prescriptive curriculum that lacks relevance for some pupils (Kinder et al. 1995, 1996, 1999a, 1999b; Dearing 1996). Alternative education programmes, which have seen massive growth in recent years, particularly in the last two years of compulsory schooling (Lovey 1989) can be seen as a response to a global problem (Glasser 1992). In Britain, alternative education programmes were acknowledged in the Elton Report (1989) as important in meeting student needs outside mainstream education. At the time it was hoped that they would support students enabling them to return to mainstream education. More recently it has become apparent that most students attending alternative programmes remain in them until the end of compulsory education. In New Zealand, however, the ideal outcome continues to be for students to re-enter the education system in a mainstream school, although for those who are 15, other positive outcomes include entering a training programme, or finding a job (O'Brien et al. 2001).

Advocates of alternative curricula argue that if other educational opportunities are provided for students at risk of failure they will be able to succeed and that such alternatives are necessary to meet the needs of all students.

An international perspective on alternative curricula

Alternative curricula in the developed world are many and varied, ranging on a continuum from informal, individual work experience, through to formalized curricula. Even within the USA, where 48 states define alternative education, definitions vary tremendously (Martin and Brand 2006). In Ohio, local school boards offer alternative schooling for K-12 students who are suspended, truanting, experiencing academic failure or exhibiting disruptive behaviour. In California, governing boards provide expelled students with access to alternative programmes operated by the district, the county superintendent of schools or a consortium of districts (Martin and Brand 2006). Such variation is not seen as problematic, since historically, alternative curricula are based on the tenet that different individuals learn in different ways (Morley 1991) and that there is no single best approach to education.

In New Zealand alternative education refers to programmes which are operated as a result of community collaboration. The Ministry of Education establishes contracts with schools to provide a given number of places for young people, aged 13.5 to 15 years who have become alienated from the education system. Generally schools work with community partners who provide the alternative programmes (O'Brien et al. 2001).

Young people engaged in these programmes are likely to have:

- been out of school for two terms or more;
- had multiple exclusions (urban – more than one school, rural–one plus other factors);
- a history of dropping out of mainstream schooling after being reintegrated; and
- dropped out of the Correspondence School after enrolment as an 'At-Risk Student' (O'Brien et al. 2001).

Programmes have a managing school, and a manager or coordinator, who is responsible for a 'cluster' of schools in the immediate area, known as a 'consortium'. The manager can be the principal of the school or a nominated staff member. Providers deliver the alternative programmes for the consortium. Alternative education provision can include school-based programmes set within a segregated unit; community-based programmes; or individual placements for young people with, for instance, a local employer. The staff of the alternative education programmes may include trained teachers, community and youth workers.

In the USA it has been estimated that there are 10,900 alternative public schools and programmes for at-risk students. As of October 2000, the number of individuals enrolled in these alternative school programmes was 612,900, or 1.3 per cent of all public school students (National Center for Education Statistics 2001). Aron (2006) draws attention to promising models of alternative provision in the USA which include Career Academies, Twilight Academies, Jobs Corp, Youth Build USA, Gateway to College and Open Meadow Alternative School. Career Academies provide small learning communities for 30 to 60 students. Students stay in these communities for two to four years with the same teachers and follow a curriculum that includes academic and career-oriented courses. Additional input to the programme is from community resources and local employers. Twilight Academies provide an after-school programme over a four/five-week period with the aim of reintegrating the pupil back into school.

Alternative curricula in the UK

In England, alone, 75,000 young people participated in education outside mainstream secondary schools in 2003 whether in Local Authority (LA) managed or brokered alternative provision (QCA 2004). The provision included that provided by Pupil Referral Units; hospital teaching services; home tuition services; virtual (or e-) learning centres, and provision commissioned by the LA from Further Education colleges; training providers; employers; voluntary sector organizations; community services; youth services; youth offending teams, and other local agencies.

Students accessing alternative provision at Key Stage 4 in England include:

- those already permanently excluded from school;
- those presenting challenging behaviour at risk of exclusion;
- students with very poor attendance at Key Stage 3;
- students who were ill, in hospital or with particular medical needs, including those with psychiatric problems;
- young carers;
- pregnant schoolgirls and young mothers;
- highly mobile students (such as travellers, refugees, asylum seekers, young people whose families are in crisis);
- students in and out of custody; and
- school refusers and school phobics (QCA 2004).

As elsewhere, in England, the government has supported alternative curriculum initiatives and encouraged schools to offer more options for pupils aged 14–16 years (DfEE/QPID 1998; QCA 1998a, 1998b; Statutory Instruments 1998). Specifically included are changes to the mode of study, the content of the curriculum, the teaching and learning context, and the nature of assessment. In practice, this means that students might spend more time developing key skills, spending part of the week at college, in training or with an employer learning vocational or pre-vocational skills, or attending community activities designed to promote personal and pro-social skills. Examples of work-related programmes include Manchester's Mpower programmme and AC2001 (Charlton et al. 2004). Charitable organizations have also provided alternative curricula places, such as the Prince's Trust. However, the quality of the curriculum across such provision remains uneven (Ofsted 2003).

Cullen and colleagues (2000) propose that there are three main types of alternative programmes: satellite, extension and complementary, however, in practice the distinctions are often less clear cut. A satellite programme is separate provision for a group of identified pupils with problems: there is little relationship or impact on the normal curriculum. Complementary programmes are available to all pupils in some schools as an externally provided vocationally oriented option. Extension programmes, by contrast, offer an individualized approach that seeks to compensate for perceived weaknesses in the breadth of content or style of delivery of the National Curriculum. Differences are also apparent in the location of the provision whether off- or on-site at the school.

The remainder of this chapter sets out in detail four examples of good practice in developing alternative provision. Although the types of provision, the model of delivery, and the location are different, common characteristics are shared. These reflect findings from the international and UK literature.

- Most alternative curricula provision is small in size (Arnove and Strout 1980; Bryk and Thum 1989; Natriello et al. 1990; Young 1990; Quinn et al. 1999; Tobin and Sprague 1999; Hallam et al. 2003; Kendall et al. 2003; Aron 2006).
- There is an emphasis on one-on-one interaction between teachers and students, with teachers adopting the role of firm but kind facilitators (Arnove and Strout 1980; Tobin and Sprague 1999; O'Brien et al. 2001; Hallam et al. 2003, 2007; Kendal et al. 2003).
- Importance is placed on creating a supportive environment (Arnove and Strout 1980; Case 1981; Bryk and Thum 1989; Young 1990; Tobin and Sprague 1999; O'Brien et al. 2001; Hallam et al. 2003; Kendall et al. 2003).
- Students are presented with opportunities for success that are relevant to their future (Arnove and Strout 1980; Natriello et al. 1990; Hallam et al. 2003; Kendal et al. 2003; Martin and Brand 2006).
- Alternative curricula permit greater flexibility in structure than traditional mainstream curricula with an emphasis on student decision-making (Natriello et al. 1990; Hallam et al. 2003, 2007; O'Brien 2003; Aron 2006; Martin and Brand 2006). This flexibility also means that it is possible to address individual student needs in the structure of the day (Shaw 1998; Hallam et al. 2003, 2007).

On-site alternative curriculum: an extension programme

As part of the Behaviour Improvement Programme (BIP), LAs were encouraged to develop alternative curricular provision. In one LA, provision was made at an off-site centre within walking distance of the school. The teacher in charge continued to teach a small number of lessons in the mainstream school. The centre was a joint venture with the Youth Service, who owned the building and provided a full-time Youth Worker. In the opinion of parents as well as staff, the centre had managed to retain pupils within the education system who might otherwise have been permanently excluded. At the time of the visit the centre had twelve Year 10 pupils and six Year 11 pupils. For some Year 10 pupils who had been regular excludees and who said they 'couldn't wait to leave school' and 'lessons are boring', the prospect of a work-related programme in Year 11 was really important. This, in most cases, consisted of one day of work experience, one day at a college course and three days in school. The latter became tolerable because of the work-related programme. Details of some of the pupils' experiences are provided in Box 8.1.

Box 8.1 Alternative curriculum

Case study: Pupils attending an alternative curriculum centre

Brian had been excluded from school and spent all his time at the centre. Rick had been bordering on fixed-term exclusion on a regular basis. His parents had been in constant receipt of phone calls and letters from school and admitted that Rick was always in trouble. He was described as 'messing about' and being confrontational with teachers. He attended the centre on a regular basis and participated in everything. His courses included motor mechanics and woodworking and the ASDAN programme.

All the students interviewed were keen to attend college in Year 11 – Brian to take courses in building, Rick to take an electrician's course and Lucy to study sports and leisure. In addition they were to undertake literacy and computer work. Rick was also going to take art and maths at school as this was possible for students on a part-time basis and was seen as useful socially. Rick's father wanted him to go back to school full-time but Rick indicated that he couldn't sit and do all the curriculum work and that the centre allowed him to stop work for a few minutes which he couldn't do in school. Rick's attitude had changed since being in the centre: he was more settled and his parents were happy that he was attending, and had the opportunity to gain qualifications in Year 11, but remained concerned that he was not actually in school, which they felt might affect the perceptions of future employers. However, Rick had remained on the school roll and had an entitlement to school reports and a Record of Achievement, the latter giving him some self-confidence. His parents were convinced that if Rick had not been able to attend the centre he would have been permanently excluded from school and become involved with crime.

Lucy was a persistent truant, disliking everything about school. The learning mentor referred her for placement at the centre and attempts were being made to gain Lucy access to a 'Positive Futures' course and assist her in getting a qualification as a lifeguard which she badly wanted (Hallam et al. 2005).

The parents of these students had given up hope of their children staying in education but as a result of the work of the centre there had been no Key Stage 4 exclusions. There were plans to extend the curriculum by having maths and English subject teachers teaching there. Critical factors in the success of the centre included:

- the more relaxed atmosphere which enabled pupils to talk to members of staff at any time;
- pupils being treated with respect. All the students had aspirations and the centre gave them an opportunity to realize them in a way in which their school did not;
- pupils being encouraged in their work and attempts being made to raise self-esteem. This included setting targets, which in some cases were very challenging, for example, five GCSEs Grades *A–C;
- links with the school, the opportunity to undertake some lessons there and receive careers advice, other external opportunities for personal development; and
- staff working hard at building relationships with parents, making home visits and parents seeing the impact on their children.

Initiatives within a community: a satellite programme

Re-Entry is a community-based initiative with an educational bias. It aims to enable young people excluded or truanting from school to embark upon a programme leading to their return to mainstream education, or accessing a training programme. Funding from the BIP enabled the charity to set up their fourth base in a house which had been empty for two years. As with other alternative provision, student numbers were small. At any one time eight pupils attended Re-Entry, specialist tutors undertaking the teaching and community mentors working on issues relating to poor attendance, the aim being to get students back to school or to find them a place in college. Staff built up relationships with individual pupils and all the people who were involved with them worked to get to know the community and recruited community members to assist in the renovation of the house. Funding came from different local agencies, members of the community helped, as did pupils from the youth inclusion project. The approach adopted was to try to understand the whole community, and to support the young people to encourage the community to grow and develop. A mentor development officer trained people in the community and this constituted an important element of the work.

When young people were referred they were interviewed with their families and key workers. Referrals came from a wide range of different agencies. Pupils agreed to the centre rules, had a two-week trial and then entered into a partnership plan with the centre, the pupil and his/her parents signing this. Pupils attended for two terms only as the provision was seen as providing a bridge to other forms of education. Many of the pupils had been out of school for as long as two years and they and their parents tended to have rejected the need for education. Unlike much alternative provision, Re-Entry catered for Key Stage 3 and 4 students although the two groups attended separately each doing two days at the centre, one day on a joint off-site activity and two days on a placement. Tuition was provided in mathematics, English, and drug and sexual awareness. There were links with the police through a citizenship programme and with other services for placements. Staff maintained links with schools and key workers. Pupils were set specific targets and progress was monitored half-termly. Staff also ran after-school clubs in primary and secondary schools, particularly focusing on social interactions and Circle Time and worked in playgrounds helping pupils to learn a range of games. Sixty–seven students had progressed through the programme in the year prior to the study. Of these 18 went on to college, 15 returned to school, 4 had left the LA, 13 had moved on to another provider and some were referred back to the LA. Overall, the project provided a positive means of re-engaging some students with education (Hallam et al. 2005). In common with other alternative curricular provision stress was placed on building up effective relationships, setting relevant targets, providing a variety of activities, and offering a more relevant curriculum.

Skill Force: a complementary programme that operates on school premises

Skill Force started as a pilot scheme in two counties in England in 2000 and at the time of its evaluation had 23 teams throughout the UK (Hallam et al. 2003). The stated mission of Skill Force is to: reawaken enthusiasm for life through education; build self-worth, and through that families and communities; and reduce truancy, exclusion, unemployment and criminal records. The specific aim of the programme is to develop citizenship and improve the employability of the students helping them achieve their full potential by: improving students' behaviour and attitude to learning; reducing truancy and exclusions; remotivating students within schools; and providing students with vocational qualifications that employers would recognize and value.

Skill Force's core programme offers a wide range of activities which focus on team building, problem solving and raising self-esteem through the teaching of programmes such as the Duke of Edinburgh's Award scheme. The programme is delivered by instructors with appropriate military and civilian qualifications mainly selected for their experience of working with young people. The military systems approach to training of the instructors enables them to deliver a course that is practical, flexible and relevant.

Students selected for Skill Force typically drop two GCSE subjects which equate to around two half days of instruction a week. The programme takes place within school hours and operates under school rules. The Skill Force curriculum was devised in conjunction with senior teachers and developed within schools to provide a course based around work-related learning that future employers recognize. The programme is principally based upon the ASDAN key skills award but also utilizes other awards, certificates and qualifications such as the Duke of Edinburgh Award, St John's Ambulance Young Lifesavers Certificate and the OCR Certificate in Preparation for Employment. The activities undertaken place emphasis on student learning in practical situations. Students are given responsibility for their learning and have the opportunity to make choices about what they learn. The core of the Skill Force programme is the provision of alternative curricula for Key Stage 4 students, although some Key Stage 3 students have been included. The teams offer a range of activities typically including residential trips, sports, outdoor pursuits, community/environmental projects and classroom work. Students also learn practical life skills. Whatever activity is undertaken it is documented and contributes to the ASDAN folder. There are a limited number of Skill Force places in each school and more students want to participate than there are places available. Box 8.2 gives parents' account of their children's experiences of Skill Force.

Box 8.2 Parents' perceptions of the impact of an alternative curriculum

Case study: Parents' perceptions of the impact of Skill Force on their children

> Peter really liked Skill Force and I'm glad he's in it. He's not keen on school. Skill Force is the only time he gets up and goes in. He's benefited from it. It's calmed him down. He went on a camping holiday. He really enjoyed it – they did things like water sports that kids like doing – not education like school work, but at least they're learning about something. They do basic activities. There's a more relaxed atmosphere. He's on a part-time timetable because of his behaviour but he's had brilliant marks in Skill Force. I'm glad he enjoys it and attends at those times. He only goes to two other lessons apart from Skill Force at the moment. This will be the case until they sort out a place at college after the summer. He'll tell you if he's done something really good. It's the only thing he talks about with us from school. He's more grown up in Skill Force. He messes about in the other lessons. He is a totally different child. He rang us every day from his trip and told us what he'd been doing. He'd be out of school for definite if he hadn't attended Skill Force. It has been an incentive to be at school for a certain number of lessons because he's doing something he's enjoying.
>
> *(Peter's mother)*

The Team leader explained that Tracey's family had experienced a lot of difficulties (including bereavement) during the year, and Tracey had missed many months of schooling to help support her mother through the problems. She had particularly low self-esteem, was overweight and not naturally sporty or keen on the outdoors. She was one of six sisters, and helped to bring up her siblings. Her initial reaction to the residential course was negative, and she would not take part in activities, but the mentor persuaded her to stay a second day, and she was 'fantastic' by the end. Her mother described how:

> 'Tracey's been going through lots of problems. Skill Force has helped. It's been fantastic. She's got the mentors to turn to if she's got problems. The residential trip was her first time away from home. She really enjoyed it. I lost a granddaughter and a lot of other bad things have happened. I've been depressed. Tracey's been through a lot. Skill Force has been fantastic. She's coming back to her original self. She'd been showing attitude to teachers, which wasn't like her. She's a very deep person.

> Now she's getting better. She really enjoyed the climbing and all that – she sent me a postcard after the first half day to say that everything was OK and rang me every night too. Skill Force is bringing her back out of herself'.
>
> (*Hallam et al. 2003*, p. 85)

Overall, the programme provided a successful alternative to the National Curriculum for these disaffected pupils (Hallam et al. 2003, 2007). It was perceived as successful by the students because:

1. The curriculum was practical and the written work which was required was seen as meaningful. Students were given opportunities to express themselves, write about their own experiences and draw on a range of other artefacts, for instance, photographs.
2. They were offered the opportunity to gain qualifications. All students attained a first aid qualification soon after beginning the course. For some students this was the first formal educational success that they had achieved. The other qualifications on offer were also seen as useful for their future employment. The students wanted to engage with what they described as 'the real world' and perceived the Skill Force curriculum as more relevant in this respect.
3. The Skill Force personnel treated them as adults, allowed the pupils to call them by their first names, and relationships with them were respectful. This contrasted sharply with their interactions with teachers in school.
4. Curriculum delivery acknowledged their aspirations to adulthood and enabled them to demonstrate what they could do rather than providing them with opportunities which only enabled them to demonstrate failure.
5. Many of the students were able to develop relationships with the Skill Force personnel which facilitated them in talking about difficulties in their personal circumstances, for instance, there were examples where students had been deterred from running away from home.
6. The delivery of the programme was flexible. It was adapted to take advantage of local circumstances and also the needs of the pupils.
7. There was consistent use of rewards and consequences. Students were made aware that if their behaviour was good and they completed their work a reward would follow. If they did not, there would be no reward. The rewards were simple, for instance, undertaking a sporting activity or going for a walk. This contrasts

with most school regimes where there are few rewards for low-attaining students and consequences are seen in terms of punishment.

8. As the behaviour of each individual had consequences for the whole group, there was considerable peer pressure. This reinforced the focus on developing team work and social and communication skills, which the students often lacked at the start of the programme.

Not all students responded well to the Skill Force programme and some dropped out. Skill Force personnel believed that they were more successful with students at risk of exclusion than those whose behaviour had already deteriorated beyond that point. Other students who benefited were those lacking in confidence, perhaps because they had been bullied, and those with poor attendance. The Skill Force teams worked with students to build on their strengths and support them in overcoming their difficulties. The focus on team work was crucial in this process. The emphasis on learning to work with others contrasted with most of the students' prior experiences in school.

Pivotal to the success of Skill Force in supporting young people was effective integration into the schools in which they operated. Skill Force personnel and school staff worked together. Critical was that school staff understood the nature of the programme and were made aware of the requirements of Skill Force. The support of the senior management team and the presence of an effective Link Teacher were crucial for Skill Force personnel to become integrated into the work of the schools. Successful integration occurred where schools and Skill Force worked towards an agreed behaviour policy; were jointly able to resolve practical difficulties over accommodation and timetabling; had a clear understanding of the requirements of each other and of how both parties operated; and Skill Force staff attended school staff meetings and were seen as members of staff who made a wider contribution to school life. Where this commitment was lacking and Skill Force was perceived as a 'bolt-on' extra, there was potential for misunderstandings to occur between school and Skill Force staff with subsequent consequences for students. Particularly important was the role of the Link Teacher in facilitating the day-to-day running of the programme and ensuring good communication. That school staff and pupils held Skill Force in high regard was important since without this it is unlikely that the programme would have been a success.

Notschool.net: an e-learning satellite programme

Notschool.net was designed as an online learning community and resource for vulnerable and disaffected young people who were not engaging with any other form of conventional or alternative education. It began with a research phase in 1998, funded by the Department for Education and Skills (DfES) and ran with participants from Essex, Sussex and Glasgow in September 2000. Since then the project has been rolled out to 24 LAs predominantly within England. At the request of the DfES, the focus has been on expanding into LAs engaged in BIP: approximately 70 per cent of participants now come from inner-city BIP LAs. Until August 2005 Notschool.net was managed by a team at Ultralab and based at the University of East Anglia since then, at the behest of the DfES, an educational charitable trust named TheCademy has been formed to disseminate the Notschool.net model and apply aspects of this model to inclusion practice.

The stated aims of Notschool.net are to:

- re-engage teenagers in learning;
- provide a secure, non-threatening environment without fear of failure;
- rebuild confidence, self-esteem and social skills; and
- provide a bespoke pathway into further education, lifelong learning and further qualifications.

The project consists of a website which is described as a community for learning. Rather than being described as students, the participants in Notschool.net are referred to as a community of researchers and are supported by a team of personal mentors, subject experts and virtual 'buddies'. Typically, the mentors are qualified part-time teachers who work with six researchers to develop and facilitate individualized learning plans. Buddies are young people who have participated in the Notschool.net community but on reaching school leaving age have remained to support and offer encouragement to researchers. Subject experts provide curriculum content and resources across a range of subjects. They work through dialogue with the mentors and researchers in order to facilitate the researchers' learning. The software enables debating, polls, and other methods of interactive communication to encourage collaboration. The learning activities cover a broad range and academic interests are rated as highly as other pursuits. Researchers have explored mathematics, literacy, dance, saxophone playing, juggling and the environment (Duckworth 2001, 2005).

All LAs participating in the project operate with a team of two or three who are responsible for running Notschool.net within their LA. The teams comprise a project leader, an administrator and a technician. They are responsible for recruiting and training mentors and buddies, processing referrals, providing computers and Internet connections, and monitoring their cohort within the Notschool.net community. Box 8.3 describes the impact of Notschool.net.

Box 8.3 The impact of an alternative distance learning curriculum

---

Case study: The impact of Notschool.net

One young person (in a children's home) was set up with Notschool-.net in a Midlands LA. House moves followed to other parts of the country and then back to the original place. In each place the same LA arranged for Notschool.net to be available. As a result the young person received national accreditation from Notschool.net and started at a college. The children's service from the Midland's LA visited the boy in his new home and were in daily contact online and on the phone. Another young person had a real interest in computers and as a result of Notschool.net had been engaged in work experience setting up and configuring computers. He took up an apprenticeship with a computer firm. Other young people designated as school phobic and 'uneducable' benefited from the initiative and demonstrated that they could benefit from education, just not that on offer in school. The scheme was transforming for families since the computer was there for all. The impact extended to siblings and parents. Despite the fact that Notschool.net put expensive equipment into really deprived homes the equipment was used with care (Hallam et al. 2005).

Endnote

The findings from the projects reviewed here demonstrate the importance of providing an appropriate curriculum and motivational assessment procedures in stimulating enthusiasm for learning. This can lead to re-engagement with education and a reduction in indiscipline. Important is that the curriculum is relevant to young people's needs and aspirations and that relationships develop which enable staff to provide much needed guidance and pastoral support. Although different types of alternative curricula have been described both in the UK and internationally, there are common factors that affect success. Programmes need to be clearly introduced to staff, parents, students, and governors so that they have a clear understanding of their aims and operation. As programmes become established they need to have a high profile and involve past students in promotional activities. Students need to be selected with care, groups need to be balanced and students must want to participate. Programme staff should be involved in the selection procedures. Programmes are more successful where participants are at risk rather than already highly disaffected.

Where provision is offered in schools, programmes need to operate adopting the disciplinary systems of the school while having clear boundaries, rewards and punishments themselves. Programme staff need to understand the systems within which they are working at school, LA and agency level, and recognize that there are differences in culture between schools, LAs and different agencies. Schools need to recognize the needs of programmes in relation to space, resources and timetabling. Programme and school staff need to work closely together, good communication between school and programme staff is crucial. Programme staff need to be integrated into the day-to-day working of the school, for example, through attending staff meetings or meetings with Heads of Year. Programmes must have the full support of the senior management team and key staff must be appointed within the school to provide appropriate links with the programme staff. Programme staff need to have up to date information about programme participants.

Chapter summary

- It is important to provide pupils with a curriculum and assessment procedures which are perceived as relevant and which enhance motivation. For some pupils this will need to be an alternative to the National Curriculum.
- Common factors that contribute to the success of alternative curricula include:
  - the development of trusting relationships between 'staff' and 'students' including mutual respect;
  - a negotiated curriculum which matches the needs of learners;
  - students being given responsibility for their own learning;
  - the counselling and mentoring role of 'staff' who have time to help;
  - the development of a learning community;
  - praising and rewarding what young people can do;
  - real achievement and qualifications as recognized and valued by the young people;
  - adopting a problem solving approach; and
  - the commitment and qualities of the 'staff'.

Further reading

Cullen, M.A., Fletcher-Campbell, F., Bowen, E., Osgood, J. and Kelleher, S. (2000) *Alternative Education Provision at Key Stage 4*. Slough: NFER/LGA.

Hallam, S. and Rogers, L. with Rhamie, J. et al. (2003) *Evaluation of Skill Force.* London: Institute of Education.

Ofsted (2003) *Key Stage 4: Towards a Flexible Curriculum.* London: The Stationery Office.

References

American Youth Policy Forum (AYPF) (2000) *High Schools of the Millennium: Report of the Workgroup.* Washington, DC: AYPF.

Arnove, R. and Strout, T. (1980) Alternative schools for disruptive youth. *The Educational Forum*, 44: 452–71.

Aron, L.Y. (2006) *An Overview of Alternative Education.* Washington, DC: National Center on Education and Economy.

Ball, S. (1993) Education, Majorism and the curriculum of the dead. *Curriculum Studies*, 1: 195–214.

Bayliss, V. (1999) *Opening Minds: Education for the 21st Century. The Final Report of the RSA Project: Redefining the Curriculum.* London: RSA.

Blyth, E. and Milner, J. (1994) Exclusion from school and victim blaming. *Oxford Review of Education*, 20(3): 293–306.

Bridges, L. (1994) Exclusions how did we get here? in J. Bourne, L. Bridges and C. Searle (eds) *Outcast England: How Schools Exclude Black Children*, pp. 1–17. London: Institute of Race Relations.

Bryk, A. and Thum, Y. (1989) The effects of high school organization on dropping out: An exploratory investigation. *American Educational Research Journal*, 26: 353–83.

Burkett, E. (2002) *Another Planet: A Year in the Life of a Suburban High School.* New York: HarperCollins.

Case, B. (1981) Lasting alternatives: A lesson in survival. *Phi Delta Kappan*, 62(8): 554–7.

Charlton, T., Panting, C. and Willis, H. (2004) Targeting exclusion, disaffection and truancy in secondary schools: An evaluation of an alternative curriculum for older pupils. *Emotional and Behavioural Difficulties*, 9(4): 261–75.

Cullen, M.A., Fletcher-Campbell, F., Bowen, E., Osgood, J. and Kelleher, S. (2000) *Alternative Education Provision at Key Stage 4.* Slough: NFER/LGA.

Davie, R. (1996) Preface, in K. David and T. Charlton (eds) *Pastoral Care Matters: In Primary and Middle Schools*. London: Routledge.

Dearing, R. (1996) *Review of Qualifications for 16–19 Year Olds: Full Report*. London: SCAA.

Department for Education and Employment (DfEE), Quality and Performance Improvement Division (QPID) (1998) *Funding Sources for Projects for Disaffected Young People* (QPID Study Report No. 69). Sheffield: DfEE.

Department for Education and Skills (DfES) (2003) *14–19: Opportunity and Excellence*. London: DfES.

Duckworth, J. (2001) *Evaluation of the Notschool.net Research Project Initial Pilot*. Exmouth: Cutters Wharf Consultants.

Duckworth, J. (2005) *Notschool.net Evaluation*. Exmouth: Cutters Wharf Consultants.

Eccles, J.S., Midgley, C. and Adler, T.F. (1984) Grade-related changes in school environment: Effects on achievement motivation, in J.G. Nicholls (ed.) *Advances in Motivation and Achievement*, pp. 283–331. Greenwich, CT: JAI Press.

Elton Report (1989) Committee of Enquiry into Discipline in Schools *Discipline in Schools*. London: HMSO.

Fredricks, J.A. and Eccles, J.S. (2002) Children's competence and value beliefs from childhood to adolescence: Growth trajectories in two 'male-typed' domains. *Journal of Developmental Psychology*, 38: 519–33.

Glasser, W. (1992) *The Quality School: Managing Students Without Coercion*. New York: Harper Perennial.

Hallam, S. and Rogers, L. with Rhamie, J. et al. (2003) *Evaluation of Skill Force*. London: Institute of Education.

Hallam, S., Castle, F. and Rogers, L. with Creech, A., Rhamie, J. and Kokotsaki, D. (2005) *Research and Evaluation of the Behaviour Improvement Programme*. Research Report 702. London: DfES.

Hallam, S., Rogers, L., Rhamie, J. et al. (2007) Pupils' perceptions of an alternative curriculum: Skill Force. *Research Papers in Education*, 22(1): 43–63.

Harland, J., Moor, H., Kinder, K. and Ashworth, M. (2002) *Is the Curriculum Working? The Key Stage 3 Phase of the Northern Ireland Curriculum Cohort Study*. Slough: NFER.

Hattam, R. (2004) Poor prospects for public schooling. *Adelaide Review*, 15 October.

Hilton, Z. (2006) Disaffection and school exclusion: Why are inclusion policies still not working in Scotland? *Research Papers in Education*, 21(3): 295–314.

Hodgson, A. and Spours, K. (1997) *Dearing and Beyond: 14–19 Qualifications, Frameworks and Systems*. London: Kogan Page.

Kendall, K., Kinder, K., Halsey, K., Fletcher-Morgan, C., White, R. and Brown, C. (2003) *An Evaluation of Educational Alternatives. Research Report 403*. London: DfES.

Keys, W. and Fernandes, C. (1993) *What Do Students Think About School? Research into the Factors Associated with Positive and Negative Attitudes Towards School and Education*. Slough: NFER.

Kinder, K., Harland, J., Wilkin, A. and Wakefield, A. (1995) *Three to Remember: Strategies for Disaffected Pupils*. Slough: NFER.

Kinder, K., Wakefield, A. and Wilkin, A. (1996) *Talking Back: Pupil Views on Disaffection*. Slough: NFER.

Kinder, K., Wakefield, A. and Wilkin, A. (1997) *Exclusion: Who Needs It?* Slough: NFER.

Kinder, K., Kendall, S., Halsey, K. and Atkinson, M. (1999a) *Disaffection Talks: A Report for the Merseyside Learning Partnership Inter-Agency Development Programme*. Slough: NFER.

Kinder, K., Wilkin, A., Helen, M., Derrington, C. and Hogarth, S. (1999b) *Raising Behaviour 3: A School View*. Slough: NFER.

Lannes, D., Rumjanek, V., Velloso, A. and de Meis, L. (2002) Brazilian schools: Comparing students' interests with what is being taught. *Educational Research*, 44(2): 157–79.

Le Métais, J. (2002) *New Zealand Stocktake: An International Critique*. Auckland: National Institute of Education Policy Research/Ministry of Education.

Lovey, J. (1989) *Teaching Troubled Adolescents*. London: David Fulton.

Martin, N. and Brand, B. (2006) *Federal, State, and Local Roles Supporting Alternative Education*. Washington, DC: American Youth Policy Forum.

Morley, R.E. (1991) *Alternative Education: Dropout Prevention Research Reports*. Clemson, SC: National Dropout Prevention Centre. (ERIC Document Reproduction Service No. ED 349 652).

Morris, J.T. (1996) Excluded pupils: The mismatch between the problem and solutions. *Journal of Emotional and Behavioural Difficulties*, 1(2): 35–8.

National Center for Education Statistics (2001) *District Survey of Alternative Schools and Programs, FRSS 76*. Washington, DC: US Department of Education.

Natriello, G., McDill, E. and Pallas, A. (1990) *Schooling Disadvantaged Children: Racing Against Catastrophe*. New York: Teachers College Press.

Nicaise, I. et al. (2000) Success for all? Educational strategies for disadvantaged youth in six European countries, in: G. Walraven, C. Parsons, D. Van Veen and C. Day (eds) *Combating Social Exclusion through Education*, Leuven/ Apeldorm: Garant.

O'Brien, P., Thesing, A. and Herbert, P. (2001) *Alternative Education: Literature Review and Report on Key Informants' Experiences*. Report to the Ministry of Education. New Zealand, Ministry of Education.

Ofsted (2003) *Key Stage 4: Towards a Flexible Curriculum*. London: The Stationery Office.

Organization for Economic Co-operation and Development (OECD) (2001) *Knowledge and Skills for Life: First Results from PISA 2000. Executive Summary.* Paris: OECD.

Qualifications and Curriculum Authority (QCA) (1998a) *Disapplication of the National Curriculum at Key Stage 4: Guidance for Schools*. London: QCA.

Qualifications and Curriculum Authority (QCA) (1998b) *Learning from Work Experience: A Guide to Successful Practice*. London: QCA.

Qualifications and Curriculum Authority (QCA) (2004) *Designing a Personalised Curriculum for Alternative Provision at Key Stage 4*. London: QCA.

Quinn, M.M., Rutherford, R.B. and Osher, D.M. (1999) *Special education in alternative education programmes*. Reston, VA: ERIC Clearinghouse on disabilities and gifted education.

Rudduck, J., Chaplain, R. and Wallace, G. (eds) (1996) *School Improvement: What Can Pupils Tell Us?* London: David Fulton.

Shaw, H. (1998) *Improving Achievement*. Wellington: Ministry of Education.

Smith, C. (1996) Special needs and pastoral care: Bridging a gap that shouldn't be there. *Support for Learning*, 11(4): 151–6.

Statutory Instruments (1998) *Education, England and Wales. The Education (National Curriculum) (Exceptions at Key Stage 4) Regulations 1998 (SI 2021)*. London: The Stationery Office.

Tobin, T. and Sprague, J. (1999) Alternative education programs for at-risk youth: Issues, best practice and recommendations. *Oregon School Study Council Bulletin*, 42: 4.

Webb, R. and Vulliamy, G. (2004) *A Multi-agency Approach to Reducing Disaffection and Exclusions from School. Research Report 568.* London: DfES.

Woolnough, B. (1994) Changing pupils' attitudes to careers in science. *Physics Education,* 31(5): 301–8.

Young, M. (1998) *The Curriculum of the Future: From the New Sociology of Education to a Critical Theory of Learning.* London: Falmer Press.

Young, T. (1990) *Public Alternative Education.* New York: Teachers College Press.

9 Supporting at-risk children

This chapter considers the ways that children at risk of being excluded from school for poor behaviour can be identified and how they can be supported in mainstream education. This includes initiatives developed internationally and in the UK, including the role of key workers and learning mentors, Behaviour and Education Support Teams, nurture groups, Learning Support Units and transition work.

Background

Under the Dakar Framework (UNESCO 2000) governments from around the world reaffirmed their commitment to achieving Education for All by the year 2015. Among the key goals were that by 2015 every child in the world would be able to attend and complete primary school, that by 2005 as many girls as boys would be attending school and that there would be improved early childhood care and education, especially for the most vulnerable children. While attendance has increased, education remains beyond the reach of many children, particularly girls. In 2005, it was estimated that 60 million girls and 40 million boys were out of school (Global Campaign for Education 2005)

While some of these pupils have been excluded from school, many have never been given the opportunity to attend school at all. Reasons for this are complex. In countries such as China, Egypt and India poverty is an issue as are the demand for school fees and other related costs of education. Even where formal tuition fees have been abolished, for instance in Africa, the costs associated with education (e.g. books, uniform and transport), mean that education is prohibitively expensive for many families (Human Rights Watch 2005a). Many children with HIV are prevented from accessing education. In Romania, for example, fewer than 60 per cent of children with HIV attend any form of schooling (Human Rights Watch 2006). Inequalities remain in relation to gender, and in many countries the education of girls is not seen as a priority: this is particularly prevalent in sub-Saharan Africa (Human Rights Watch 2005a). Children with disabilities are also often denied access to education. In Uganda children with a disability or suspected of being infected with HIV/AIDs are often chased away from school. Problems also exist when children are required to work, whether this be part- or full-time. While child labour might be most prevalent in India and Bangladesh, girls as young as 5 are reported working for 100 or more hours a week without rest breaks or days off in Morocco (Human Rights Watch 2005b).

In signing the Salamanca declaration, the international community adopted the term 'inclusive education', although this has not led to a formally fixed and stable use of the term (Vislie 2003). Inclusion has been implemented at different levels, embraces different goals, is based on a range of different motives, and reflects varied classifications of special educational needs and varied service provision (Peters 2003). In developing countries, for instance, India and Africa, the main struggle continues to be in providing education for the majority. In practice, poor countries lack the resources and do not have the necessary experience to support children at risk of school exclusion (Panayiotopoulos and Kerfoot 2007).

Where children are in full-time education, poor or disruptive behaviour can lead to exclusion; indeed, aggressive behaviour is the main reason for exclusion among primary children (Parsons et al. 1994; Hayden 1997). In the UK, exclusion for disciplinary matters, such as unacceptable behaviour, occurs disproportionately. Boys, those from deprived areas, young people identified with special educational needs and those who are 'looked-after' are over-represented. In many cases excluded pupils have high levels of unmet educational and/or social needs (Hayden et al. 1996). The expression of violent, aggressive or disruptive behaviour is frequently linked to these needs and can be seen as one of the ways in which disaffection manifests itself. Emotional difficulties may lead to poor behaviour, and need to be addressed as early as possible (DfEE 1997). The more extreme a pupil's difficulties in relation to education, the more investment will be needed in resolving personal and social issues before formal educational needs can be addressed (Parsons et al. 2001). Relevant too is evidence that early intervention is of paramount importance if the emotional and behavioural difficulties of young children are not to develop into mental health problems, adolescent delinquency and/or adult criminality (Farrington and West 1990).

Identifying children at risk of exclusion

Definitions of 'at-risk' children are problematic as there is no consistency between them (Moore 2006) or indeed what the child is 'at-risk' of. For instance, in the USA there is a greater concern with dropout rather than exclusion (Wombler et al. 1997). Possible definitions of 'at-risk' include: students who have experienced difficulty or failure in their careers as learners (Presseisen 1991); children and adolescents who are not able to acquire and/or use the skills necessary to develop their potential and become productive members of society (Redick and Vail 1991); young people who are chemically dependent, suicidal, pregnant or economically disadvantaged; those from minority groups; runaways; or school dropouts (Kleese and D'Onofrio 1994). Barr and Parrett (2001) argue that regardless of the labels attached to at-risk students teachers have always identified them as disinterested, disruptive students who refuse to learn. In many countries some groups of children are more at risk of dropping out, for instance, in the USA those of Hispanic descent and students from low-income families. Worldwide, students with disabilities have the greatest risk of dropping out (Lehr et al. 2004a). Within Europe, a review of 15 countries that supported inclusion found that pupils with emotional, social and/or behavioural difficulties were regarded as presenting the greatest challenge. This included unmotivated and disaffected pupils (Meijer 2001).

Critical is that the right children are identified and targeted for interventions. Unfortunately, this has not always been the case. A recent USA White Paper (Archive Incorporated 2006) indicated that one of the causes of interventions yielding poor results is that they have not targeted the pupils most in need of support. So what systems have been put in place to facilitate effective identification?

Check and Connect, a dropout intervention programme in the USA takes referrals from school staff that are then reviewed by a team usually comprising the school principal, a nurse, teacher and Check and Connect monitor. A primary indicator is poor attendance with other referral criteria including low levels of parental support for learning, sibling history of excessive absence or dropout, inconsistent completion of school work, passive classroom presence, or other academic or behavioural problems (Lehr et al. 2004b).

Within the UK the Department for Education and Skills's (DfES 2003a) guidance for the setting-up of Behaviour and Education Support Teams (BESTs) states that as part of the referral criteria the child should be exhibiting early indications of emotional or behavioural problems, including those coming to the attention of staff due to attendance issues or risk of exclusion, or be at risk of developing them. Evaluations of the effectiveness of BESTs suggest that the criteria adopted in relation to 'at-risk' are rather broad and vary across different teams. Halsey et al. (2005) found that in the majority of BESTs the criteria for 'at-risk' covered children showing early indications of attendance, behaviour, emotional well-being, mental health or exclusion issues (e.g. children receiving support from a learning mentor, those who lack confidence or have low self-esteem). In such cases, the purpose of the referral was for early intervention and prevention work. Alternatively, four BESTs developed referral criteria based on case complexity where problems were already established and other support had been accessed and was unsuccessful. Examples included pupils with one or more fixed-term exclusions and pupils continuing to experience behavioural problems, despite additional support.

In the Behaviour and Improvement Programme (BIP) one Local Authority (LA) implemented, SLEUTH, a data tracking programme for monitoring positive and negative behaviour. This was used to analyse pupil behaviour and identify pupils 'at-risk'. For those at risk of exclusion there was an on-site centre staffed by a full-time behaviour mentor and an LA person from the BIP management team. The centre supported 12 pupils who were placed on a flexible timetable spending some time in mainstream school and some in the behaviour support suite.

In another LA, a three-tier system of identification evolved alongside tracking and monitoring. Pupils were categorized according to set criteria as they moved through the three-tier continuum. At one end of the continuum was fixed-term exclusion, at the other was reintegration. This three-tier system was linked to a multi-agency approach, with each tier being associated with support from particular agencies. As the child moved further up the tiers, key workers became progressively more involved, both inside and outside of school. This process was facilitated by the expansion of multi-agency services. Box 9.1 provides an example.

The development of effective identification and tracking systems has become increasingly important in England with the introduction of multi-agency partnerships as involved professionals need to share information about children across a range of services (GHK Consulting et al. 2004).

Box 9.1 Identifying and working with at-risk pupils

Case study from the Behaviour and Improvement Programme: identifying and working with at-risk pupils

At-risk children were identified using criteria relating to exclusion, attendance and risk of engaging with crime. Three possible tiers of risk were identified requiring increasing levels of support from schools in partnership with relevant agencies as appropriate. This included children identified for intervention through the Special Educational Needs (SEN) Code of Practice. Named key workers supported children at each of these tiers.

- Level 1 included targeted support within the local school from a range of relevant professionals;

- Level 2 provided intensive support with the local school from a range of relevant professionals;
- Level 3 required rapid response from a range of agencies as appropriate.

Schools ensured every 'at-risk' pupil had a key worker. A learning mentor or sports coach/drama specialist was identified to work with 'at-risk' pupils providing an appropriate role model in terms of gender and race. The system for signing off 'at-risk' pupils varied from school to school. In cases of attendance problems, pupils were signed off when attendance improved to an average level. In the case of being at risk of exclusion pupils remained on the list unless there was a major improvement in their behaviour or alternative provision, such as an augmented curriculum, was in place. Pupil involvement in crime proved more problematic to deal with.

Although the focus of this chapter is identifying children at risk of exclusion and interventions that have been put in place to offer support, a range of protective and resilience factors have also been identified which support children regardless of the situation in which they find themselves. Similarly to at-risk factors, resilience factors can operate at the level of child, family and community. Thus, for instance, family resilience factors might include consistent discipline, affection and support for education. Relevant is the balance between risk and protective factors. Viewed in this way interventions can be seen as an attempt to shift the balance from vulnerability to resilience (Werner 1990) (see Chapter 2 for more details of risk and resilience factors).

Interventions to support children at risk from exclusion

In countries able to provide support for children at risk of exclusion, there is consensus that prevention and early intervention are key to preventing the escalation of problems in adolescence and early adulthood. In the USA the No Child Left Behind Act (2001) increased the focus on student dropout and highlighted the need for interventions for those at risk of school failure. Numerous programmes have been implemented and developed to prevent students from dropping out (Lehr et al. 2004a; Lever et al. 2004). Although practices vary, they have included counselling services, mentoring programmes, tutoring, attendance monitoring and after-school programmes (Lehr et al. 2004a). Programmes for young children have included those to promote social and emotional competence, and school readiness and reading skills to prevent academic failure (Lehr et al. 2004b). Important is the work of Communities in Schools (CIS): a large-scale dropout prevention programme that delivers resources to almost one million students in over 3000 schools across the country (CIS 2006). CIS works on the principal of five basics that every child needs and deserves:

1. A one-on-one relationship with a caring adult.
2. A safe place to learn and grow.
3. A healthy start and a healthy future.
4. A marketable skill to use upon graduation.
5. A chance to give back to peers and community (CIS 2006).

There are clear parallels here with the aims of *Every Child Matters* (DfES 2003b) in the UK. Across the USA, the services in place for CIS vary among different states and communities but all address specific needs, including academic support, mentoring, health care, summer and after-school programmes, alternative education models, career development and family strengthening. Dropout prevention strategies are tailored to the needs of individual students and all programmes involve the local community.

The FUTURES Programme, another example from the USA, centres on effective collaborative partnership between the business community, employment training systems, mental health and public school systems (Lever et al. 2004). Students at risk of dropping out are identified in the ninth grade and then follow a five-year programme that supports them through the transition to high school to post-secondary education or employment. For the first year of the programme students attend smaller classes and are taught by specially trained teachers. Thereafter students attend some classes by FUTURES teachers but are reintegrated into the larger school environment. Key aspects of the programme include mentoring, monitoring of attendance, smaller classes, tutoring, life skills training, leadership development, career preparation, work experience, problem solving and incentives for positive achievement. Throughout the duration of the programme students have access to mental health support (Lever et al. 2004).

In the UK, the Green Paper, *Excellence for all Children Meeting Special Educational Needs* (DfEE 1997), drew attention to the increasing number of children with emotional and behavioural difficulties who were perceived as failing, and indicated a need to find new ways of tackling their difficulties early, before they lead to underachievement, disaffection and, in too many cases, exclusion from mainstream education. Studies of disaffected young people (Ball et al. 2000) indicate that many of their difficulties can be traced back to problems, such as social, emotional or educational dilemmas that were inadequately appreciated or addressed during their years in primary education (Macrae et al. 1997). Concern for pupils with emotional and behaviour problems continues and has been manifest in most government policies that have had as their aim the retention of pupils in school. In developing policies to support children at risk, there has been an increase in multi-agency initiatives the aim being that different services work with children in a coherent manner (DfES 2004a, 2005a). Children and young people with additional needs require high quality multi-agency assessment; a wide range of specialist services available close to home; and effective case management by a lead professional working as part of a multidisciplinary team.

The rest of this chapter describes different interventions that have as their focus preventative work with children at risk of exclusion for poor behaviour.

Behaviour and Education Support Teams

A short section is included here on the work of BESTs, since in practice members of the teams were part of all the other interventions that follow in this chapter. A distinctive feature of the work of the BESTs was the careful attention given to the support that individual pupils needed. In some cases a short-term intervention was successful, but in others it was apparent that pupils would require long-term work since the nature of their problems was extremely complex. BESTs differed in whether the intervention was undertaken by one person or whether there were many layers of support.

As with programmes in the USA, the work of BESTs often involved counselling. In one secondary school a strong focus of the work of the BEST was on counselling, which had been outsourced to a single agency. Approximately 180 pupils had been referred to the BEST, not including those who had been targeted for after-school activities. Of these 100 had received counselling. For some pupils the counselling brought about change in a relatively short space of time. In many cases, while the focus of the counselling was on particular behavioural issues, there was also a positive impact on attendance and schoolwork. An example is provided in Box 9.2.

Box 9.2   Counselling

Case study: BEST year-long counselling support for anger and self-harm

Yvonne was in Year 7 and reported enjoying school. She received regular support from the counsellor and used the time to talk about any problems that she was having in school or at home. Prior to this she had been engaged in incidents of self-harm, often became extremely angry, bottled up emotions, and had been involved in many fights. The relationship with her mother was extremely difficult and pupils within the school would 'wind her up' encouraging her to fight with another pupil. The sessions with the counsellor gave Yvonne time to talk about her feelings, and she was made aware of when other pupils might be 'encouraging' her to become aggressive. The self-harming had stopped:

> I used to do this because I got stressed out all the time, I was angry about everything. Cutting myself was a bit of a release. Now I can talk about things, they are not all bottled up inside me. When I first came I was rather shy and didn't know what to do. Now I come every week, but if I have a problem I can drop in at any time. Since being here, everyone has said that I don't get angry so often. Now if I have a problem, rather than having an argument, I calm down and then sort it out. Before I used to get into lots of arguments and fights. Also, my friends don't wind me up anymore, since they know that I am not going to get involved in fights. Before, in the morning I used to think, I don't want to go to school, and I used to pretend to be sick so that I didn't have to come. Now I want to come to school. My attendance has improved, since I used to have a lot of days off before. Now, if my Mum says I can't go to school, I feel really disappointed. Before I never wanted to do my homework, but now I do it well. I had parents' evening the other week and the teachers were really pleased. My school work has improved, my relationship with my Mum has improved and my attendance has improved.

There is evidence that increasing numbers of children are being excluded as a result of anger management problems (Humphrey and Brooks 2006). Anger management interventions featured strongly in the small group work of BESTs. Groups generally ran for between six to eight weeks and were reported to be successful by teachers and pupils. In most cases pupils also received individual support from the BEST or a key worker. In one primary school an anger management group ran over two terms. This was facilitated by the BEST Educational Social Worker and targeted at nine boys from Years 4 to 6. Although the group focused on anger management, issues around social skills, peer mentoring and how to cope in different situations were explored. The learning mentor commented on how much the boys had enjoyed the group and indicated that their behaviour had improved significantly. An example of change in one pupil is given in Box 9.3.

Box 9.3 Anger management

Case study: BEST group and individual support for anger management and behaviour

Chris came to the UK in Year 3, having previously lived in Jamaica. He missed the fishing, the lifestyle, his grandmother and his friends. Initially, in the UK his family had lots of different temporary accommodation, which was unsettling. His level of literacy was very poor and it was difficult for him to communicate effectively with his peers or his teachers. Prior to the BEST intervention he had been excluded several times in Year 5. The learning mentor reported that:

> He found it difficult to interact with other children, his guard was always up and the fights were quite ferocious. He used to run away from situations, which was better than a fight, but you then had to run around school looking for him. He would be in a corner, pulling at his hair, pulling at his jumper and you would have to do breathing exercises with him to gradually calm him down.

In Year 5 Chris worked with a BEST social worker individually and in a group. The group work included anger management, issues around social skills, peer mentoring and how to cope in different situations. In Year 6 Chris received support from the BEST counsellor. Chris continues his story:

> School is a lot better because in Year 3 it was OK and Year 4 was OK but in Year 5 things went really badly. I used to get really angry and get into lots of fights. Once I was excluded for a few days and had to stay at home. I don't get so angry now and I don't start a fight. I just walk away. Last year I had some help from David (a social worker from BEST) and this year I've been seeing Emily (a BEST counsellor). I've really enjoyed seeing Emily. She's a really nice lady and it has been good to talk with her. It has been really helpful to have someone to talk to who isn't a teacher. Today we get our SATs results and I'm hoping to get 4 in all of them (he did). I have lots of friends now and I enjoy playing football with them. My favourite subject is maths because I like it and I like doing the times-table. I'm hoping that I can make a new start in my secondary school.

Chris was to receive an award at the end of term for the progress he had made in relation to behaviour and attainment.

One unusual intervention involved a series of drama workshops that ran after school where pupils worked on radio plays. Pupils were referred through Heads of Year to the BEST. One aim of the radio play was to give the pupils the opportunity to consider the impact their use of language had on other people, what they conveyed by their tone of voice and expression. The workshops were reported to have helped the pupils to gain confidence and to reflect on how they were perceived by others.

Also valuable was that BESTs were able to offer specialist support to troubled children much more quickly than had previously been possible. In one LA the presence of a speech and language therapist working with groups of six children at Key Stage 1 had been particularly appreciated as there was a 66-week waiting list for individual therapy and pupils with communication difficulties became frustrated leading to poor behaviour.

Important to the success of BESTs was that they worked closely with all school staff, established effective communication systems, and tailored their activities to the needs of particular schools.

Nurture groups

Increasingly, attention has turned to implementing early interventions with young children and their families. The Head Start programme launched in 1965 in the USA is targeted at low-income young children aged up to 5-years old and aims to prepare disadvantaged young children early enough for them to be successful in school. Sure Start, launched in 1998 in the UK was based on the Head Start programme. It is run through local communities and seeks to achieve better outcomes for those involved by increasing the availability of childcare for all children, improving children's health, education and emotional development and supporting parents in their role and in developing employment aspirations. Programmes are aimed at children under 4 and groups run throughout the UK. The Better Beginnings, Better Futures project was developed in Ontario from 1990. Unlike Sure Start and Head Start the project works with two groups of children: those up to the age of 4 and those aged from 4 to 8 in which a pre-school programme integrates with a primary school programme. The emphasis in all projects is on a community-based strategy that focuses on the social-emotional functioning of young children.

Originating in Enfield in 1970, nurture groups have become an important intervention for primary school pupils exhibiting social, emotional and behavioural difficulties (Colwell and O'Connor 2003; Cooper and Tiknaz 2005; Doyle 2005; Hallam et al. 2005; Ofsted 2005). Although beginning in England, nurture groups now form an important intervention in primary schools in Scotland (Gerrard 2005) and are being developed in Canada and

New Zealand. Drawing on concepts derived from Bowlby's attachment theory, the underlying rationale of nurture groups is that if children can experience interactions with significant others they will acquire age-appropriate behaviours and develop a sense of self that is conducive to healthy social, emotional and cognitive development (Colwell and O'Connor 2003).

Typically, nurture groups consist of 10 to 12 pupils and two members of staff, usually one teacher and one teaching assistant. Important to the success of the groups is the selection of pupils so that there is a balance of difficulties between them (Cooper and Tiknaz 2005; Hallam et al. 2005). This echoes findings from other interventions with at-risk pupils already described, for instance, among students selected for Skill Force. Pupils in the nurture group spend time in their own class, since the aim is to enable them to reintegrate full-time into mainstream education. The amount of time spent in the group varies, although this is usually between two and four terms (Cooper and Tiknaz 2005). Good practice nurture groups have regular reintegration evaluations to monitor progress (Hallam et al. 2005).

In BIP, nurture groups were established in a number of LAs. The children in these nurture groups had extremely difficult home circumstances and the group provided stability in terms of a safe routine. Nurture group staff reported differences in the behaviour of the children after the weekends and holidays and expressed particular concern about the long time away from school in the summer (Hallam et al. 2005). On starting the group many of the children had no way to express their emotions and required support with speech and language. Particularly important to the nurture group was the establishment of regular routines with highly structured timetables and clear boundaries for pupils (Ofsted 2005). Nurture group classes have special environments and are costly since most have kitchen areas, dining tables, areas for eating, and comfortable areas in addition to teaching areas. An important part of the day is the focus on meal times and times for sharing news. For many of the pupils in the BIP nurture groups this was their first experience of sharing a meal. Typically, pupils arrive at 9.30 am, and over breakfast have a news session so that they learn to share information. They prepare breakfast, and wash and dry the pots. As a result of these breakfast-time activities, their social skills tend to improve. One child, on her first day, grabbed pieces of fruit and immediately started eating them as she was so hungry. Subsequently, she realized that breakfast would be available every day and was less anxious to guzzle the food. Staff reported evidence of real change in the pupils. They learned to share and learned about their emotions. For example, in one news session one little boy said, 'I've got some news but it's very bad and it's going to take me a long time to tell you'. Later in the day he managed to communicate his news (Hallam et al. 2005). Staff acknowledged that if the children had not been in the nurture class they would have 'just gone by the wayside' (Hallam et al. 2005). Box 9.4 provides an example case study.

Box 9.4 Participation in a nurture groups

Case study: illustration of change following participation in a nurture group

One child on arrival at the class did not speak, would not respond when called, and spent a lot of time crying. She snatched toys and would not give them up unless they were physically removed. After membership of the group she was able to listen to and concentrate on a story lasting 15 to 20 minutes. She settled down in her own class, asked questions, and her language improved dramatically with the use of complete sentences demonstrating clarity of thought. The support provided for her speech and language development was successful. She made rapid improvement and it became clear that she had the ability to learn and retain information. This had previously been in doubt (Hallam et al. 2005).

There is growing evidence that nurture groups can be successful and that skills can transfer from the nurture group to the classroom (Colwell and O'Connor 2003; Cooper and Tiknaz 2005; Gerrard 2005; Hallam et al. 2005; Ofsted 2005). However, there are few long-term evaluations, although Iszatt and Wasilewska (1997) followed-up children who had attended a nurture group two years previously, and found that 83 per cent did not need any additional support.

Where nurture groups have been less successful this has been related to a lack of effective staff training, lack of clarity about the aims, and an inappropriate balance of problems in the children selected to take part. The high level of resourcing required for nurture groups means that tensions have been reported among other school staff (Hallam et al. 2005). Like any intervention in schools to improve behaviour this needs to be considered at school level. Important too, is that strong links are made with staff teaching in the mainstream so that effective reintegration is possible.

Key workers

In the UK, pupils identified as at-risk of exclusion are assigned a key worker. This is a named person with an established relationship with the child or someone who is involved in a specific intervention (DfES 2004b). The key worker acts as a point of contact for the child and family and as an interface between various agencies and the client. In more complex cases where more than one practitioner or agency is involved one aspect of the role is to coordinate support from the other professionals. Given the range of people appointed as key workers and their different levels of qualifications it is important that they work with children at-risk up to the limits of their own competence (DfES 2004b).

In the BIP a number of LAs expressed concern about the clarity of the role of key workers (Hallam et al. 2005). Across the programme, a range of staff undertook the role, for instance, home liaison workers, Connexions workers, learning mentors, members of BEST and form tutors. The allocation of key workers depended on arrangements within the LA. These varied from being tightly structured with careful monitoring and record keeping of progress to being relatively informal. In some cases key workers were allocated on the basis of expertise in relation to the nature of the difficulty that the child was experiencing (e.g. behaviour problems, bereavement, immigration difficulties). In some schools the Lead Behaviour Professional (LBP) worked with all pupils who were at-risk, taking responsibility for monitoring their progress. Regular meetings were usually held to assess the progress of pupils.

In one LA schools used a wide range of adults as key workers ranging from Senior Leaders, Heads of Year, teachers, teaching assistants, learning mentors and Social Inclusion Assistants, the latter mainly appointed through BIP funding. In another LA, the composition of the multi-agency teams determined who became the key worker. The LBPs and the multi-agency teams attempted to identify the 'right' person to work with each child. In another LA, LBPs identified children as high, medium or low risk. Key workers and LBPs met monthly to discuss issues and to establish how progress could be managed strategically. In secondary schools where there were large numbers of children it proved difficult to make meaningful plans and the BIP coordinator had to support schools.

In one school, the BEST coordinator developed solution-focused training for people acting as key workers. Initially this was rolled out to teachers, but was cascaded down to Learning Support Assistants who worked with students in classrooms. The expectation was that all form tutors would act as key workers for any BIP students who were in their tutor group. Within the school there was also an expectation that at a minimum meetings between the student and their key worker would last for one hour and that they should be held at least fortnightly, although once a week was seen as more desirable. Indeed, some students needed more support than this. The success of the approach was in part attributable to the training that the key workers had received.

Learning mentors

The mentoring of students has become widespread in many countries, for instance, Australia, Canada, Israel, Sweden, the UK and the USA (Miller 2002; Colley 2003; Ayalon 2007), although there are wide variations in practice between countries. Research in the USA on the impact of mentoring with disadvantaged students is more advanced (Hall 2003; Reid 2007) in part because programmes, for instance, Big Brother, Big Sister have existed for over 90 years (Hall 2003) and now employ more than a quarter of a million community volunteers (Colley 2003). Also popular has been the use of undergraduate students in the mentoring of pupils at-risk, for instance, GEAR-UP in the USA, which works with 16–19-year-olds at risk of disaffection. In Israel one-fifth of the undergraduate student population serve as mentors (Miller 2002) and a similar approach is being adopted in Sweden.

In the UK, much interest has focused on learning mentors operating with disaffected pupils in primary and secondary schools. Learning mentors were introduced in 1999, as part of the Excellence in Cities (EiC) initiative and their use has extended through other educational programmes including Beacon Schools, Education Action Zones (subsequently Excellence Clusters, EC), and the Behaviour Improvement Programme. Learning mentors in these paid roles differ from the voluntary mentors found in community programmes such as Big Brother, Big Sister. It is estimated that 12,000 EiC/EC mentors are in place across the primary and secondary sectors (DfES 2005b), although the actual number of mentors is much higher since many posts are funded through alternative funding streams or paid for directly through school budgets in non-EiC/EC areas. Although Hall (2003) reviewing the literature on learning mentors criticized the lack of evaluation, recent research has demonstrated a positive impact. Ofsted (2003) reported that the most popular and successful strand of the EiC was learning mentors, while Hallam and colleagues (2005) found that their work was particularly important in primary schools, reducing staff and headteacher stress by supporting at-risk pupils, improving behaviour and freeing up staff time. Learning mentors were sometimes employed directly by schools or were sometimes members of BESTs.

The role of learning mentors in the UK is to support schools in raising standards through raising pupils' achievement, breaking down barriers to learning, improving attendance and reducing exclusions. Guidance from the DfES (2005b) suggests that there are three main strands to their work:

1. To provide a complementary service that enhances existing provision in order to support learning, participation and encourage social inclusion.

2. To develop and maintain effective and supportive mentoring relationships with children, young people and those engaged with them.
3. To work within an extended range of networks and partnerships to broker support and learning opportunities and improve the quality of services to children and young people.

A particular strength of the role of learning mentors is the flexibility offered in enabling them to focus on particular needs as necessary. There were many instances of learning mentors having involvement with Learning Support Units (LSUs), and of LSUs being used to support pupils at risk of exclusion during the transition period from primary to secondary school. Learning mentors worked individually with pupils or with small groups. As part of the BIP (Hallam et al. 2005), one primary school learning mentor set up a 'Popcorn Club' that ran every Friday. This included special activities for some pupils. It proved so popular that all of the children wanted to participate so a weekly reward system was introduced whereby well-behaved pupils' names were put into a raffle for the available places. A cool-off room also provided a place where pupils could talk to the learning mentor alone. In another LA the learning mentor spent time in the nursery on a regular basis in support of children at risk of exclusion. Breakfast clubs, run by learning mentors, were also important since many children did not have breakfast at home.

In one secondary school, support was given by the BEST learning mentor to a small group of Year 7 boys with personal and family difficulties. The boys indicated, 'we needed help'. One, who lived with a guardian and did not see his family had 'run off'. Two pupils had been excluded, one for four days and the other for five. They had been invited to spend two double lessons per week for eight weeks with a BEST worker who 'sits down and talks and listens'. The pupils were able to walk out of lessons where they felt uncomfortable and find the learning mentor. There had been an agreement of confidentiality and the boys 'let their feelings out instead of them building up inside'. They reported that 'sometimes teachers don't listen to your problems'. Health-related issues, such as smoking and alcohol abuse were discussed and one of the boys admitted that he was inclined to go 'too far' in class. He felt pressured in maths and had to try very hard to keep his temper. His behaviour had improved since attending the sessions and he wanted them to continue. Box 9.5 gives an example of an intervention by a learning mentor.

Box 9.5 Learning mentor intervention

Case study: a short-term single-level intervention from the BEST senior learning mentor

Natalie began experiencing difficulties during Year 7 at school and at home. She refused to complete homework, was rude to the teachers and as she said, 'things were becoming difficult'. Her mother approached the school and Natalie was assigned to the senior learning mentor from the BEST. She had weekly one-to-one sessions where she was able to talk through problems, and was given the opportunity to reflect on her behaviour both in and out of school. Now in Year 8, she spoke about how things had changed for her, how she was a 'different person', and that her behaviour, attitude and approach to school and home were different. Without the opportunity to spend time with the learning mentor, Natalie felt that her behaviour would have become much worse and that she may, ultimately, have been excluded.

The success of the work of learning mentors was based upon the development of supportive relationships, the opportunity for pupils to discuss problems, and the provision of flexible access if problems occurred during the school day. The key element of the role was the availability of an individual in school in a non-teaching role who could support children, and act as a link with parents. Where learning mentors were less effective, problems arose because of a lack of role definition and clarity and inadequate training (Hallam et al. 2005).

Transition from primary to secondary school

Transition from primary to secondary school can be a particularly difficult time for students at risk of exclusion from school (Osler et al. 2001). Groups of pupils at-risk include those eligible for free school meals, pupils with special educational needs, pupils less fluent in English, and pupils from some ethnic groups (Galton et al. 1999). Research from the USA indicates that pupils with behavioural problems also find the transition to secondary school more difficult (Berndt and Mekos 1995).

In response to this, support programmes for students at risk have been established in several countries (Holmes 2000; McElroy 2000; McGee et al. 2003). In the USA, students at risk of school failure have been provided with programmes that offer additional academic and personal support (McGee et al. 2003) which may include individual counselling, advocacy, tutoring, and efforts to increase parental involvement. In New Zealand, schools have used vertical grouping and mixed-ability classes to assist pupils with adjustment to secondary school (McGee et al. 2003). Other strategies include additional pastoral support, buddying with older pupils and mentoring. Crucial is that students at-risk receive support prior to transition (McGee et al. 2003), and longer periods of post-transition support as they may still be experiencing anxieties well into the first year (Stradling and McNeil 2000; Ward 2000).

In the UK, buddying schemes are developing whereby pupils perceived as at-risk during the immediate transfer period are linked with Year 7 pupils in their new school and provided with a learning mentor in the primary school (Galton et al. 2003). The learning mentors work with the same pupils following transfer to secondary school. The use of learning mentors in this way was a feature of the BIP. Some Year 6 pupils identified by the BEST were also supported at the secondary LSU (see Box 10.1 in Chapter 10 for an example).

The key elements of good practice in the support of pupils at risk of exclusion during the transition process include:

- beginning the intervention prior to transition;
- involvement of the primary school SENCO and effective liaison with the secondary school SENCO;
- effective transfer of information and understanding of the pupils' needs so that support structures are in place from day one in the secondary school;
- continuing the transition programme in the secondary school to allow time for the pupil to settle in; and
- use of the LSU to support the pupil.

Box 9.6 illustrates the value of transition work.

Box 9.6 Different perspectives on the impact of transition work

---

Case study: The value of transition work

The primary school perspective

Mike was identified as 'at-risk' during the transition period as he had emotional and behavioural difficulties and was very withdrawn despite having considerable intellectual capabilities. The primary SENCO described him as very needy and indicated that he required support.

> Effective liaison work took place with the secondary SENCO, appropriate support was discussed and put in place for Mike from day one of the secondary school and critically he was able to build up a good relationship with the transition worker

over a period of time. Without this intervention he would not have attended school, he would have disappeared from the system.

The secondary school perspective

Mike continues to be isolated in school. He is on the Gifted and Talented list as well as having emotional needs. Family life is very difficult and he gets very little support from his mother. There were major problems with him starting secondary school since he did not have the uniform. Because of the transition worker we found out about this. We managed to get some money to fund his uniform from the LA. If it wasn't for this he probably would not have started at all. He is a very big boy and stands out immediately, without a uniform this would have been even worse. He is a very bright lad and is involved in lots of extra-curricular activities. I feel very positive about his future. (SENCO)

Mike's perspective

It's all about moving from primary to secondary school and all the changes. It's about being in a big school and being worried about being bullied. In my primary school I was afraid that I was going to be bullied – I thought they would flush my head down the toilets. I was worried about making friends. I like the lessons and the teachers. I also like the trips. If I hadn't had this support I would have gone off track, I would have been bad. I want to go to college when I finish school and then go to university. Then I want to get a job possibly in a bank. Year 7 has been much better than I thought. I've not been in too much trouble this year, overall my attendance has got better but I did have one slip – I had four weeks off. I've also been excluded once this year and spent the time in the LSU. I got into trouble because of a spray gun, it was an accident but it was dangerous. I don't think I'm going to get excluded next year, or at least I hope I don't. I think the transition work was a good thing and that everyone should do it. It made a real difference in terms of my behaviour, having someone to talk to. I haven't really got into any fights this year, I don't get as stressed as much. It's because I've had someone to talk to.

Learning Support Units

Learning Support Units (LSUs) are school-based centres for pupils who are disaffected, at risk of exclusion, or vulnerable because of family or social issues. Originally called in-school centres they have been successful in reducing permanent exclusions (Hallam and Castle 1999). The Department for Education and Employment (DfEE) used the outcomes of the Evaluation of the Behaviour and Discipline Pilots (Hallam and Castle 1999) to develop guidance in *Social Inclusion: Pupil Support* (DfEE 1999a) and in the *Excellence in Cities* document (DfEE 1999b). LSUs were one strand of development within the *Excellence in Cities* policy and were integrated with the BIP in many areas to provide more focused support for behaviour and to support pupils with their learning. In broad terms, LSUs provide short-term teaching and support programmes that are tailored to the needs of pupils who need help in improving their behaviour, attendance or attitude to learning. The aim is to keep pupils in school and working, and to provide opportunities for issues that might be concerning them to be tackled. It is intended that pupils are reintegrated back into mainstream classes as soon as possible.

Particularly important is that LSUs are an integral part of the whole-school behaviour and attendance policy (DfES 2005c) since the LSU needs to support and change the behaviour of pupils and staff for whole-school impact (McSherry 2004; Steer Report 2006). The aim of the LSU is to provide targeted support for specific priorities in the school's behaviour strategy. For this reason there is no one model for LSUs that will suit the needs of all schools (DfES 2005c).

LSUs are not:

- a facility for long-term respite care;
- a 'sin bin' or dumping ground;
- a 'catch-all' facility to compensate for lack of other provision;
- an isolated 'bolt-on' provision;
- a place of punishment;
- a provider of education for excluded pupils in BIP schools; or
- a quick route to exclusion (DfES 2005c).

Similarly to alternative curriculum interventions (see Chapter 8) the numbers of pupils attending LSUs at any one time is generally small, usually varying between 2 and 12 pupils (McSherry 2004; Kendall et al. 2005). Pupil attendance can vary, with some pupils attending full- or part-time, the latter spending the remaining time with their class. It is common for pupils to attend during those lessons with which they have particular difficulties. Important is having clear links between the curriculum followed in the LSU and the mainstream class to assist with reintegration. LSUs have been successful in improving behaviour and attendance (Ofsted 2006).

While provision in LSUs remains variable (Ofsted 2006; Steer Report 2006) common features of successful provision include:

- well organized learning environments;
- a varied programme of activities with a good balance between teaching and curriculum programmes and activities to support emotional and behavioural needs;
- attention given to improving pupils' literacy;
- support offered to help pupils to develop better learning strategies;
- clear entry and exit criteria;
- thorough assessment of pupils;
- systematic monitoring and evaluation;
- effective liaison between the LSU manager, class teachers, tutors, year heads, parents and outside agencies;
- support from the senior management team; and
- pupils allowed to return to the LSU if they need further support and as a drop-in facility.

Box 9.7 provides an example of the nature of provision.

Box 9.7 Learning Support Unit

Case study: LSU provision

Dominic was excluded for a number of times when in Year 8 and as a result began spending time in the LSU. His father was contacted and it was explained that Dominic would benefit from being in the LSU as he was having difficulty in coping with the main stream classroom environment. Now in Year 9, the time spent in the LSU has gradually been reduced and Dominic only goes there when the class is studying Modern Languages (three lessons each week). He was reintegrated into mainstream lessons when new topics were being started. He still uses the LSU occasionally when he is experiencing difficulties. He reported that the LSU was very supportive and sensed that he would have been excluded if this provision had not been in place. During the LSU sessions he worked on specific curriculum areas and attended a small group that focused on enhancing self-esteem. Dominic reported that he was motivated to work now and hopefully get good GCSEs. In his mock SATs he had achieved level 5 in science and English and level 6 in mathematics.

Endnote

Where countries are able to adopt an inclusive approach to education most have put in place interventions to support children at risk of exclusion for poor behaviour. Such provision may be for individual pupils or for groups of pupils and may involve support from a single adult or, in more complex cases, a multi-agency team. While there is variation in the provision offered, there is a consensus that early intervention is crucial and that the support offered needs to be tailored to the needs of the individual. The research evidence and the case studies described in this chapter suggest that interventions can support children, providing them with opportunities to talk through their problems and reflect on their behaviour, and offering strategies to enable them to cope when things are going less well. Success depends on a range of factors including intervening as soon as problems arise; being clear about responsibilities; setting up effective monitoring, tracking and communication systems; having clear criteria for identifying children at-risk; and matching the needs of the child to the most appropriate intervention. Children at-risk require a caring environment, personal supportive attention from staff to enable relationships to develop and opportunities for success. Provision needs to be sufficiently flexible to meet changing needs and reintegration needs to be carefully planned.

Chapter summary

- Support for at-risk children may be provided for individuals or groups and may involve support from a single adult or in more complex cases a multi-agency team.
- Successful support depends on:
  - having clear criteria for identification of at-risk children;
  - early intervention;
  - strategies being tailored to meet the needs of the individual;
  - children being given an opportunity to talk through their problems, reflect on their behaviour and develop a range of coping strategies;
  - staff having a clear understanding of their role;
  - effective monitoring;
  - good communication;
  - the provision of a safe, caring environment;
  - personal attention from staff to enable relationships to develop;
  - flexibility;
  - providing students with opportunities for success; and
  - carefully planned reintegration routes.

Further reading

Boxall, M. (2002) *Nurture Groups in Schools*. London: Paul Chapman.

Hallam, S., Castle, F. and Rogers, L. with Creech, A., Rhamie, J. and Kokotsaki, D. (2005) *Research and Evaluation of the Behaviour Improvement Programme. Research Report 702.* London: DfES.

McSherry, J. (2004) *Learning Support Units: Principles, Practice and Evaluation.* London: David Fulton.

Miller, A. (2002) *Mentoring for Students and Young People: A Handbook of Effective Practice.* London: Kogan Page.

References

Archive Incorporated (2006) *Identifying Potential Dropouts: Key Lessons for Building an Early Warning Data System A Dual Agenda of High Standards and High Graduation Rates.* A White Paper prepared for Staying the Course: High Standards and Improved Graduation Rates, a joint project of Achieve and Jobs for the Future, funded by the Carnegie Corp. of New York.

Ayalon, A. (2007) A model for teacher mentoring of poor and minority children: a case study of an urban Israeli school mentoring programme. *Mentoring & Tutoring,* 15(1): 5–23.

Ball, S.J., Maguire, M. and Macrae, S. (2000) *Choice, Pathways, and Transitions Post-16: New Youth, New Economies in the Global City.* London: Routledge-Falmer.

Barr, R.D. and Parrett, W.H. (2001) *Hope Fulfilled for At-risk and Violent Youth: K-12 Programs that Work.* Boston, MA: Allyn and Bacon.

Berndt, T.J. and Mekos, D. (1995) Adolescents' perceptions of the stressful and desirable aspects of the transition to junior high school. *Journal of Research on Adolescence,* 5: 123–42.

Colley, H. (2003) Engagement mentoring for 'disaffected' youth: A new model of mentoring for social inclusion. *British Educational Research Journal.* 29(4): 521–42.

Colwell, J. and O'Connor, T. (2003) Understanding nurturing practices: A comparison of the use of strategies likely to enhance self-esteem in nurture groups and normal classrooms. *British Journal of Special Education,* 30(3): 119–24.

Communities in Schools (CIS) (2006) *Communities in Schools Annual Report 2006: Addressing America's Dropout Crisis One Child at a Time.* Alexandria, VA: Communities in Schools Incorporated.

Cooper, P. and Tiknaz, Y. (2005) Progress and challenge in nurture groups: Evidence from three case studies. *British Journal of Special Education*, 32(4): 211–22.

Department for Education and Employment (DfEE) (1997) *Green Paper: Excellence for All Children Meeting Special Educational Needs*. London: The Stationery Office.

Department for Education and Employment (DfEE) (1999a) *Social Inclusion: Pupil Support* (Circular 10/99). London: The Stationery Office.

Department for Education and Employment (DfEE) (1999b) *Excellence in Cities*. London: The Stationery Office.

Department for Education and Skills (DfES) (2003a) *Good Practice Guidance for Behaviour and Education Support Teams*. London: The Stationery Office.

Department for Education and Skills (DfES) (2003b) *Every Child Matters*. London: The Stationery Office.

Department for Education and Skills (DfES) (2004a) *Every Child Matters: Change for Children*. London: The Stationery Office.

Department for Education and Skills (DfES) (2004b) *Final Guidance for Excellence Clusters on the Behaviour Improvement Programme (BIP)*. London: DfES.

Department for Education and Skills (DfES) (2005a) *Higher Standards for All*. London: The Stationery Office.

Department for Education and Skills (DfES) (2005b) *Supporting the New Agenda for Children's Services and Schools: The Role of Learning Mentors and Co-ordinators*. London: The Stationery Office.

Department for Education and Skills (DfES) (2005c) *Guidance for Establishing and Managing Primary and Secondary Learning Support Units (LSUs)*. London: The Stationery Office.

Doyle, R. (2005) 'I hate you. Please help me': A case study from a classic Boxall nurture group. *Pastoral Care in Education*, 23(1): 3–11.

Farrington, D. and West, D.J. (1990) The Cambridge Study in Delinquent Development: A long-term follow-up on 441 London males, in G. Kaiser and H.J. Kerner (eds) *Criminality: Personality, Behaviour, Life History*. Berlin: Springer Verlag.

Galton, M., Gray, J. and Rudduck, J. (1999) *The Impact of School Transitions and Transfers on Pupil Progress and Attainment*. *Research Report 131*. London: The Stationery Office.

Galton, M., Gray. J., Rudduck. J. et al. (2003) *Transfer and Transitions in the Middle Years of Schooling (7–14): Continuities and Discontinuities in Learning. Research Report 443.* London: DfES.

Gerrard, B. (2005) City of Glasgow nurture group pilot scheme evaluation. *Emotional and Behavioural Difficulties*, 10(4): 245–53.

GHK Consulting, Holden McAllister Partnership and IPSOS Public Affairs (2004) *The Reintegration of Children Absent, Excluded or Missing from School. Research Report 598.* London: The Stationery Office.

Global Campaign for Education (2005) *Missing the Mark: A School Report on Rich Countries' Contribution to Universal Primary Education by 2015*, April 2005.

Hall, J.C. (2003) *Mentoring and Young People: A Literature Review.* Edinburgh: Scottish Council for Research in Education.

Hallam, S. and Castle, F. (1999) *Evaluation of the Behaviour and Discipline Pilot Projects (1996–99) Supported under the Standards Fund Programme. Research Report 163.* London: The Stationery Office.

Hallam, S., Castle, F. and Rogers, L. with Creech, A., Rhamie, J. and Kokotsaki, D. (2005) *Research and Evaluation of the Behaviour Improvement Programme. Research Report 702.* London: DfES.

Halsey, K., Gulliver, C., Johnson, A., Martin, K. and Kinder, K. (2005) *Evaluation of Behaviour and Education Support Teams. Research Report 706.* London: The Stationery Office.

Hayden, C. (1997) *Children Excluded from Primary School: Debates, Evidence, Responses.* Buckingham: Open University Press.

Hayden, C., Sheppard, C. and Ward, D. (1996) Primary school exclusions evidence for action. *Educational Research*, 38(2): 213–25.

Holmes, G. (2000) Education Connect: An innovative approach to transition. *Principal Matters*, 45: 2–5.

Human Rights Watch (2005a) *Failing Our Children: Barriers to the Right to Education.* Chicago, IL: Human Rights Watch.

Human Rights Watch (2005b) *Inside the Home, Outside the Law Abuse of Child Domestic Workers in Morocco.* Human Rights Watch Index No. E1712.

Human Rights Watch (2006) *'Life Doesn't Wait': Romania's Failure to Protect and Support Children and Youth Living with HIV.* Human Rights Watch Index No. D1806.

Humphrey, N. and Brooks, A.G. (2006) An evaluation of a short cognitive-behavioural anger management interventions for pupils at risk of exclusion. *Emotional and Behavioural Difficulties*, 11(1): 5–24.

Iszatt, J. and Wasilewska, T. (1997) Nurture groups: An early intervention model enabling vulnerable children with emotional and behavioural difficulties to integrate successfully into school. *Educational and Child Psychology*, 14(3): 121–39.

Kendall, L., O'Donnel, L., Golden, S. et al. (2005) *Excellence in Cities: The National Evaluation of a Policy to Raise Standards in Urban Schools 2000–2003. Research Report 675A*. London: The Stationery Office.

Kleese, E.J. and D'Onofrio, J.A. (1994) *Student Activities for Students at Risk*. Reston, VA: National Association of Secondary School Principals.

Lehr, C.A., Johnson, D.R., Bremer, C.D., Cosio, A. and Thompson, M. (2004a) *Essential Tools: Increasing Rates of School Completion*. Minneapolis, MN: National Center on Secondary Education and Transition.

Lehr, C.A., Sinclair, M.F. and Christenson, S.L. (2004b) Addressing student engagement and truancy prevention during the elementary school years: A replication study of the Check and Connect model. *Journal of Education for Students Placed at Risk*, 9(3): 279–301.

Lever, N., Sander, M.A., Lombardo, S. et al. (2004) A dropout intervention programme for high-risk inner-city youth. *Behavior Modification*, 28(4): 513–27.

McElroy, C. (2000). Middle School programs that work *Phi Delta Kappan*, 82(4): 277–279.

McGee, C., Ward, R., Gibbons, J. and Harlow, A. (2003) *Transition to Secondary School: A Literature Review*. Wellington: Ministry of Education.

Macrae, S., Maguire, M. and Ball, S.J. (1997) Whose 'learning' society? A tentative deconstruction. *Journal of Education Policy*, 12(6): 499–509.

McSherry, J. (2004) *Learning Support Units: Principles, Practice and Evaluation*. London: David Fulton.

Meijer, C.J.W. (2001) *Inclusive Education and Effective Classroom Practices*. Odense: European Agency for Development in Special Needs Education.

Miller, A. (2002) *Mentoring for Students and Young People: A Handbook of Effective Practice*. London: Kogan Page.

Moore, K.A. (2006) *Defining the Term 'At Risk'*. Washington, DC: Child Trends.

Ofsted (2003) *Excellence in Cities and Education Action Zones: Management and Impact*. London: Ofsted.

Ofsted (2005) *Managing Challenging Behaviour*. London: Ofsted.

Ofsted (2006) *Evaluation of the Impact of Learning Support Units.* London: Ofsted.

Osler, A., Watling, R. and Busher, H. (2001) *Reasons for Exclusion from School. Research Report 244.* London: The Stationery Office.

Panayiotopoulos, C. and Kerfoot, M. (2007) Early intervention and prevention for children excluded from primary schools. *International Journal of Inclusive Education*, 11(1): 59–80.

Parsons, C., Benn, L., Hailes, J. and Howlett, K. (1994) *Excluding Primary School Children.* London: Family Policy Studies Centre.

Parsons, C., Godfrey, R., Howlett, K., Hayden, C. and Martin, T. (2001) Excluding primary school children: The outcomes six years on. *Pastoral Care*, 19(4): 4–15.

Peters, S. (2003) *Inclusive Education: Achieving Education for All by Including Those with Disabilities and Special Education Needs.* Geneva: World Bank.

Presseisen, B.Z. (1991) At-risk students: Defining a population, in K.M. Kershner and J.A. Connolly (eds) *At-risk Students and School Restructuring*, pp. 5–11. Washington, DC: Office of Educational Research and Improvement.

Redick, S.S. and Vail, A. (1991) *Motivating Youth At Risk.* Gainesville, VA: Home Economics Education Association.

Reid, K. (2007) The views of learning mentors on the management of school attendance. *Mentoring & Tutoring*, 15(1): 39–55.

Steer Report (2006) *Learning Behaviour: The Report of the Practitioners' Group on School Behaviour and Discipline.* London: DfES.

Stradling, R. and McNeil, M. (2000) *Moving On: The Process of Transition from Primary to Secondary School.* Inverness: Highland Heath Board of Scotland.

UNESCO (2000) *The Dakar Framework for Action, Adopted by the World Education Forum.* Paris: UNESCO.

Vislie, L. (2003) From integration to inclusion: Focusing global trends and changes in the western European societies. *European Journal of Special Needs Education*, 18(1): 17–35.

Ward, R. (2000) Transfer from middle to secondary school: A New Zealand study. *International Journal of Educational Research*, 33: 365–74.

Werner, E. (1990) Protective factors and individual resilience, in S. Meisels and J. Shonkoff (eds) *Handbook of Early Childhood Interventions.* New York: Cambridge University Press.

Wombler, M.N., Hall, H.C. and Turner, J.P. (1997) Middle school vocational teachers' knowledge of the characteristics of at-risk learners. *Journal of Vocational and Technical Education*, 14(1). Available online http:// Scholar.lib.vt. edn/ejournals/JVTE/v14n1/JVTE-5. html (12 Feb. 07).

10 Approaches to exclusion

When children are excluded from school they must be provided with alternative educational opportunities. This chapter explores a range of ways that this has been undertaken, through the use of learning mentors, the sharing of provision between schools, alternative school timetables, and other means.

Introduction

As we saw in Chapter 1, rates of exclusion in Britain, the USA and Australia saw major increases during the 1990s. In 2003/04, in England, 1.3 million pupil days were spent out of the classroom due to fixed-term exclusion (DfES 2005). Around 13 pupils in every 10,000 were permanently excluded from schools, most commonly for persistent disruptive behaviour but also for verbal abuse, threatening behaviour or assault (DfES 2005). The main provision for permanently excluded pupils in England is in Pupil Referral Units (PRUs). While the standards of education in PRUs have improved (Ofsted 2005), attendance remains poor and less than half of the pupils gain a single General Certificate of Secondary Education (GCSE). The notion that pupils would be reintegrated back into the mainstream after being in a PRU has not been enacted in most cases and most PRUs have long waiting lists contributing to the 10,000 students who have disappeared from school rolls entirely (Ofsted 2005).

Exclusion is regarded as the ultimate sanction for challenging behaviour in schools, although schools have different thresholds for what is considered acceptable behaviour. It is financially costly, and there has been a consistent failure to achieve a high standard of alternative provision for those outside mainstream education. Teachers are rarely in favour of excluding pupils, believing that it is either ineffective or has negative effects, although most feel that it is essential to be able to remove a pupil from school for a short period (Reed 2005).

Until recently in England, the government required that all pupils excluded from school for more than 15 consecutive days received full-time and appropriate education. However, a survey in 2004 found that there was some disparity in the understanding of the number of taught hours required to fulfil this requirement. Although the majority of Local Authorities (LAs) in the sample were usually able to meet the full-time provision requirement, there were a minority that were struggling to do so, particularly for primary school pupils. LAs used a wide range of agencies and other services to provide full-time education. College placements and those with other agencies tended to be less expensive than providing a place in a PRU (Atkinson et al 2004). From September 2007 the law changed to require LAs to arrange full-time education from and including the sixth day of a permanent exclusion (DfES, 2007); this in response to recommendations from the Steer Report (2006).

Getting pupils into full-time alternative education takes time. In 2000, the average time between permanent exclusion and a placement in alternative provision was over three months and over 14 per cent of pupils waited more than six months for a place (Daniels et al. 2003). LAs participating in the Behaviour Improvement Programme (BIP) were required to provide education on the first day of exclusion. Although this was difficult to implement it ensured that children were not out of school for long periods of time. Later sections in this chapter provide examples of how this was achieved.

Pupils' and family's experiences of exclusion

When children are excluded from school they experience feelings of rejection, feel that they have been treated unfairly and have been labelled as a troublemaker, and often have a strong sense of injustice, believing that there are inconsistencies in the ways that pupils are treated. They often face serious difficulties at home as their parents are frequently angry and upset. Their families report increased stress and feelings of helplessness, many already coping with multiple disadvantage (Cohen et al. 1994; Cullen et al. 1996; Cullingford and Morrison 1996; De Pear and Garner 1996; John 1996; Hayden 1997; Kinder et al. 1997; Brodie 1998; Kinder et al. 1999).

Munn and colleagues (2000) identified five stages following exclusion:

1. Immediate – strong negative feelings of rejection, fear, injustice.
2. Initial reaction at home – angry reaction from parents, further punishment.
3. During time out of school – boredom, missing out on school work, missing out on time with school friends, negative reputation in the community.

4. On return to school – negative reaction of peers, negative reputation among teachers, difficulties catching up with school work.
5. Long-term – fear that being excluded would negatively affect job prospects.

Families typically expressed irritation with the child, as the exclusion caused them inconvenience, and dealing with the system created stress and frustration. In addition, the mother and siblings were frequently stigmatized (Munn et al. 2000). In most cases the exclusion was the result of more than one incident, and pupils and parents generally felt that an alternative punishment which kept the child in school would have been better.

In the UK African-Caribbean children are far more likely to be excluded from school than White pupils. Research on the impact of this on their lives has shown that for many exclusion acts as a critical incident, making them reassess their behaviour and renew their determination to succeed in getting qualifications. Most subsequently return to education or find employment, although some receive no further education or engage in a variety of alternative provision. They report exclusion to be traumatic, leading to a loss of dignity and self-respect, and generating a sense of injustice, as punishments for Black students seem more severe than for White, raising awareness of the way that race affects the way they are and will be seen by others in the future. After the immediate reaction to the exclusion a resilient sense of self develops with a positive Black identity that motivates them to disprove official expectations of them. The support provided by their immediate and extended family, friends and the voluntary sector is crucial to their successful transition into education and employment. Their families generally find the support from statutory resources to be inadequate but the emotional support and advice about careers, employment, and assistance with advocacy and representation, and the practical educational alternatives and help with reintegration into mainstream education offered by the voluntary services are viewed as particularly beneficial (Wright et al. 2005).

Variability between schools in levels of exclusion

Issues relating to intake account for much of the variation in school's behaviour outcomes, in particular community factors, for instance, educational aspiration, levels of self-esteem and levels of conflict within the population from which the school draws. High levels of pupil mobility and casual admissions are also important explanatory factors because of settling-in issues, and disproportionate numbers of children arriving who have been excluded from other schools, or who have emotional and behavioural problems and disrupted personal histories. Schools facing intake challenges are vulnerable, particularly when LA spending fails to recognize their greater need (Reed 2005). Despite this, schools in the same catchment area have widely different levels of exclusion. Policies on when to exclude vary greatly from the 'three strikes and you're out' approach to those which advocate either fixed-term or permanent exclusion only in response to bringing offensive weapons or intruders onto school premises. While written policies are often similar, there is significant variation in interpretation, consistency and flexibility (Reed 2005).

Variability in exclusion levels between similar schools reflects differences in the levels of behaviour threshold set, the degree of flexibility in schools' behaviour policies, the use of legitimate alternatives to exclusion, and the use of informal exclusion. Variation in the level of a school's official exclusions does not necessarily relate to variation in behaviour outcomes or inclusiveness of practice. Major factors affecting school's thresholds include the level of challenge presented by pupils, the pressure the Head is under to improve the school, and the levels of priority given to academic outcomes (Reed 2005). Schools reporting no or few exclusions have been shown to emphasize parental involvement and do not view pupils of low socio-economic status as being disadvantaged (Sammons et al. 1997; Munn et al. 2000). They tend to emphasize praise and reward systems in managing behaviour, have structured breaks and lunchtimes, and involve pupils in decision-making (Munn et al. 2000). Table 10.1 sets out the key differences in ethos between high- and low-excluding schools.

Many schools do everything that they can to avoid excluding pupils. However, even within these schools teachers feel the need to retain the power to remove a pupil for a short period to give respite for the rest of the class, although internal exclusion is often perceived as fairer and more effective than fixed-term exclusion. In some schools temporary informal exclusion is a day-to-day norm. It is viewed as necessary to managing working relationships within the school without creating a lengthy bureaucratic process (Reed 2005). While it is often carried out in the interests of the child to avoid the stigma of exclusion, it removes from parents and carers any rights they may have to challenge the school's decision.

Table 10.1 School ethos and exclusion

Encouraged exclusion	Discouraged exclusion
Beliefs about school, teaching and pupils	
Narrow definition of teacher's job, focused on subject knowledge, exam results	Wide remit, including persona and social development of pupils, as well as exam results
Academic goals prominent	Social and academic goals
Acceptable pupils were those who arrived willing to learn and came from supportive homes	Acceptance of a wide range of pupils, including those with learning and other difficulties
The curriculum	
Academic curriculum, pressure on pupils, lack of differentiation	Curriculum flexible and differentiated
Personal and social development curriculum lacks status	Personal and social development curriculum highly valued
Potential of informal curriculum for motivating less academic pupils not realized	Informal curriculum, lively and covering a wide range of activities, such as sport, drama, art, working in the local community
Relations with parents	
Parents expected unquestioningly to support the school	Time and effort spent involving parents in decision-making about their children
Decision-making about exclusion	
Hierarchical decision-making separating pastoral support staff from those with responsibility for maintaining discipline	Decisions informed by a network of staff with a range of perspectives on the pupil
Tariff systems leading to automatic exclusion	Flexible system, behaviour evaluated in context
Pastoral support staff expected to meet needs of all pupils	Pastoral support staff an information source on decisions
Learning/behaviour support expected to remove troublesome pupils and solve problems	Learning/behaviour support a source of support and ideas for mainstream staff

Source: Derived from Munn et al. (2000).

Reducing the need for exclusion

The role of the Special Educational Needs Coordinator (SENCO) is seen as particularly important in reducing exclusions as many excluded children have learning or behaviour difficulties. Implementing an inclusive and multicultural curriculum which motivates pupils from all backgrounds has also been suggested as a means of reducing exclusions. Indeed, secondary schools with low exclusion rates frequently develop alternative flexible curriculum arrangements for vulnerable pupils at Key Stage 4 (Osler et al. 2001). As the highest rates of exclusion are in Year 9, attention also needs to be given to the Key Stage 3 curriculum.

Schools which have focused on improving behaviour as a means of reducing exclusions have found the following effective:

- well integrated in-class support for teachers;
- having a clear, well understood set of behaviour expectations;
- consistent but fair use of rewards and light touch sanctions;
- strongly established, well staffed learning support units and mentoring support;
- strongly embedded multi-agency support; and
- a strong commitment to inclusion (Reed 2005).

Schools successful in maintaining low levels of exclusion offer individualized support as a preventative measure rather than waiting until exclusion is needed. The work of Behaviour and Education Support Teams (BESTs) can be highly effective in this respect. Similarly Bagley and Pritchard (1998) described a three-year small-scale project where social workers worked in a primary and linked secondary school which served a deprived area with high rates of unemployment, poverty and crime, and high rates of exclusion from school. The programme was successful in significantly reducing rates of self-reported theft, truancy, bullying, drug use and exclusion. In the project the multi-agency team (senior Education Welfare Officer (EWO), Project Social Worker, project teachers in the schools) worked intensively with troubled children referred by teachers. They supported and counselled teachers and visited families ensuring the maximum possible inter-agency coordination and financial and social service benefits for the family. Counselling was provided for the family and child with a focus on child protection issues, transition to secondary school, bullying, truanting, health education, community development, interagency collaborative and school exclusions.

Similar preventative work was undertaken in the Behaviour Improvement Programme by the BESTs (see Chapter 9). It can also be implemented through the Extended Schools Programme (see Chapter 4). In providing support schools need to consider the nature of the pupil's difficulties. If a pupil is misbehaving because of problems at home bringing about change will require a different intervention to a child who is behaving badly because the curriculum is inappropriate, or they are being bullied.

Alternatives to exclusion

The main alternatives to exclusion are the use of PRUs, collaborative arrangements between schools, varied provision in clusters of schools, internal exclusion centres, external centres, setting up an alternative school day, managed moves to another school, and alternative educational provision. The BIP required LAs to provide full-time education from the first day of exclusion. This proved particularly challenging (Hallam et al. 2005).

Educational provision for fixed-term exclusions and the first day of exclusion

First-day response centres set up as part of BIP were felt by teachers to be an improvement on sending children home (Reed 2005). However, some LAs have difficulty in meeting the requirement for providing full-time alternative education after 15 days so voluntarily providing full-time education on the first day of exclusion is unlikely (Atkinson et al. 2004). As the average length of fixed-term exclusions is 3.8 days many children are deprived of full-time education for much of the time that they are excluded (DfES 2005). As those who are permanently excluded often have several prior experiences of fixed-term exclusion they inevitably miss out on a substantial proportion of their education.

LAs participating in BIP were committed to the provision of full-time education on the first day of exclusion. While most LAs had well established provision for long-term exclusion short- and medium-term provision proved problematic for a range of reasons and expensive to implement.

Overall, there was considerable variability in the way that LAs provided first-day education for excluded pupils. The arrangements made included:

- the use of the PRU;
- reciprocal exchanges between schools;
- the setting-up of internal exclusion centres;
- the setting-up of LA centres;
- buying in outside agencies to make provision;
- adopting a flexible school day for excluded pupils; and
- monitoring work undertaken at home.

There were differences in the type of arrangements made in secondary and primary schools. The following sections provide examples.

The use of Pupil Referral Units for short-term exclusion

In some LAs, the PRU took on the task of providing education on the first day of exclusion. In one LA, schools provided fixed-period provision for days 1 and 2, pupils then went to the PRU. Schools could send pupils to the PRU for the first two days but had to provide staff to ensure the necessary support. Transport to the PRU was generally provided by the LA. In the PRU, primary and secondary school pupils were separated from each other and from the long-term PRU students. While students attended the PRU they were monitored, weekly reviews were held, and systems of targets and individualized work set in place. Schools received an end-of-placement report about attendance, work and behaviour. In theory schools should have set work to be completed while the pupils were attending the PRU but in practice the work set was often inappropriate and did not support an improvement in behaviour. The PRU staff tried to provide a more appropriate curriculum and aimed to develop pupils' social and team working skills. All the pupils participated in an anger management course, although three days was not sufficient for this to be completed. While the system generally worked well, some of the pupils expressed a preference for staying at the PRU rather than returning to mainstream school and it proved difficult to predict the numbers of students attending at any one time.

At primary level, one LA organized first-day provision centrally through an extension of the primary PRU provision. The primary schools liased with the Behaviour and Learning Support Service to implement this. Where pupils did not attend the PRU or where the exclusion was long-term, the Education Welfare Service took responsibility for providing education at home.

Collaborative arrangements between schools

Another solution to ensuring appropriate provision for excluded pupils is for schools to collaborate. In the future it is anticipated that schools will work together with Children's Services through Children's Trusts to identify potentially challenging pupils early on and plan the provision that they need. Some help will be provided through Extended Schools. Examples of such cooperation were identified in the evaluation of BIP.

In one LA, a school made an arrangement with the local grammar school. Excluded pupils were required to attend there, spending the day working in the library with a learning mentor who collected work from the excluding school for the pupil to complete. This provision could be made for up to five days, after which work was sent home. This acted as a strong deterrent and was responsible for much improved behaviour. In another LA, an arrangement was made between two partner schools on a reciprocal basis. An 'Exclusions Learning Support Assistant' was employed as the link person, and accompanied the pupils to the other school and acted as a mentor. There were also plans to make a part-time teaching appointment based partly in school and partly in the PRU. In another LA, secondary schools were paired and provision arranged via 'managed pupil exchange'. This worked well and most pupils responded positively. At primary level, one LA designated six primary schools as centres which each offered provision on a termly rota basis. Each school was allocated funding for a full-time learning mentor to support this initiative.

Responsibility devolved to schools

In some LAs the responsibility for arranging education for the first day of exclusion was devolved to schools. Schools typically set up internal exclusion centres, sent pupils to work with external agencies or to other schools, or arranged for work to be supervised at home. They were given funding to support this. The model was reported by schools to work well except for pupils whose behaviour was extreme and who had displayed violence, particularly towards members of staff.

Varied provision in clusters of schools

In many LAs the provision varied between clusters of schools. In one LA each cluster developed its own provision, with the PRU providing places for those young people whose behaviour could not be managed within the locally organized provision. Dealing with exclusion in this way led to an increasing recognition that the young people belonged to the school, not an individual teacher, and that they should be maintained in the school community rather then handed on to another institution. Each cluster adopted a different approach. One created an Internal Exclusion Unit which was used for those children at risk of exclusion who were perceived as likely to benefit from several days in fairly isolated provision, and children who had been formerly excluded. In this cluster, pupils in Years 5 and 6 in linked primary schools also used the internal exclusion centre. In another cluster, there was a base in a secondary school to which excluded pupils at primary or secondary level were transported. The third cluster had internal provision which was not directly connected to the school. The primary schools worked together, each identifying a room for excluded pupils with children being sent to a different school for the period of their exclusion. In the fourth cluster a room was identified in a community space which catered for primary and secondary pupils. Primary pupils spent the morning there, returning to the excluding primary school in the afternoon with support from a member of staff. Similarly, in another LA, five primary schools jointly funded a Learning Centre. This enabled two children from each school to attend in the mornings, returning to school in the afternoon. This hugely benefited both the pupils and the schools concerned. An example of the experience of one pupil is given in Box 10.1.

Box 10.1 Transfer to secondary school

Transfer from primary to secondary school for an excluded pupil

One Year 6 pupil, who had been permanently excluded from a primary school was taken into the Learning Support Unit (LSU) at the secondary school for three afternoons a week prior to his transfer there. This was in addition to attending an Exclusion Centre for two days. The experience of exclusion was described as 'having knocked the confidence out of him'. He settled in well at the LSU and his mother indicated that this would benefit his transition to secondary school and provide him with greater access to learning mentors. Other vulnerable Year 6 pupils identified by the BEST were also supported there. Supportive visits were made to the home by the BEST Child and Adolescent Mental Health Service (CAMHS) worker and the learning mentor.

In another LA some schools employed additional support staff, usually learning mentors, some set up exclusion bases within school, while others made partner arrangements. One school offered education before school for two hours then after school for three hours. Some set up an in-school exclusion unit before formal exclusion took place, others set up a 'nurture' room for pupils thus removing the punitive element. In primary schools these rooms often served a dual purpose enabling staff to develop different methods of working interactively and creatively with children. These arrangements were successful as schools were less likely to exclude pupils when they continued to have responsibility for them after the exclusion had taken place. Overall, children did not like attending the units and this acted as a deterrent reducing the numbers of exclusions.

A similar approach was adopted in another LA. Measures included parental supervision of set work with monitoring visits by school staff; excluded pupils receiving education on the school site; some education taking place on-site but out of the normal school day; and some sharing of excluded pupils with neighbouring schools. These arrangements ensured that the children's education was not interrupted. Children were no longer able to regard exclusion as an unofficial holiday. Schools found the concept of supporting pupils philosophically sound, but the administration of the system was challenging. Overall, exclusions did reduce but in some cases this created issues with staff and the parents of victims who viewed exclusion as a significant punishment which was not being used.

Internal exclusion centres

Several schools developed internal exclusion centres. For instance, one secondary school had a new purpose-built centre, the Alternative Centre for Education (ACE), which was additional to and different from the Learning Support Unit (LSU). Pupils in Key Stages 3 and 4 were referred to the centre rather than being excluded. The LSU focused on long-term preventative work while ACE provided short-term tuition. A software package was used to identify pupils at-risk. If three teachers expressed concern about a child, he/she would receive intervention through the centre.

The internal exclusion processes in one school included pupils receiving an official exclusion letter and parents being telephoned to inform them of the situation. Parents chose whether the child attended the centre or stayed at home. The exclusion room had a range of curriculum resources and classes began at 9.30 am. Pupils were off-site during the lunchtime break which was set at a different time to the rest of the school and when they returned they stayed until 4 pm, later than the rest of the school. Exclusion rates were high since the school had a zero tolerance policy relating to strong language and if pupils accrued 30 conduct slips or were engaged in fighting they were excluded. The school viewed the procedures as highly successful in dealing with short-term exclusions. Where pupils were perceived as being at risk of long-term exclusion the LSU developed individual programmes to work through specific issues. The exclusion centre acted as a deterrent as pupils were reluctant to return to it.

Some LAs provided internal provision for the first days of exclusion through LSUs but this was relatively ineffective because the practice was not sufficiently distinctive from the normal role of the LSU. Primary schools frequently did not have a physical exclusion centre but learning mentors, Pupil Support Officers, or members of the BESTs supervised pupils on-site. In some cases one learning mentor was shared between a cluster of schools, in other cases schools were allocated, or provided additional funding, to have a learning mentor in each school.

External centres for fixed-period exclusions

Some schools created their own off-site provision, often in a nearby building. This alternative provision was able to meet the needs of the students providing small group teaching, multiprofessional staffing, and work-related learning. Close proximity to the main school meant that pupils could return to the mainstream for some lessons, although there was a danger that the centre came to provide permanent education for some pupils rather than attempting to reintegrate them into the mainstream. In some cases such off-site provision was set up jointly with other schools.

Several LAs set up centres external to schools to provide pupils with education on the first day of exclusion. One LA leased Youth Centre premises staffed by Youth Workers. The centre developed resources for projects and students usually stayed for between 2 to 14 days, although the average stay was 6 to 7 days. The centre had capacity for up to 12 pupils. This sometimes led to problems when several new pupils turned up simultaneously. There were also issues related to antagonism between pupils when they came from different schools. The centre also accommodated pupils who had not been excluded but needed a break from mainstream school and specific help with literacy skills. There were very few re-referrals to the centre. Success was perceived to lie in providing the pupils with an opportunity and the space to talk. Following attendance at the centre each pupil was provided with a report to assist in their reintegration. The provision was flexible and well supported by schools. Centre staff noted that there were differences in the lengths of time schools sent pupils for similar incidents and in the amount of information they provided. The existence of the centre meant that exclusion came to be perceived by pupils as a punishment whereas in the past it was viewed as an opportunity to spend a few days at home. It became a useful tool in managing behaviour because pupils did not wish to be re-referred. Parents reacted positively and took exclusions more seriously.

In another LA, a similar system was developed. The Youth Service offered provision for education on the first day of exclusion in a designated centre. Pupils were offered activities ranging from anger management to homework support and ICT opportunities. This was effective for the pupils that attended, but the centre's location and travelling difficulties meant that many did not do so. Communication with pupils after they returned to school was difficult and they often felt quite isolated. The geographical location made developing stronger links with the schools problematic.

Another LA enlisted the services of a voluntary organization, Community Links, to cater for pupils on the first day of exclusion. Pupils attended when exclusion was for more than three days. Sessions were held in church premises and there were up to 18 pupils in any single week. There were four staff, one teacher and three youth workers. The students did curriculum work until lunchtime (English, maths and ICT) and then participated in social activities to encourage teamwork. If pupils misbehaved they had to work all afternoon. Parents and pupils were required to sign a code of conduct and rules were explained and agreed. The staff had links with schools prior to the exclusion but not when the pupils returned to school. The system acted as a deterrent and pupils wanted to go back to school. Pupils were pleased with the amount of work that they had completed and this raised self-esteem. While working at the centre behaviour generally improved. Some children and their parents preferred the education on offer at the centre to that in school. The centre was not successful with all pupils and some continued to be placed in a PRU.

At primary level, in one LA, Pupil Development Centres (PDC) were set up with the intention of preventing exclusion in Key Stage 1 and 2 pupils. Three boys in the Key Stage 2 PDC had experienced fixed-period exclusions in the past, including one excluded for drug and solvent abuse. The PDC functioned on a part-time basis for four sessions, as there was a wish to avoid pupils being out of the classroom on a full-time basis. Much of the work undertaken was concerned with the development of life skills for pupils at risk of becoming disaffected. Developing linguistic skills and raising self-esteem were the priorities.

Changes in the timing of the school day

Some schools innovatively rearranged the school day requiring pupils to attend at different times to the other children. For instance, in two extended schools with a continental day from 8.00 to 1.30 the first-day provision for excluded pupils was in the afternoon from 1.30 to 6.00. Work was supervised by learning mentors. In another LA, secondary schools operated a 'flexible day' for fixed-period exclusions. The length and timing of this was left to schools to organize, with pupils attending possibly from mid-afternoon until 5.30–6pm (these being the prime times identified by the police for crimes being committed). This was an expensive arrangement as it was necessary for pupils to be supervised by two adults. However, it was regarded as a strong deterrent. Pupils found the work very intensive and figures for fixed-period exclusions for one of the schools operating the system reduced dramatically over a one-year period from 119 to 18. Another school set up an after-school group. This was very successful in cutting down the number of exclusions.

The challenge was providing staffing. There was also an outreach tutor, an extension for the LSU, and alternative timetables for Year 11 pupils.

One secondary school dramatically reduced fixed-period exclusions through the use of a Time Out room. This isolated pupils from their peers during break and lunch times. A system of 'Extra Time' learning was also used which involved the pupils coming to school from 3 to 6 pm. The extended day system allowed pupils at risk of permanent exclusion to remain in education at school, while at the same time 'giving the school, the kid and the parents a break'. One Year 8 pupil, who had problems at home brought his younger brother to the Time Out room and the system also attracted Year 10 persistent absentees and was being considered as a way of getting them back into school. The extended day was staffed on a rota basis organized by the senior management team.

Managed moves

Some schools arranged through the LA a move to another school to enable the child to make a fresh start. Such moves are intended to prevent exclusions when all other options have been exhausted (Reed 2005). Some charitable organizations offer support for such managed moves.

Alternative educational provision

There is a lack of high quality alternative provision for excluded pupils and many continue to fall through the gaps in the system, although increasingly charitable institutions are offering support. An Ofsted report in 2003 indicated that much Key Stage 4 alternative provision had poor or uneven curriculum provision and in the weakest of projects the young people were merely kept out of harm's way. To improve the quality of such provision, guidance has now been issued relating to the minimum standards required of alternative provision outside of mainstream schools. Examples of good practice have been provided in Chapter 8.

The role of the voluntary sector

There is an expectation that in the future the charitable sector will play an increasing role in providing alternative educational opportunities. Indeed a range of initiatives have already been developed (for a review see Goodall 2005). However, there is a lack of coordination in the way that they help schools. Goodall's report provides an analysis of the kinds of activities that charities can offer to support disaffected young people and the relative costs of each. The report argues that social support can achieve real and lasting change for vulnerable young people and their families. However, supporting preventative work alongside existing educational provision is effective and less costly than providing alternative provision (see Table 10.2). Independent alternative provision should only be used when all other measures have failed.

Table 10.2 Relative expense of different types of charitable support

	Indicative cost per young person	Key outcomes
	Social support	
Emotional Health (e.g. Antidote, The Place2Be)	£115 per annum	Improved school environment Improved well-being of teachers and pupils Increased behaviour and attainment at whole-school level Better behaviour, emotional well-being and peer relations among individual pupils
Support networks within school (e.g. Childline in partnership with schools, the Children's Society's Genesis Project, Family Service Units)	£210–£2900 per annum (depending on intensity of need and level of work with parents outside of school)	Improved well-being for individual children experiencing difficulties Improved school response to at-risk children Improved relationship between school and parents Identification and resolution of difficulties in the home
Community-based support (e.g. Chance UK, Friends United Network)	£2500–£4900 per annum (depending on the length of the programme and level of disaffection)	Development of new skills for children which work as protective factors Provision of appropriate role model for children Improved relationship between parent and children and between child and peers Improved behaviour, attendance, and attainment at individual level

Advising parents		
Advice on education policy to professionals and parents (The advisory Centre for Education, IPSEA)	£90 per call to helpline	Increased understanding of education system Increased awareness of rights and the ability and confidence to assert those rights Improved ability for parents to act as advocate for their children Improved education for children
Alternative provision		
In-school programmes (Skill Force, the Prince's Trust xl network)	£830 per annum	Increased motivation and engagement in school Improved self-esteem, confidence and behaviour among individuals Improved attendance and attainment
Provision for pupils outside mainstream education (Include, Community Links, NACRO, Cheltenham Community projects, Fairbridge, Kids Company, Extern, Right Track)	£6500–£9500 per annum (depending on facilities on offer; level of need among pupils and geography)	Provision of education and life skills Reduction in barriers to learning (e.g. housing or substance misuse issues) Reduced social exclusion
Helping the state		
Providing solutions to truancy and exclusion at a national level (e.g. Inaura, Save the Children, Advisory Centre for Education, the Learning Challenge)	£130–£890 per annum (depending on services offered)	Improved response on the part of the education system to at-risk pupils Offer a greater voice to truanting and excluded children and their parents

Source: Derived from Goodall (2005).

Endnote

There are long-term detrimental consequences for pupils who are excluded from school which also have considerable costs for the state. While exclusion for most students and their families is traumatic it does not appear to act as a deterrent. The time spent out of full-time education can place already vulnerable students at risk of involvement in crime and has a negative impact on their educational opportunities in the short- and long-term. Initiatives developed as a result of the Behaviour Improvement Programme indicate that there are alternatives which can act as a deterrent without disrupting children's education. While it is to be hoped that preventative measures at the level of the school, the family and the individual pupil will reduce the need for exclusion, where these are not successful it is important that children's engagement with full-time education is maintained while their problems are addressed, whether this is internally within schools or on the basis of schools collaborating.

Chapter summary

- Exclusion from school is regarded as the ultimate sanction for challenging behaviour but teachers are rarely in favour of it although they feel that the sanction is necessary.
- Local Authorities are required to provide full-time education from and including the 6th day of exclusion. LAs in the BIP were required to provide full-time provision on the first day of exclusion. This was effective in enabling vulnerable children to continue their education.
- Excluded pupils feel rejected and often feel that they have been treated unfairly. Exclusion creates stress for their families and feelings of helplessness.
- There is considerable variability among schools with similar characteristics in their levels of exclusion. These differences reflect school ethos.
- Most schools offer preventative support to pupils perceived to be at risk of exclusion.
- Alternatives to exclusion include managed moves to other schools, attendance at off-site centres run by the LA or the school, attendance at on-site centres, and the provision of an alternatively timed school day.
- Preventative work provided alongside mainstream education is effective and much less costly than providing alternative education following exclusion.

Further reading

Goodall, E. (2005) *School's Out? Truancy and Exclusion: A Guide for Donors and Funders*. London: New Philanthropy Capital.

Reed, J. (2005) *Toward Zero Exclusion: An Action Plan for Schools and Policy Makers.* London: Institute for Public Policy Research.

References

Atkinson, M., Johnson, A., Wilkin, A., Johnson, F. and Kinder, K. (2004) *Good practice in the provision of full-time education for excluded Pupils.* Slough: NFER.

Bagley, C. and Pritchard, C. (1998) The reduction of problem behaviours and school exclusion in at-risk youth: an experimental study of school social work with cost-benefit analysis. *Child and Family Social Work.* 3: 219–26.

Brodie, I. (1998) *Exclusions from School.* London: National Children's Bureau.

Cohen, D., Richardson, J. and Labree, L. (1994) Parenting behaviours and the onset of smoking and alcohol use: A longitudinal study. *Pediatrics*, 20: 368–75.

Cullen, M.A., Johnstone, M., Lloyd, G. and Munn, P. (1996) *Exclusion from School and Alternatives: Three Reports to the Scottish Office.* Edinburgh: Moray House.

Cullingford, C. and Morrison, M. (1996) Who excludes whom? The personal experience of exclusion, in E. Blyth and J. Milner (eds) *Exclusion from School: Interprofessional Issues for Policy and Practice.* London: Routledge.

Daniels, H., Cole, T., Sellman, E., Sutton, J., Visser, J. with Bedward, J. (2003) *Young People Permanently Excluded from School. Research Report 405.* London: DfES.

De Pear, S. and Garner, P. (1996) Tales from the exclusion zone: The views of teachers and pupils, in E. Blyth and J. Milner (eds) *Exclusion from School: Interprofessional Issues for Policy and Practice.* London: Routledge.

Department for Education and Skills (DfES) (2005) *Permanent Exclusions from Schools and Exclusion Appeals, England 2003/2004.* London: DfES.

Department for Education and Skills (DfES) (2007) *Providing Full-time Education from the Sixth Day of any Fixed Period Exclusion: Implementation and Good Practice Guidance for Schools, including PRUs.* London: DfES.

Goodall, E. (2005) *School's Out? Truancy and Exclusion: A Guide for Donors and Funders.* London: New Philanthropy Capital.

Hallam, S., Castle, F. and Rogers, L. with Creech, A., Rhamie, J. and Kokotsaki, D. (2005) *Research and Evaluation of the Behaviour Improvement Programme. Research Report 702.* London: DfES.

Hayden, C. (1997) *Children Excluded from Primary School: Debates, Evidence, Responses.* Buckingham: Open University Press.

John, P. (1996) Damaged goods? An interpretation of excluded pupils' perceptions of schooling, in E. Blyth and J. Milner (eds) *Exclusion from School: Interprofessional Issues for Policy and Practice.* London: Routledge.

Kinder, K., Wakefield, A. and Wilkin, A. (1997) *Exclusion: Who Needs It?* Slough: NFER.

Kinder, K., Kendall, S., Halsey, K., and Atkinson, M. (1999) *Disaffection Talks: a Report for the Merseyside Learning Partnership Inter Agency Development Programme.* Slough: NFER

Munn, P., Lloyd, G. and Cullen, M.A. (2000) *Alternatives to Exclusion from School.* London: Paul Chapman.

Ofsted (2005) *Managing Challenging Behaviour.* London: Ofsted.

Osler, A., Watling, R. and Busher, H. (2001) *Reasons for Exclusion from School. Research Report 244.* London: DfEE.

Reed, J. (2005) *Toward Zero Exclusion: An Action Plan for Schools and Policy Makers.* London: Institute for Public Policy Research.

Sammons, P., Thomas, S. and Mortimore, P. (1997) *Forging Links, Effective Schools and Effective Departments.* London: Paul Chapman.

Steer Report (2006) *Learning Behaviour: The Report of the Practitioners' Group on School Behaviour and Discipline.* London, DfES.

Wright, C., Standen, P., John, G., German, G. and Patel, T. (2005) *School Exclusion and Transition into Adulthood in African-Caribbean Communities.* York: Joseph Rowntree Foundation.

Section 3
Improving Attendance

11 Whole-school approaches to attendance

This chapter identifies how schools and Local Authorities can develop strategies for improving attendance for the whole school population. It considers how schools can develop reliable systems for monitoring attendance; the role of electronic attendance systems; the importance of follow-up on the first day of non-attendance; the work of Education Welfare Services in addressing whole-school attendance issues; and the role of senior managers and teachers. It also addresses broader issues relating to improving the physical, social and learning environment in the school.

Introduction

As we saw in Chapter 2, the reasons that children do not attend school are many and varied (Easen et al. 1997; Hallam and Roaf 1997; Malcolm et al. 2003). Some are considered legitimate by schools, while others are not. The term truancy has been used to include all unauthorized absence from school and in the UK all kinds of regional expressions have developed, for instance, mitching, skiving, bunking off, dodging, wagging, sagging, dolling, slamming, bobbing and cutting.

During the 1990s schools in England were required by government to report their levels of attendance (authorized and unauthorized). Following this, some schools focused on reducing unauthorized absence (leading some schools to massage figures). There is now a recognition that the focus should be on improving overall attendance. This requires considerable time and effort and is not always successful (Ofsted 2004a; Hallam et al. 2005). To improve attendance schools have to address the causes of absence. Steps which can be taken to support this process with individual persistent truants will be considered in Chapter 12. The following sections consider whole-school approaches that can contribute.

Making a commitment to improving attendance

In order for a school to improve attendance there needs to be strong leadership and the commitment of all members of staff, including support staff, so that systems can be agreed and applied. Crucial is the consistency with which staff implement policy. Pupils respond if they know that the consequences for particular behaviours will be applied consistently across the school. Attendance and punctuality need to be expected and demanded by all teachers, and concentration, effort and high standards once students are in class. Senior managers need to monitor and have close and detailed knowledge of the way that practices are implemented across the school, giving a strong lead to heads of department or faculties, stressing the importance of consistency in approach to attendance, and the need for high quality teaching (Hallam 1996; Reid 1999).

Improving attendance also requires a commitment in relation to staff time. Pastoral staff need sufficient time to be able to undertake their tasks properly, there should be a time allowance for meetings, and the develop-ment of efficient systems of communication (Hallam 1996).

Governors also need to demonstrate commitment. They can play a direct role in relation to parents and pupils, as members of attendance panels or in counselling pupils. Regular visits to see the school at work enable governors to see for themselves which policies work in practice (Hallam and Roaf 1997).

Raising the profile

An early step in improving attendance is to raise its profile. Schools can adopt a number of strategies to achieve this. For instance, they might organize competitions among the students to design posters or leaflets to be displayed in school, and other places within the local community as parents frequently report lacking information about attendance, how to improve it, and the kinds of support that may be available (Dalziel and Henthorne 2005). Headteachers of schools that perform well on attendance indicate that it is important to maintain a continuing high profile for attendance issues over time (National Audit Office 2005).

Undertaking an audit

When schools take a decision to focus on improving attendance they need to establish the particular issues that affect attendance in their school. They need to understand why children are not attending and generate ideas for change. This means listening to pupils, attempting to understand their point of view, and valuing their perspectives. Without this it is impossible to create a coherent school community. Audits are very effective in establishing particular areas where attention is required (Hallam et al. 2005; Ofsted 2005a, 2005b). As with behaviour audits discussed in Chapter 3, an attendance audit can be undertaken in a variety of ways, but the more inclusive it is in terms of participants the better the quality of the information that will be collected. It is crucial that the children themselves are involved. Data on the days of the week, times of year, particular groups of children or classes where attendance is poor enable patterns to be identified. In secondary schools data also need to be collated regarding lesson attendance. Improvement requires planning based on evidence and an honest appraisal of the issues. Everyone needs to be involved in this, staff, governors, external agencies, parents and pupils (Hallam 1996; Ofsted 2001).

The day-to-day management of attendance

Attendance policies

Headteachers need to ensure that there is a clear policy on attendance and that teachers, pupils and parents are aware of it and know and understand its contents. It should include sections on lesson attendance and term-time holidays. Attendance procedures also need to be established and documented in such a way that parents are aware of them. This may mean them being translated into other languages. Once policy and practices are agreed staff must apply them consistently (Hallam 1996; Reid 1999; Ofsted 2001).

Monitoring attendance

If schools wish to improve attendance they have to be able to monitor it effectively. Registration systems need to be effective and data collated systematically. Many schools now employ administrative staff with responsibility for entering attendance data into computer systems or managing electronic registration. In the most sophisticated systems teachers input data with a personal digital assistant which transmits results by radio waves to a central personal computer. This generates a list of parents of pupils who are absent enabling school administrative staff to telephone the parents. Where calls are not answered the system generates letters to parents. Some systems automatically generate phone or text messages. Whatever system is adopted parents should be required to make contact with the school on the first day that their child is absent. If they do not do this the school should contact them. Particulary at primary level this ensures that children are safe. It also immediately establishes if pupils are truanting. The systematic follow-up of unexplained or inadequately excused absence is absolutely vital for improving attendance. Parents can be contacted by telephone, paging or text messages. If this does not produce a response a home visit may be required from a member of the support staff or Education Welfare Service (EWS) (Hallam 1996; Reid 1999).

Whatever systems of registration are adopted procedures and processes need to be regularly monitored by senior managers. The roles of senior managers, pastoral heads of year, and form tutors need to be clearly defined. Those with pastoral roles need to know pupils well and be able to liaise with parents, other support staff the Behaviour and Education Support Team (BEST), the EWS, and other agencies (Hallam 1996; Reid 1999; Hallam et al. 2005).

Electronic registration where a register is taken at every lesson can act as a deterrent for post-registration truancy. Such systems are not available in all schools at the moment (National Audit Office 2005) but schools are optimistic about the benefits that they will bring. The monitoring of lesson attendance reveals where there are issues with particular classes, subjects or teachers, which can then be addressed. If electronic systems are not available, teachers can take lesson registers. These then need to be checked against records of pupil absence for the day. This is time consuming and teachers are often reluctant to do it on a regular basis. It is more realistic if lessons are relatively long. This also reduces the extent to which pupils have to move around within the school during the day, times when there are many opportunities to misbehave or abscond. Other alternatives include having randomly timed, but frequent spot checks carried out by a senior member of staff, and the checking of school premises, particularly hidden away places, where truants might congregate. To discourage pupils leaving school premises restricting the number of entrances and insisting that pupils sign out is helpful. Some schools restrict pupils from leaving the premises particularly at lunchtime unless they have a specific written parental request to do so. To promote good behaviour a range of interesting lunchtime activities can be arranged (see Chapter 4).

Punctuality

Schools need to have clear guidelines for monitoring lateness and for when lateness becomes non-attendance. Latecomers almost invariably disrupt lessons, Schools also need to ensure that children move efficiently between lessons. Where teachers follow agreed procedures for transitions between lessons and supervise corridors, punctuality is improved. Keeping pupils on the premises at lunchtime also helps.

Creating a positive school ethos

The physical environment

The physical environment of the school is important in encouraging attendance because it sends messages about whether the people working in it are valued. Involving pupils in creating an attractive environment is important for them to respect it. School facilities which have been found useful in promoting attendance are outlined here:

- a pleasantly decorated parents' room;
- a quiet study room;
- a quiet room where pupils can meet with professionals from outside the school;
- an indoor games room;
- a social area for each year group;
- a designated girls-only room;
- clean and well maintained toilet facilities; and
- a place of safe storage for pupils' belongings (Hallam 1996).

Parental access to the school is very important, including signposting to the reception area which should be pleasant and welcoming with a seating area, information about the school, and displays of pupils' work. Access for the disabled, signposted car parking and labelled toilet facilities are also important.

The school grounds provide places where pupils skipping lessons can go to avoid detection and can also be the site of bullying incidents. Areas where pupils can undertake different activities can be set up taking account of age differences. Also playgrounds can be zoned to separate different types of activities (see Chapter 4). Areas where behaviour may be troublesome or where there is bullying can be identified and security increased. Similar procedures apply where there is vandalism. Security to ensure that the school is safe also assists in keeping pupils in school. An audit provides an opportunity to explore these issues establishing how outdoor facilities are currently used; areas where bullying occurs; the kinds of sporting activities that pupils would like to undertake; other facilities that pupils would like outdoors; and the effectiveness of outdoor supervision (Hallam et al. 2005).

The general maintenance and cleanliness of the school is important for health and safety in addition to ensuring the morale of staff and pupils.

Attention needs to be paid to lighting, heating and ventilation. Displays and decoration provide interest and some can be designated for pupils' own use.

Social relationships in school

The social climate of the school is critical in engendering a suitable environment for learning. If children are afraid of being bullied and there is constant disruption in and out of lessons the possibility of effective learning taking place will be considerably reduced. The reduction of incidents of bullying and the improvement of the social climate of the school depend on mutual respect. Ofsted (1993) recommend that school behaviour policies should include as one of their aims the encouragement of self-discipline. This requires that schools try to encourage greater openness in classrooms, promote good teacher–pupil relationships, engender high self-esteem in pupils, and create the kind of social and learning environment in which pupils will wish to participate. Bringing about this kind of change requires commitment (Ofsted 1993). In primary schools the Social and Emotional Aspects of Learning (SEAL) programme has attempted to engender this type of change (see Chapter 7).

Bullying

Pupils only feel secure from bullying where staff are overtly vigilant and where senior managers take action when it is necessary. Pupils should be encouraged to report all incidents of bullying which should then be thoroughly investigated. Engaging pupils in discussions about bullying can have a considerable effect in countering it. In some schools older pupils are trained to support younger pupils who perceive that they are being bullied. Such pupil mentors need to be aware of their own limitations and understand the need for some issues to be referred to teachers. Some schools are assisted in mediation by voluntary agencies or the police. See Box 4.3 in Chapter 4 for an example of a restorative justice intervention for bullying involving police in schools. Most schools welcome guidance on these matters but some find it difficult to sustain staff awareness. Most parents have concerns about the effects of bullying and recognize the demotivating and damaging effect it has. They feel that schools are generally responsive once contacted, although not all problems are resolved to their satisfaction. In such cases there is a feeling of injustice.

Olweus (1997) outlines a programme of actions that schools can take to reduce bullying. The programme is based on four key principles:

1. The school environment should be characterized by warmth, positive interest and involvement from adults.
2. There should be clear limits to unacceptable behaviour.
3. In cases of violations of limits and rules, non-hostile, non-physical sanctions should be consistently applied (this requires monitoring of students' behaviour).
4. Adults should act as authorities at least in some respects.

An audit can be used as a means of increasing awareness of bullying and gathering knowledge about it. Once the extent of the problem is known teachers and parents need to take responsibility and make it clear that bullying is not acceptable. There must be clear rules about bullying and teachers must operate consistent sanctions if it occurs. They should also praise compliance with the rules.

The learning and working environment

An important element in whole-school approaches to improving attendance is the quality of learning in the school. An orderly atmosphere, good behaviour and regular attendance are prerequisites to effective learning. In Chapter 7 strategies were presented to improve classroom behaviour; this in the context of adopting strategies in the classroom to enhance motivation to learn. If the focus is only on improving behaviour and attendance the outcomes for pupils remain unsatisfactory as in the long-term they need to develop skills which will support them in employment and throughout their lives. The learning environment, both physical and motivational, has to be considered. Schools where pupils' achievements are celebrated, however small, encourage pupils to be self-motivated and self-disciplined, reducing the need for staff to police their behaviour and attendance.

Pupils spend the majority of their time at school in the classroom. It is therefore crucial that the learning environment is conducive to working. Unsuccessful classroom practices are those that discourage students from becoming involved in their work. Motivating pupils is one of the most vital tasks of a teacher. The TARGET programme sets out ways of doing this (Epstein 1989; Ames 1992). The details are set out in Table 11.1. Implicit in this formulation is the assumption that teachers will have high expectations of all their pupils.

Table 11.1 Motivating pupils in the classroom

Engaging classrooms
- In what ways can classrooms encourage a positive style of learning and motivation?

Tasks
- Design activities that make learning interesting and that involve variety and personal challenge.
- Help learners establish realistic goals. With short-term goals, students view their class-work as manageable and they can focus on their progress and what they are learning.
- Help students develop organizational and management skills and effective task strategies. Students, especially those with learning difficulties need to develop and apply strategies for planning, organizing and monitoring their work.

Authority
- Give students opportunities to participate actively in the learning process via leadership roles, choices and decision-making.
- Help students develop the skills that will enable them to take responsibility for their learning.

Recognition
- Recognize individual student effort, accomplishments and improvement.
- Give all students opportunities to receive reward and recognition.
- Give recognition and rewards privately so that their value is not derived at the expense of others.

Grouping
- Provide opportunities for cooperative group learning and peer interaction.
- Use heterogeneous and varied grouping arrangements.

Evaluation
- Evaluate students for individual progress, improvement and mastery.
- Give students opportunities to improve their performance.
- Vary the method of evaluation and make evaluation private.

Time
- Adjust task or time requirements for students who have difficulty completing their work.
- Allow students opportunities to plan their schedules and progress at an optimal rate.

High quality teaching and learning

Good teaching provides the best incentive for attendance at school (Ofsted 2001). It is crucial where pupils have limited concentration, ill-developed social skills and poor literacy. Clarity and consistency are key to the effective management of pupils and are reflected in clear routines, expectations, objectives, instructions, explanations, examples, structure, discipline and language. These issues were addressed at the whole school level in Chapter 3 and at the classroom level in Chapter 7. Learning across the school is more effective when all teachers are consistent in the way that they deal with different pupils and situations and the way that they manage behaviour in the classroom by controlling entry and seating, giving instructions and explanations, using interesting material and activities, challenging and supporting pupils, keeping them on task, and responding fully to their work. Good teachers also address weak basic skills systematically and help pupils to work independently and efficiently (Ofsted 2005c). If teachers within a school work together to provide a high quality of teaching behaviour, attendance will improve.

The curriculum and extra-curricula activities

The curriculum must be relevant to retain pupils' interest in learning. Recent relaxation of the National Curriculum provides schools with opportunities to ensure that pupils value what they are learning. Where there are early signs of disaffection, including increased absence, schools can adapt the curriculum to provide flexibility. Work-related programmes are often effective in re-engaging disaffected students (see Chapter 8).

Provision of extra-curricular activities which offer support for learning are particularly important in the period leading into high stake examinations. Activities before school can improve attendance and punctuality, for instance, breakfast clubs, ICT activities. Homework clubs can also provide facilities for those children whose home environment may not be conducive to doing homework and foster a positive attitude towards school (Hallam 2004). Setting up activities during lunchtime assists schools in encouraging pupils to remain on site and helps staff in managing pupils in playgrounds and dining areas.

Informal opportunities for learning, through a range of after-school clubs and a variety of extra-curricular activities provide pupils with opportunities to develop self-confidence and skills. Where schools have extensive and well focused extra-curricular activities relationships between teachers and pupils often benefit (Ofsted 2001). Opportunities for pupils to display their abilities in other areas apart from the formal classroom contribute to their developing self-esteem. Sport, drama, music, residential outdoor activities, trips abroad all help pupils to understand themselves and others better (Ofsted 2001). The teachers who give their time for these activities are held in high esteem by students, and recognize that being involved with students outside the classroom helps them to get to know the students and manage them better in class.

Catching up with work

Very few schools systematically address the need of pupils to catch up on learning missed during absence even where guidance in staff handbooks indicates that this should be done. There are rarely practical procedures at departmental level which enable pupils who have been absent for lengthy periods of time to make up the work that they have missed. This can lead to frustration and may lead to further non-attendance (Hallam and Roaf 1997).

Providing opportunities for students to seek help and support

Pastoral organization in schools has been relatively neglected in recent years. Those staff involved with it experience considerable pressure on their time. A major contribution of a number of recent government initiatives including the Behaviour Improvement Programme (BIP) has been in raising the status of pastoral care and issues relating to behaviour and attendance. Schools now employ a range of pastoral support staff and have easier access to a wide range of outside agencies (Hallam et al. 2005). For instance, illustrations of the work of BESTs are given in Chapters 3, 4, 6, 7 and 9 and the support offered by learning mentors is discussed in Chapters 5 and 9.

Meeting pupil needs

Pupils' needs change as they get older. For instance, there is evidence that in Year 7, the excitement and anxiety of starting a new school tend to overshadow everything else. At this stage the school functions as a social centre and the complexities of the pupils' social world leads to a preoccupation with things other than learning. In Year 8, school life becomes more routine and students want to be treated more as adults. In Years 9, 10 and 11 as external examinations approach the emphasis changes to a greater focus on learning (Harris and Rudduck 1993).

For younger pupils it is important to ensure that:

- playgrounds are safe environments;
- lunchtimes are staggered to minimize contact and possible friction between young and older pupils; and
- ancillary staff on duty at lunchtime have appropriate training.

Older pupils benefit from:

- an acceptance that they need time and space for themselves and the facilities to make this possible;
- the setting up of youth clubs in lunch breaks;
- being allowed to set up their own social activities;
- evening social activities where youth workers are available;
- access to homework clubs; and
- being given some responsibility for the monitoring of behaviour.

Rewards for students

Schools can reward students for good or improving attendance. Rewards can be made at the individual, class or year group levels. Senior staff can draw attention to the issue of good attendance during assemblies, parents' meetings and in published information citing it as a prerequisite for good progress. Attendance figures can be prominently displayed in public places and form tutors can encourage high attendance by promoting constructive competition among tutor groups. Pupils can also be given attendance targets and rewards if they are met (Schulz 1987; Reid 1999). While detentions and removal of privileges are frequently used as a means of improving attendance, rewards are more effective.

Staff issues

Training for staff

The role of the form tutor is crucially important in influencing individual pupils and in building their identification with the school community but few receive training for this work (Ofsted 2001; Reid 2003). Where form tutors also teach the class that they tutor, the relationship is even more powerful. Tutorial time does not always have a focus and is sometimes treated casually by staff, although some tutors design activities to develop a range of social, speaking and listening skills. The day gets off to a better start if tutor groups have clear focus (Ofsted 2001).

Increasingly, administrative staff are involved in dealing with the day-to-day routine issues of attendance. They need to develop a range of skills in relation to data analysis and dealing with parents, who may sometimes be confrontational (Hallam 1996).

Teachers do not always realize the extent to which they need to adapt their teaching and use of materials to meet the special educational needs of children. Special Education Needs Coordinators (SENCOs) have a crucial role in providing guidance and support for teachers in particular in appreciating the implications of individual education plans. The assessment of Emotional and Behavioural Difficulties is also rare in schools, which can pose particular problems when pupils are admitted to schools after Year 7. Staff need to be trained in such assessment processes.

Working with other agencies

The role of the Local Authorities and Education Welfare Services

Evaluations of the work of Education Welfare Services (EWS) have established wide differences in practice (NFER 2002, 2003). In 2002/03 Ofsted (2004b) indicated that most LAs provided a satisfactory EWS but that support was good in only a third of English LAs. Much of the work of EWSs has been devolved to schools. Typically, Education Welfare Officers (EWOs) are physically located in schools but managed by the LA. Schools decide on the priorities. The tasks undertaken by EWOs include telephoning parents on the first day of absence, visiting parents of persistently absent pupils, and developing the schools' attendance strategies.

Minimal occupational standards for EWOs have been devised (TAG 2004) but their role in many LAs and schools is not clear particularly as schools have employed learning mentors and Home–School Link workers who undertake many of the traditional roles of EWOs. One issue concerns the equity of support which schools receive from EWSs, some schools receiving more support than others. Tensions can also arise between schools and EWSs when schools are thought to authorize absence too easily (Malcolm et al. 2003).

Where EWSs work constructively with schools on policies and procedures rather than focusing on case work, schools develop the skills to manage attendance issues better. EWOs are only then required to help with more complex cases. Schools are better supported by EWSs:

- when there is a formal contract between the school and the EWS;
- when the EWS helps in identifying attendance problems in the school;
- where the school knows the days or hours allocated and timetables pastoral staff time accordingly;
- when there are clear initial and first-day responses to absence;
- when preventative strategies involving all pupils in the school are developed;

- when early intervention schemes are implemented;
- when pupils are targeted when their attendance falls below a certain level;
- when the school uses the EWO after its own systems are exhausted;
- when there is a balance between individual case work and group work;
- where appropriate interdisciplinary and multidisciplinary links are fostered; and
- where school and service action is supported by action in the courts (Atkinson et al. 2000; Ofsted 2001).

EWOs usually work well with school staff, particularly pastoral heads, and are often successful in effecting short-term change in difficult cases. The key difficulty for EWOs is the lack of sufficient time to meet needs. Schools need to have effective systems in place to manage attendance only calling on EWOs for very difficult and complex cases (Ofsted 2001).

The role of the police

In England, the police have become involved in dealing with truancy, working closely with LAs and schools on truancy sweeps; challenging young people's attitudes to criminal behaviour; developing youth participation in community projects; and setting up schemes to alert police to the proximity of truants in shops. Schools have been encouraged to designate a teacher as a liaison officer with local police. Truancy sweeps consist of patrols of public areas by small teams typically comprising EWOs and police officers and sometimes involving school staff, Connexions and Youth Offending Teams. Truancy sweeps can be useful in identifying pupils who need support and getting them back to school. They can discourage pupils from skipping school, raise the profile of school attendance in the community, and provide an opportunity to draw various agencies together to tackle absence. They also have a role in highlighting parentally condoned truancy. Truancy sweeps have demonstrated that as many as 30 per cent of pupils are out of school with their parents. The sweeps are seen to be effective in the short term in raising awareness but there are concerns about the long-term impact. Principal Education Welfare Officers believe that they are undertaken too frequently and are not cost effective (Reid 2006).

Although the focus here is on attendance, in Chapter 4 the wider role of police in schools was discussed in relation to Safer School Partnerships.

Improving links with the community

Whatever the circumstances in a community its members are generally interested in promoting the well-being of the young people within it.

Schools can work in partnership with the community to promote and encourage attendance and achievement at school. Local residents often have concerns regarding pupils' behaviour when they are out of school. Schools can act to reduce fears and promote good relations by encouraging pupils to undertake work in the community. This can take a variety of forms depending on local circumstances and need. Schools might contribute towards entertainment in care homes for the elderly, local hospitals or undertake charitable activities. Work experience can also be valuable in forging links with local industry and in the community, for example, in children's nurseries, other local schools, medical centres, libraries, family centres. The school can also encourage the local community to use the school as a centre for their activities. Full Service Extended Schools have a role to play in offering wider services to the community (see Chapter 4).

Truancy watch schemes have been developed where police, local businesses and shopkeepers promote community involvement in improving school attendance. The evidence indicates that such schemes can be effective in the short term.

Working with other schools

Liaison between primary and secondary schools is particularly important in relation to attendance. Patterns of absence established in the primary school tend to continue in the secondary school. Information from the primary school regarding pupils' attendance can therefore be important for taking preventative measures. The links established between parents and school at primary level also need to be continued on transfer. General links between primary and secondary school can be promoted by:

- joint artistic and musical productions (e.g. concerts, musicals);
- presentations given at primary schools by subject specialists;
- primary visits to secondary schools for special projects;
- work experience undertaken in other local schools;
- liaison on curriculum matters; and
- joint planning in relation to school transfer.

Also relevant are whole-school approaches to transition (see Chapter 3) and individual support for those at risk of exclusion during the transition period in Chapter 9.

Key features of primary schools successful in improving attendance

Evaluations of the Behaviour Improvement Programme (Hallam et al. 2005; Ofsted 2005a) indicated there were key features of primary schools in the most deprived areas that were successful in improving behaviour and attendance. These included: undertaking an audit; using the data derived from the audit to inform practice and the deployment of staff and other resources; providing appropriate training for staff; and drawing on the skills of other professionals to work with parents and pupils (particularly BESTs). These schools undertook preventative work particularly working with parents, maintaining contact with them on a daily basis; creating a secure environment; and enhancing relationships through support/befriending groups. They offered support through nurture groups and a quiet place; rewarded good behaviour and attendance through allowing children an opportunity to choose activities; worked with other schools and the LA to share successful strategies; and valued children's academic and social achievements.

Key features of secondary schools successful in improving attendance

The secondary schools from extremely deprived areas that improved attendance as a result of their involvement in the Behaviour Improvement Programme focused on learning in addition to attendance (Hallam et al. 2005; Ofsted 2005b). These schools had effective leadership, and data from the audit, alongside other data, were used to identify weaknesses. Informed and honest discussion took place to develop and agree strategies, improved monitoring and evaluation systems were introduced, and an inclusive philosophy was established throughout the school that changed the staff and pupil culture and challenged assumptions about behaviour and attendance. There were clearly articulated expectations, which were rigorously enforced by the Head teacher and senior staff. Funding was focused to provide support for pupils where it was needed and staff worked closely with other professionals. The Behaviour Improvement Programme was not effective in all schools. In some cases the situation deteriorated because of ineffective senior management, high levels of staff turnover, weak teaching and inconsistency in implementing behaviour and attendance strategies (Ofsted 2005b).

What Local Authorities can do

Local Autorities achieve the greatest success in raising the level of pupils' attendance when they give a clear strategic lead to schools in encouraging them to make attendance a key issue; produce supporting documentation about improving attendance for schools; use data on absence rates to identify needs and target resources; and expand the EWS and deploy officers flexibly and according to need (Atkinson et al. 2000; Ofsted 2001).

Endnote

Improving attendance at school is not easy. It takes time and considerable effort to bring about change and even more effort to sustain the improvement over time. It is, however, worthwhile as the strategies implemented at whole-school level enhance the working environment in the school and have benefits in relation to the overall school climate, social relationships, learning and subsequently attainment.

Chapter summary

- Improving attendance at school requires time, effort and the commitment of all staff.
- Initiatives need to focus on children's need for safety, a one-to-one relationship with a caring adult, developing marketable skills, and a chance to give back to the community.

Steps towards improving attendance include:

- – raising the profile;
- – undertaking an audit and acting on its findings;
- – developing a policy and ensuring it is known and understood by staff, parents and pupils;
- – monitoring attendance and punctuality and taking immediate action when it is poor;
- – creating a positive school ethos through paying attention to physical, social and learning environments;
- – ensuring that the quality of teaching is high;
- – ensuring an appropriate curriculum and a range of extra-curricula activities;
- – making opportunities available for catching up with work;
- – rewarding good attendance;
- – providing training for staff;
- – working closely with the Education Welfare Service and the police;
- – developing community links; and
- – developing relationships with other schools particularly feeder primary schools.

Further reading

Ofsted (2005a) *Improving Behaviour and Attendance in Primary Schools*. London: Ofsted.

Ofsted (2005b) *Improving Behaviour and Attendance in Secondary Schools*. London: Offsted.

Reid, K. (1999) *Truancy and Schools*. London: Routledge.

References

Ames, C. (1992) Achievement goals and the classroom motivational climate, in D. Schunk and J. Meece (eds) *Student Perception in the Classroom*. Hillsdale, NJ: Lawrence Erlbaum.

Atkinson, M., Halsey, K., Wilkin, A. and Kinder, K. (2000) *Raising Attendance 2: A Detailed Study of Education Welfare Service Working Practices*. Slough: NFER.

Dalziel, D. and Henthorne, K. (2005) *Parents'/Carers' Attitudes Towards School Attendance. Research Report 618*. London: DfES.

Easen, P., Clark, J. and Wootten, M. (1997) *Focusing on the Individual While Ignoring the Context: An Evaluation of an Attendance Project*. Newcastle: University of Newcastle, Department of Education.

Epstein, J. (1989) Family structures and student motivation: A developmental perspective, in C. Ames and R. Ames (eds) *Research on Motivation in Education, Vol. 3*. New York: Academic Press.

Hallam, S. (1996) *Improving School Attendance*. London: Heinemann.

Hallam, S. (2004) *Homework: The Evidence*. London: Institute of Education.

Hallam, S. and Roaf, C. (1997) *Here Today, Here Tomorrow: Helping Schools to Promote Attendance*. London: Gulbenkian Foundation.

Hallam, S., Castle, F., Rogers, L., Rhamie, J., Creech, A. and Kokotsaki, D. (2005) *Evaluation of the Behaviour Improvement Programme. Research Report 702*. London: DfES.

Harris, S. and Rudduck, J. (1993) Establishing the seriousness of learning in the early years of secondary school. *British Journal of Educational Psychology, 63*: 322–336.

Malcolm, H., Wilson, V., Davidson, J. and Kirk, S. (2003) *Absence from School: A Study of Its Causes and Effects in Seven LEAs. Report 424*. London: DfES.

National Audit Office (NAO) (2005) *Improving School Attendance in England.* London: The Stationery Office.

National Foundation for Educational Research (NFER) (2002) *The Evaluation of the Pilot Devolution of Education Welfare Services to Secondary Schools: Second-year Follow-Up Report.* Slough: NFER.

National Foundation for Educational Research (NFER) (2003) *The Evaluation of the Pilot Devolution of Education Welfare Services to Secondary Schools: Final Report.* Slough: NFER.

Ofsted (1993) *Education for Disaffected Pupils.* London: Ofsted.

Ofsted (2001) *Improving Attendance and Behaviour in Secondary Schools.* London: Ofsted.

Ofsted (2004a) *Out of school: A Survey of the Educational Support and Provision for Pupils Not in School.* London: Ofsted.

Ofsted (2004b) *Annual Report of Her Majesty's Chief Inspector of Schools: Standards and Quality in Education, 2002/03.* London: Her Majesty's Inspectorate.

Ofsted (2005a) *Improving Behaviour and Attendance in Primary Schools.* London: Ofsted.

Ofsted (2005b) *Improving Behaviour and Attendance in Secondary Schools.* London: Ofsted.

Ofsted (2005c) *Managing Challenging Behaviour.* London: Ofsted.

Olweus, D. (1997) Bully/victim problems in school: Facts and intervention. *European Journal of Psychology of Education,* XII (4): 495–510.

Reid, K. (1999) *Truancy and Schools.* London: Routledge.

Reid, K. (2003) A strategic approach to tackling school absenteeism and truancy: The PSCC scheme. *Educational Studies,* 29(4): 351–71.

Reid, K. (2006) The views of education social workers on the management of truancy and other forms of non-attendance. *Research in Education,* 75: 40–57.

Schulz, R.M. (1987) Truancy: Issues and interventions. *Behavioural Disorders,* 12: 117–30.

TAG (2004) *Reform of the Educational Welfare Service.* Carlisle: TAG.

12 Working with persistent absentees

This chapter considers the effectiveness of a range of strategies that have been adopted to support persistent absentees in returning to education. It considers the extent of persistent absenteeism, how different types of persistent absenteeism have been classified, and approaches to returning students to school.

Introduction

Even when schools have in place procedures which ensure good attendance for the majority of their pupils, there will be a small minority for whom unauthorized absence is a major concern. A recent study of attendance in Excellence in Cities (EiC) schools found that for a minority of pupils (just over 5 per cent) incidents of unauthorized absence amounted to up to two weeks per school year. For over 1 per cent this absence amounted to half a term or longer. Nearly half of the recorded incidents of unauthorized absence were attributable to just 2 per cent of the pupils (Morris and Rutt 2005). Even in Pupil Referral Units (PRUs), where classes are very small and there are appropriate policies and practices for monitoring and improving attendance, persistent absentees' attendance on the whole does not improve (Ofsted 2004).

Distinguishing between truancy, school refusal and school phobia

There are ongoing debates as to whether to classify those who continually refuse to go to school as truants, school refusers, social phobics, specific school phobics, or as having separation anxiety (Bernstein and Garfinkel 1986; Last and Strauss 1990; Pilkington and Piersel 1991). In the UK, there are no clear criteria for distinguishing between different types of persistent absenteeism. Educational professionals' descriptions of school refusers and school phobics overlap, although school phobia is generally seen as a subset of school refusal (Archer et al. 2003).

Early distinctions between school refusal, school phobia and truancy were made in terms of separation anxiety, conduct disorders, or whether the child tried to conceal their absence. A commonly accepted early definition of school refusal was that of Berg and colleagues (1969). This listed the following features:

- severe difficulty in attending school which often results in prolonged absence;
- severe emotional upset, indicated by excessive fearfulness;
- anxiety;
- bad temper;
- misery;
- complaints of feeling ill without obvious causes when faced with the prospect of going to school;
- staying at home with parental knowledge; and
- an absence of significant antisocial disorders (e.g. stealing, destructiveness).

However, many persistent absentees exhibit anxious and antisocial characteristics (Bools et al. 1990; Berg et al. 1993).

Another distinction has been made on the grounds of volition (Elliott and Place 1998) in that truants and school refusers are perceived as choosing not to attend school while those with school phobia may want to attend but be unable to do so. However, the clinical value of such a distinction is highly questionable (Kearney and Silverman 1993). The narrow definition of linking refusal to separation anxiety is also unhelpful as children refuse to attend school for many reasons (Pilkington and Piersel 1991; King et al. 1994). It is now accepted that each child's case should be considered individually, focusing on developing a functional analysis of non-attendance (Kearney and Sims 1997).

Parents may have difficulty in distinguishing between illnesses brought on by anxiety, for instance, abdominal pain, headaches, nausea, diarrhoea, and shortness of breath and those with underlying physical causes (Kearney and Bensaheb 2006). Severe anxiety related to attending school can also be linked to serious and long-term mental health problems and is sometimes classified as depression (Kearney 1993). Whatever the reasons for persistent absenteeism it may cause considerable distress for parents (King et al. 1996).

Group work to prevent the development of persistent absenteeism

While it is possible to return pupils to school after a period of persistent absenteeism all concerned agree that this is difficult. It is preferable to identify 'at-risk' pupils early, when patterns of non-attendance are first developing, and take preventative measures. The sooner an intervention is initiated the more likelihood there is of success. Group work can be particularly valuable in this respect. It is less time consuming than working with individuals and has the added advantage of utilizing peer pressure. It can also support pupils in developing friendships, the lack of which can be a contributory factor in persistent non-attendance (Wenzel 1991). Adopting cooperative learning techniques or the provision of social skills training can support this (Coie and Koeppl 1990; Mize and Ladd 1990).

Persistent absentees often have poor social skills resulting in poor self-esteem and expectations of poor outcomes in social situations (Spence et al. 1999). Training typically involves identifying social situations that cause anxiety or are problematic and providing opportunities to rehearse them utilizing coping strategies. For instance, Bokhurst and colleagues (1995) worked with primary school children in 12 one-hour sessions focusing on social rules, working in cooperation with others, emotional awareness, the acceptance of individual differences, relating to others and self-acceptance. Spence and colleagues (1999) suggest that this type of approach is most beneficial when combined with cognitive restructuring and graded exposure to anxiety-provoking situations.

The Primary Behaviour and Attendance Pilot (Hallam et al. 2006) included a strand where small groups of children with a range of behavioural and attendance difficulties worked with a Child and Adolescent Mental Health Service (CAMHS) worker and a member of the school support staff to develop a range of behavioural and social skills. In some cases, Local Authorities (LAs) ran parallel groups for the parents of the children. Staff working with the small groups provided examples of the impact on children's attendance:

> The group has been quite positive. One child wanted to stay at school more. This is very positive for a child who would run home often. He would find it difficult to stay on task in school. In the group he improved considerably. There were successes for children who found interacting socially very hard and would not come to school in the morning. Lunchtimes were difficult but the lunchtime club enabled children to have their problems worked through and children missed less days at school.
>
> One success story was the child who had no friends and would not go into school. A buddy system was implemented in the group

and she is now going into school on her own. Her mother is seen by the group worker on a one-to-one basis each week as the relationship between school and home had broken down.

Attendance at school was not the focus of the small group work but nevertheless improved:

> We are not doing anything to address attendance directly but if you are giving parents the skills to manage their morning routine better and to get the children up and dressed and off to school, then that addresses attendance. If the children are doing things in school that makes them valued, they want to come.

Parents also commented on the success of the programme:

> She has always been a very quiet, nervous child. She would be scared to answer a question, she would be shaking, she is really nervous and shy. She always struggled with mingling with other children, with confidence and answering questions. She used to cry going into school, not wanting to go to school. She struggles at schoolwork. The group has made her feel more confident and she has started to trust people. She loves coming to school now.

Interventions to support a return to school

Where attendance problems have become severe the local Education Welfare Service (EWS) will normally be involved and an individual action plan will be developed to return the pupils to school. Typically, the cause of the absence will be established. This will include an assessment of the school life of the individual and factors at home or in the community that may be contributing. The distinctive nature of the problems experienced by each persistent absentee means that no single solution is appropriate and programmes need to be personalized (Schloss et al. 1981). Reid (2002) found that 120 different short-term solutions were in use in the schools and LAs that he visited, in addition to a range of longer term strategies (Reid 2003, 2004). The complex nature of the problems of some persistent absentees means that multi-agency work is often necessary to successfully return them to school (Milne et al. 2002).

School factors affecting attendance

The causes of persistent absenteeism located in schools are those which cause emotional distress, typically social anxiety, change of pupil groupings, or fear of the school environment (Archer et al. 2003). The size of the school can impact on attendance, larger schools experiencing greater problems (Reynolds et al. 1980). Other factors include strict enforcement of school rules, poor relationships, poor home–school links and high institutional control of student behaviour. The school environment may be characterized by bullying, or disruption in lessons. Policies related to pupil grouping, for instance, streaming or setting can lead to a pupil being placed in a class which has a proliferation of disaffected and troublesome peers. In some schools teacher–pupil relationships are overly formal, impersonal or even hostile (Lauchlan 2003). Where toilets, corridors and playground areas are not monitored carefully and antisocial incidents are not dealt with, anxiety can be created (Blagg 1987; Last et al. 1987; Lauchlan 2003). Schools with high numbers of children refusing to attend school have high staff and student absenteeism rates, low levels of achievement, large class sizes, low staff morale, a management style that is authoritarian and rigid, and teachers who are authoritarian, anxious or eager to obtain student approval (Hersov 1985; Blagg 1987; King et al. 1995; Elliott and Place 1998).

The quality of relationships in school is a key factor in persistent absenteeism. Persistent absentees typically experience difficulties with particular teachers. Older students want to be treated as adults and truants often perceive that there is a lack of mutual respect. Peer relationships are highly significant, particularly for girls, bullying and intimidation playing a major part in their non-attendance (Nardi and Steward 2002). Transitions between primary and secondary school and from Year 9 to Year 10 are also key triggers (Davis and Lee 2006).

Another major cause of non-attendance is difficulty with schoolwork. Children with special educational needs (SEN) are more likely to have poor attendance than other students when other factors have been taken into account (Morris and Rutt 2005). The provision of Learning Support Units (LSUs) (Hallam and Castle 1999) and the employment of learning mentors to support students enhances learning and has a positive impact on attendance (Grossman and Tierney 1998; Ofsted 2004). For older students the provision of an alternative curriculum may be appropriate (see Chapter 8).

The parents of persistent absentees are generally eager for their children to attend school and be successful, but communication with schools is often poor, and schools tend to behave arrogantly in their interactions with parents. Families frequently perceive that the Education Welfare Service (EWS) is not consistently supportive, although individual Education Welfare Officers (EWOs), learning mentors, Connexions personnel, and other alternative providers are viewed as helpful. Students are frequently successfully re-engaged with education through alternative provision (Nardi and Steward 2002; Davis and Lee 2006).

If the cause of persistent absenteeism is located in the school, staff can directly implement plans to ameliorate the situation and monitor their effectiveness. The particular programme developed will depend on the circumstances of each case. Strategies which have been found to be effective, alone or in combination with others, are outlined below. They fall into two main categories related to social and learning problems:

Social problems:

- social skills training;
- special support during break times;
- counselling with a trained counsellor;
- movement to a different class;
- restorative justice programmes to deal with bullying;
- reconciliation between pupils and teachers; and
- designating an individual member of staff as a mentor.

Learning problems:

- devising a modified timetable;
- providing additional support in class;
- providing a place in a Learning Support Unit;
- arranging a work experience scheme; and
- arranging an alternative mode of attendance (part-time attendance at a Further Education College, or with an alternative provider).

Community and family factors

As we saw in Chapter 2 the circumstances of some communities contribute towards poor attendance at school. For instance, children in receipt of free school meals are more likely to have higher levels of persistent absenteeism (Morris and Rutt 2005), although some disadvantaged communities do support attendance at school. A recent study of EiC schools found lower than average levels of unauthorized absence among young people with lower levels of fluency in English, young people for whom English was not a first language but who were bilingual, and young people who were from relatively less deprived neighbourhoods (but also where unemployment was relatively high). Where ethnicity data were available lower levels of authorized absence were seen among Black African, Chinese, Indian, Black Caribbean, Pakistani, Bangladeshi and Black other minority ethnic groups (Morris and Rutt 2005).

Families living in disadvantaged communities frequently face multiple problems in their everyday lives. To address these and improve attendance at school multi-agency initiatives are required. Progress in improving attendance is usually only made when the child, family, school and relevant agencies work together. The nature of the action plan developed for any particular child will then depend to a great extent on the family. If they have been unaware of the absence they may be supportive in getting the child back to school. If they have been aware but unable to do anything about it they may be glad of school intervention. If they have passively condoned the child's non-attendance then little support can be expected, and where absence has been actively encouraged the school may expect hostility.

Schools are often the first to recognize that a child has problems at home as they frequently manifest themselves in behaviour at school. Schools are therefore in an ideal position to recognize children in need of help. This is particularly true in the case of young carers. They often do not want to reveal their problems for fear of being ridiculed or not being believed, especially when the case involves mental illness. They may also be afraid that the adult or they will be taken away. Schools routinely note the absence of parents from parents' evenings and children who frequently arrive tired or late. If they are alert to these signs they can identify young carers and offer emotional support, provide access to counselling and demonstrate flexibility with regard to homework.

Some programmes have been designed to work simultaneously with students, schools and families. For instance, a Community Intervention Project in New Zealand which aimed to re-establish regular school attendance and reduce offending provided access to a range of services that assisted with education, health, social, and recreational needs working at the level of the individual, family and the school. Fifty-nine persistent absentees were assigned mentors leading to a reduction in the number of persistent truants from 82 per cent to 37 per cent. The multi-modal and individualized nature of the intervention contributed to its success, although it was less successful for those students using drugs (Milne et al. 2002). There are strong links between non-attendance, drugs, substance abuse, smoking, drinking and exclusion (McAra 2004).

In the USA, the Truancy Reduction Demonstration Project (Colorado Foundation for Families and Children 2002) identified several components that contributed to effective reduction of persistence absenteeism. These included:

- a commitment from the school to keep 'at-risk' youth in school;
- collaboration with community resources;
- a continuum of support with meaningful incentives and consequences;
- parent involvement; and
- a built-in capacity to conduct an ongoing evaluation of the intervention programme.

Another programme which adopts a comprehensive approach is 'Check and Connect'. This focuses on relationship building, routine monitoring of attainment and attendance, individualized support, long-term commitment (at least two years) for supporting families and children, a focus on motivation and the value of education, promoting conflict resolution skills and solution-focused approaches, and providing access to and participation in school-related activities and events (Lehr et al. 2004). Multi-modal interventions such as these are generally effective (Bell et al. 1994; Sinclair et al. 1998; Milne et al. 2002; Lehr et al. 2004).

Another US programme which focused on primary-aged children and their families initially worked with 20 families whose children had missed at least 20 per cent of schooling. Letters were sent to parents/carers informing them of the number of days missed, stressing the importance of attendance and setting out the state law and the consequences of non-attendance. If this resulted in an improvement in attendance the parents were sent a congratulatory letter commending them on addressing the problem. If this was unsuccessful the student was referred to the attendance officer, and a home visit was arranged where the seriousness of non-attendance was stressed. Following this, if further intervention was deemed necessary, other services were informed and a case worker assigned. If after two weeks there was still no improvement a police officer joined the attendance officer in a home visit. If there continued to be a lack of cooperation the parents were taken to court (McCluskey et al. 2004). This intervention was successful, the initial letter and visit by the attendance officer being particularly effective.

The Behaviour and Education Support Teams (BESTs) set up as part of the Behaviour and Improvement Programme (BIP) worked with families and students adopting a multi-agency approach to dealing with attendance problems. Boxes 12.1 and 12.2 give examples of the way that they worked with persistent absentees.

Box 12.1   Case study of multiple support

Case study: multiple support for attendance, truanting and exclusion issues

Nick was a Year 9 pupil with attendance problems. He had some learning difficulties, spent time in the Learning Support Unit and received support from a learning mentor. He had been excluded twice during Year 7 and 8, for fighting, but had not been excluded in Year 9 and hoped to stay in school. He received weekly support from the counsellor to talk about issues, and his attendance, which had been poor, improved significantly. As a result of the BEST intervention he was encouraged to discuss with his father why he needed to attend school and the problems that would arise for him and his father if he did not. Nick accepted these reasons and realized that he must attend school. The regular counselling sessions and the fact that he could 'drop-in' to the BEST hut at any time meant that he had a place to go and sort out problems. This helped him to cope with any incidents that occurred during the day avoiding them escalating into something more serious. He still had problems with fighting but these were much reduced.

Box 12.2 Counselling support for bereavement and truanting

Case study: BEST counselling support

Jason's father had died and he simply did not want to attend school and began truanting either by himself or with other pupils. His attendance began to improve, when his grandmother died leading to a return of the difficulties. When his mother found out about the truanting she returned him to school, but he simply ran off again. She was concerned about his safety when he truanted alone, since she had no idea where he was or what he was doing. Following a referral to BEST from the Head of Year, Jason received individual counselling support and the school put in place a learning mentor. The mother also received counselling support from a home school liaison worker who also worked with mother and son together. This was very beneficial. Initially, Jason only attended school on the day of his counselling session. This improved his attendance from 0 to 20 per cent. He valued the opportunity to talk about what had happened and to explore issues. His mother indicated that the sessions had been very effective: 'He was never a naughty boy but was really troubled. There has been a massive improvement. Initially Jason seemed withdrawn, he didn't want to play with his friends and was truanting a lot. Now he has a lot of friends within the school. He is enjoying himself, and seems really happy and is delighted to be in school. The counsellors have been brilliant and helped Jason to open up. Without this help, I don't know where we would have been now.'

The support from the counsellor enabled Jason to return to school full time.

In the UK, to address issues in deprived communities which contribute to poor attendance, the Children's Fund was set up in 2000 as a catalyst to move forward inter-agency cooperation and child- and family-led preventative services in LAs. It aimed to strengthen communities and families as places where children and young people could develop as healthy, responsible and engaged citizens. The initiative targeted children and young people aged 5–13 considered at risk of social exclusion and provided a range of preventative initiatives (Evans et al. 2006). The particular problems raised by children and families included school exclusion, transition between schools, bullying and racism, exposure to crime and antisocial behaviour, drug abuse, poor play and leisure facilities, and poor services for marginalized groups, such as disabled children (Evans et al. 2006). The types of provision funded as part of the initiative included:

- providing safe spaces through clubs, play or specialist services;
- individual help through mentoring, counselling or therapeutic play;
- enhancing local resources such as play areas;
- support for parents;
- breakfast and homework clubs;
- after-school clubs;
- specialist support for particular groups of children and their families (e.g. deaf children, refugee and asylum children);
- support to enable disabled children to attend Brownies; and
- support for Gypsy/Traveller children to use sports and leisure services.

Evaluation of the initiative revealed a need to focus on the barriers facing particular groups rather than the groups themselves. Unmet needs were often exposed, to which the initiative was able to respond. There was variation in the implementation of the programme. Some approaches were innovative, others continued well-established practices which were valued but continued parents' dependency, while others worked holistically with families to develop children's and families' awareness and capacity to take up opportunities and resources in the community.

The services which were most valued provided:

- fast responses and early intervention to prevent problems becoming more serious;
- child-centred approaches which worked at the individual pace of the child and supported their particular needs; and
- holistic family-oriented approaches which were able to respond to the changing needs of the family over time and provide practical and emotional support for parents/carers.

Project workers signposted and supported children and parents in accessing other services, taking an advocacy role and helping to mediate between the family and other providers. This was successful in increasing children's and families' take-up of other services and opportunities in the community.

Project workers were non-judgemental, developed trusting relationships with families, and were valued as 'safe outsiders' in mediations with school professionals. For some marginal groups the link with school was considered unhelpful and did not improve accessibility or inclusiveness, although for others school-based services were highly valued and regarded as easily accessible. Parents appreciated being supported by those from similar cultural backgrounds but this was less of a concern for children. Targeted approaches helped to improve the accessibility of services for particularly marginalized groups by ensuring that services were delivered in culturally appropriate ways, with the intention that the positive identities developed would enable participants to move on to access open services and opportunities over time.

There were positive outcomes for the children relating to all of the *Every Child Matters* agenda, health, safety, enjoyment and achievement, and making a positive contribution. Children gained in self-confidence, and there were improvements in mental health, and in some cases physical health. There was a reduction in negative peer-group influence, and children experiencing racism and bullying at school developed a positive self-identity and engaged in peer support to tackle problems. Attendance and behaviour improved and children who had offended or were at risk of doing so were diverted into more positive activities. There were also reported improvements in literacy and educational achievement through homework clubs, book clubs and nurture groups. Children's expectations and aspirations for the future were raised. Opportunities for increased access to play and extra-curricular activities gave children an increased sense of purpose and facilitated new friendships reducing the isolation previously experienced. Parents and children reported improved social, communication and life skills and children valued the opportunities to participate in shaping project activities and services and developed confidence and self-esteem as well as a range of new skills as a result.

The family and parent support systems helped parents and carers to gain important practical skills, and increased confidence and emotional well-being. Relationships between families and statutory professionals improved because of the mediating role of the workers. Projects where childcare was provided were particularly valued by single parents as they were able to return to work or study. Parents with disabled children valued respite provision which enabled them to spend time with their other children or to work.

The therapeutic initiatives targeted at asylum seekers and refugees had positive short- and medium-term impact on the emotional well-being of the children. Children with limited English language proficiency were engaged in group activities, teamwork and making contact with others in verbal and non-verbal ways. These and other out-of-school and holiday activities helped the children's integration into the school environment through promoting their social and emotional skills and providing them with the confidence and trust to approach other children in the classroom or in the playground. Homework clubs provided space and support for undertaking homework, which contributed to changing attitudes and experiences of school and learning. The profile of young refugees was raised in local schools, parents received advice on dealing with school bureaucracy, and developed skills for interacting with educational professionals. The recruitment of classroom assistants and bilingual support created and developed positive home–school relationships.

Those within the community who helped with the projects saw benefits in terms of improved mental health and well-being which had an impact more widely within the family. The services developed were innovative and techniques were adopted which had not been available previously within mainstream services and schools (Beirens et al. 2006). Some of the problems identified in the community and its environs were beyond the remit of the Children's Fund, while some communities, suffering significant hardship and deprivation struggled to take up the opportunities, having insufficient capacity to enable them to develop voluntary and community sector organizations which could engage with the Children's Fund. Capacity building among smaller voluntary organizations was an important priority for many partnerships. Overall, the programme served to reveal the scale and complexity of preventative work with vulnerable children and their families. It was apparent that for agencies and services to work together strategically to meet these complex needs coordination and continuous support was needed. Services which were effective recognized the multidimensional nature of social exclusion and framed their provision accordingly. While the development of effective networks and forums seemed a helpful way of creating opportunities the pressures facing many of the services were a barrier. It was apparent that considerable effort is required to build collaborative capacity at a strategic level (Edwards et al. 2006).

The prosecution of parents for their child's non-attendance at school

In the UK, since the Education Act 1944 the parents of children of compulsory school age have been responsible for ensuring that their children attend school regularly, and can be prosecuted by LAs if they fail to do so. Under the Children Act 1989 a LA can apply for an Education Supervision Order to make itself responsible for supervising the child to ensure that the child is properly educated. Where a parent refuses to comply they can be prosecuted. When a child refuses to comply the LA can start proceedings to take the child into care. Under the Antisocial Behaviour Act 2003, LAs, headteachers and the police can issue penalty notices to parents for a child's unauthorized absence from school. LAs usually only prosecute parents when all other attempts to resolve the situation have failed and when they believe that the prosecution may bring about an improvement. Convicted parents can be fined, given a community sentence (e.g. a parenting order) or a custodial sentence. In the region of 7000 to 8000 parents are prosecuted each year (National Audit Office 2005).

A fast-track process has been developed which includes speedy access to the courts for LAs. Parents of persistent truants are given around 12 weeks to ensure that their children attend school regularly or face prosecution. This has had a positive impact in heightening the awareness of absence issues, improving procedures and attitudes towards attendance, and enhancing attendance levels in the short term, although the impact has been limited in the longer term. After five months authorized absence rates returned to previous levels, although unauthorized absence was 14 per cent lower (Halsey et al. 2004). Forty-three per cent of headteachers believed that the scheme was effective (National Audit Office 2005), although the impact was greater where attendance was not at crisis point. For more entrenched cases other strategies were required (Halsey et al. 2004).

In general, EWOs and headteachers believe that prosecution is effective, although parents do not (NFER 2003). Prosecution damages relationships between EWOs and children and can cause financial difficulties for parents. Examination of attendance data from 43 LAs found no significant relationship between the number of prosecutions and changes in absence rates casting doubt over the impact (Zhang 2004). Other research has established that where prosecutions occurred the attendance of children improved in nearly half of cases but was totally ineffective for a third (Kendall et al. 2004). Variation in the cooperation and attitudes of parents and young people as well as family relationships and behavioural issues seem to be crucial in the relative effectiveness of prosecution. The processes and procedures involved in the lead-up to court proceedings often appear to have a greater potential for effectiveness than the court-related outcomes themselves as they facilitate opportunities for dialogue and engagement between families and other involved agencies (Kendall et al. 2004).

There are widely varying levels of prosecution between LAs, from none to 7.4 prosecutions per 1000 pupils. Some prosecutions have been challenged in court under the Human Rights Act. Most Principal Education Welfare Officers are supportive of the general principle of prosecution as it makes parents aware of their responsibilities, asserts the importance of school attendance, and has a deterrent effect. High profile prosecutions and the publicity surrounding them are perceived to lead to improved attendance. Generally, fines are perceived to be ineffective. Parenting Orders are viewed by EWSs as potentially more effective (Kendall et al. 2003, 2004). Prosecution is perceived to be more successful with primary than secondary pupils, although the actual number of prosecutions increases with age peaking in Year 10. Parents, particularly of older children feel that they should not be held responsible for their children's behaviour and question whether prosecution has any impact on changing the causes of children's non-attendance.

There has been some consideration in the UK of linking benefits to satisfactory school attendance. In the USA, in the 1990s, the majority of states adopted such policies. By 1999, 40 states had exercised their discretion to do this. However, these programmes, which adopted a sanction-only approach had negligible effects on attendance, and proved costly to run. The close monitoring of attendance which accompanied the policies had the most substantial effect (Campbell and Wright 2005).

Cases where extreme anxiety underlies persistent absenteeism

A range of strategies has been adopted to address issues of extreme anxiety which preclude attendance, whether triggered by school factors or resulting from difficulties in the home (Archer et al. 2003). In some cases drug treatments have been utilized although these are controversial. They can play a part if the problems are related to separation anxiety, a general anxiety disorder or depression (King et al. 1995). Antidepressants do minimize panic attacks but often have side effects. Trials using drugs have found that pupils taking them often do no better than those receiving placebos (Elliott 1999). Pupils can be hospitalized as a last resort (Murphy and Wolkind 1996) or as an intermediary step on the way to full-time schooling (Berg 1992). However, hospitalization is extremely rare and usually limited to children suffering from extreme neurotic disturbances and clinical depression (Borchardt et al. 1994).

Another approach is to enforce a rapid return to school, a technique known as *flooding*. Comparisons of flooding with hospitalization and a more gradual return to school (systematic desensitization) have shown that flooding is effective and economical, resulting in almost all children, particularly younger children, returning permanently to school (Blagg and Yule 1984). However, it is highly confrontational and can be distressing for parents and teachers.

Some support a more gradual return to school, systematic desensitization (Garvey and Hegrenes 1966). Typically this involves progressive relaxation training, and developing a fear hierarchy of 15–20 items with the child (and parents if necessary) of increasingly fearful situations. Each situation is then paired with relaxation. Initially, the child imagines the least anxiety-provoking situation while relaxed. If anxiety is experienced the session stops.

When the child is able to imagine or experience the situation three to four times without experiencing anxiety the procedure moves to the next level until, over the course of several sessions, the situation at the top of the hierarchy can be experienced without anxiety (Morris and Kratochwill 1983). Such procedures have been shown to be effective (Barabasz 1973, 1975; Deffenbacher and Kemper 1974; Ultee et al. 1982). *In vivo* desensitization differs in that the child is presented with the anxiety-provoking situations in the natural environment rather than imagining the situations. There may be advantages for *in vivo* desensitization in that the child is making actual contact with the feared situation thus assuring the generalization of treatment gains. Involvement of parents in desensitization processes does not add value (Spence et al. 2000). An alternative approach is to gradually change behaviour using operant conditioning by reducing the incentives for remaining at home (Blagg 1987).

Kearney and Silverman (1990, 1993) recommend selecting treatment components based on assessment of the causes of the problem. Treatments should be based on whether the school refusal behaviour is negatively reinforced by avoidance of fear-provoking situations at school, avoidance of social situations, or whether the condition is positively reinforced by the receipt of attention from caregivers or tangible outcomes at home or away from home. If the school refusal behaviour is related to fearfulness or anxiety elicited by some aspect of the school setting systematic desensitization or *in vivo* desensitization procedures are appropriate (Wolpe 1958).

If non-attendance is related to the avoidance of social situations cognitive restructuring and modelling procedures may be appropriate. The goal of these is to modify school refusal behaviour by altering the child's maladaptive thoughts or beliefs that may contribute to social avoidance (Kearney and Silverman 1993). The procedures help the child to label social situations or his/her own competence more positively thus decreasing social anxiety avoidance. There is mixed evidence relating to the benefit of such cognitive-behavioural interventions (King et al. 1998; Last et al. 1998).

Modelling or behavioural skills training procedures teach the child the social skills needed to interact competently in difficult social situations. Based on social learning theory (Bandura 1969) three types of modelling are typically used: video, live and participant. In the latter procedure the child observes a model and then performs the behaviour with the aid of a therapist. This has been found to be the most effective of the three alternatives (Ollendick 1979). Role-playing social situations followed by reinforcement through praise and feedback are particularly effective (Kearney and Silverman 1990).

When school refusal behaviour is to gain attention the recommended treatment is parental training in operant conditioning techniques. Links between attention-seeking behaviour at home and separation anxiety support the appropriateness of this approach (Brandibas et al. 2004). Parents often lack the skills to deal with such problems unaided (Mansdorf and Lukens 1987) and if there is marital discord, often the cause of the child's attention seeking, the parents' failure to work together as a team may exacerbate the problem (Bernstein et al. 1990). Parents are taught how to reinforce alternative behaviours, to reduce attention for the school refusal behaviour, to attract the child's attention, and communicate clear and specific commands (King et al. 1998), to use recognition and praise when appropriate behaviours are exhibited, and to ignore tantrums and psychosomatic complaints (Blagg 1987). Parents reward the child for attending school for longer and longer periods of time and if the child is at home when they should be at school avoid giving the child attention. Such procedures are effective. Parents and child can agree rewards for attending school and negative consequences for not doing so. Rewarding attendance is effective in increasing attendance in persistent absentees (MacDonald et al. 1970) and parent training is popular and effective in treating school refusal which is underpinned by family issues (Kearney and Beasley 1994; King et al. 1998).

Returning to school after a period of absence

The longer that children are out of school the harder it becomes for them to return. Going back to school after a long period away is often traumatic. Pupils will almost inevitably face some problems. Schools can implement a range of strategies which help the child to successfully overcome these difficulties and return to a normal pattern of school attendance.

When a child returns to school after a long period of absence it is crucial that school staff are involved in the planning process. They need to be made aware of the child's circumstances and the strategies that are to be adopted to facilitate a smooth return. They need to avoid making sarcastic or discouraging remarks and should attempt to provide positive reinforcement for the return. Much hard work by EWOs can be overturned by careless and inappropriate remarks from members of staff.

Those returning to school usually experience problems in catching up with the work that they have missed. Schools can support them by:

- providing a place to carry out private study;
- negotiating a reduced timetable;
- negotiating attendance for part of the day;
- selecting core areas of the curriculum for concentrated work;
- encouraging parental support with homework; and
- providing a member of staff to give individual help.

Readjusting to school routine can be difficult. The size of the building and the number of pupils can be threatening and the organization and routine of the school may prove demanding. In addition to this the routine of getting up and leaving the house in the morning will have been lost. Schools can support pupils by arranging for them to visit the school prior to their return to overcome their initial fears. This provides an opportunity to remind them of the timetable and school rules and gives them an opportunity to meet teachers.

Pupils often feel social isolation and an inability to relate to their peer group and teachers after a long period of absence. Friendship groups may have changed and other aspects of the social makeup of their class. They may have to face constant comments and enquiries from staff and other pupils about where they have been. These can be difficult to cope with. It is helpful if staff and other students can be supportive. Staff need to be made aware of the pupil's imminent return and of any special arrangements that have been made. Discussion in the tutor group about the child's return may also help. The child also needs to be prepared for possible problems. Role-play can be useful in this respect.

Providing a mentor who is able to offer regular daily contact has proved to be an extremely effective way of supporting pupils returning to school after a long absence. The pupil can report to the mentor initially twice a day with more contact if there are difficulties. The mentor needs to be someone with whom the pupil can relate easily. In some cases counselling may be appropriate. This may be a member of staff, a teaching assistant or learning support assistant, a school counsellor, a youth worker, or a professional such as an EWO.

For a persistent absentee with anxiety problems one or two appropriate buddies can provide peer support and assist the pupil's reintegration into school life. Pupils can also be given class responsibilities which are rewarding and encourage reintegration. If anxiety is connected with being in a crowded or turbulent environment students can enter the school through a different entrance, register separately, and leave early. Teachers should be made aware of the child's circumstances and be prepared to be flexible if the child seems not to be coping with the current situation.

In some schools reintegration units have proved successful in supporting a phased re-entry to school. Such units offer small group work and operate in less formal circumstances often with a reduced timetable and reduced overall attendance. If it is not possible to provide a Support Unit a designated member of staff can be given responsibility for overseeing reintegration. Whatever the specific arrangements that are made progress during a child's return to school needs to be monitored. Time needs to be made available for meetings with involved school staff, support services, the child and the parents.

Chapter summary

- Schools which have appropriate policies and practices for improving attendance and provide a supportive environment will still have some children who experience difficulties with attendance.
- Categorizing different types of persistent absenteeism is difficult because the underlying causes are complex. An individual plan needs to be devised for each child based on the particular circumstances prevailing.
- Group work can be effective in preventing attendance issues from becoming persistent through promoting the development of social skills and enhancing confidence and self-esteem.
- Issues in school that may need to be addressed include poor relationships, bullying, difficulties with school work, or combinations of these.
- Issues relating to particular communities and family dysfunction or stress require multifaceted interventions with a range of agencies working together.
- Prosecution of parents seems to have limited impact on attendance but the processes which lead up to it can facilitate discussion of the issues and the development of appropriate remedial strategies.
- Treatment for problems relating to acute anxiety can be addressed through drugs, flooding or systematic desensitization techniques, cognitive restructuring, modelling, or parental training in operant conditioning.
- Whatever the cause of the persistent absenteeism, children require support on their return to school. Staff need to be involved in planning. Students need to be given opportunities to catch up on missed work, and to undertake a pre-visit. The provision of an adult mentor, a peer buddy, a phased period of gradual attendance, or support in a reintegration unit will support the child.

Further reading

Edwards, A., Barnes, M., Plewis, I. and Morris, K. (2006) *Working to Prevent the Social Exclusion of Children and Young People: Final Lessons from the National Evaluation of the Children's Fund*. London: DfES.

Halsey, K., Bedford, N., Atkinson, M., White, R. and Kinder, K. (2004) *Evaluation of Fast Track to Prosecution for School Non-attendance. Research Report 567*. London: DfES.

Lauchlan, F. (2003) Responding to chronic non-attendance: A review of intervention approaches. *Educational Psychology in Practice*, 19(2): 133–46.

References

Archer, T., Filmer-Sankey, C. and Fletcher-Campbell, F. (2003) *School Phobia and School Refusal: Research into Causes and Remedies*. Slough: NFER/LGA.

Bandura, A. (1969) *Principles of Behaviour Modification*. New York: Holt, Rinehart and Winston.

Barabasz, A.F. (1973) Group desensitization of test anxiety in elementary school. *Journal of Psychology*, 83: 295–301.

Barabasz, A.F. (1975) Classroom teachers as paraprofessional therapists in group systematic desensitization of test anxiety. *Psychiatry*, 38: 388–92.

Beirens, H., Mason, P., Spicer, N., Huges, N., and Hek, R. (2006) *Preventative Services for Refugee and Asylum Seeking Children. A final report from the National Evaluaiton of the Children's Fund*. London: DfES.

Bernstein, G. A., and Garfinkel, B. D. (1986) School phobia: The overlap of affective and anxiety disorders *Journal of the American Adademy of Child Psychiatry*, 25, 235–241.

Bell, A.J., Rosen, L.A. and Dynlacht, D. (1994) Truancy intervention. *Journal of Research and Development in Education*, 27: 203–11.

Berg, I. (1992) Absence from school and mental health. *British Journal of Psychiatry*, 161: 533–6.

Berg, I., Butler, A., Franklin, J., Hayes, H., Lucas, C. and Sims, R. (1993) DSM-III disorders, social factors, and management of school attendance problems in the normal population. *Journal of Child Psychology and Psychiatry*, 34(7): 1187–203.

Berg, I., Nichols, K. and Pritchard, C. (1969) School phobia, its classification and relationships to dependency. *Journal of Child Psychology and Psychiatry*, 10: 123–41.

Bernstein, G.A., Garfinkel, B.D. and Borchardt, C.M. (1990) Comparative studies of pharmacotherapy for school refusal. *Journal of the American Academy of Child and Adolescent Psychiatry*, 29: 773–81.

Blagg, N. (1987) *School Phobia and Its Intervention*. London: Croom Helm.

Blagg, N. and Yule, W. (1984) The behavioural intervention of school refusal: A comparative study. *Behaviour Research and Therapy*, 22: 119–27.

Bokhurst, K., Goosens, F.A. and De Ruyter, P.A. (1995) Social anxiety in elementary school children: The effects of a curriculum. *Educational Research*, 37: 87–94.

Bools, C., Foster, J., Brown, I. and Berg, I. (1990) The identification of psychiatric disorders in children who fail to attend school: A cluster analysis of a non-clinical population. *Psychological Medicine*, 20: 171–81.

Borchardt, C.M., Giesler, J., Bernstein, G.A. and Crosby, R.D. (1994) A comparison of inpatient and outpatient school refusers. *Child Psychiatry and Human Development*, 24: 255–64.

Brandibas, G., Jeunier, B., Clanet, C. and Fouraste, R. (2004) Truancy, school refusal and anxiety. *School Psychology International*, 25(1): 117–26.

Campbell, D. and Wright, J. (2005) Rethinking welfare school attendance policies, *Social Service Review*, March: 1–28.

Coie, J. and Koeppl, G.K. (1990) Adapting intervention to the problem of aggressive and disruptive rejected children, in S.R. Asher and J.D. Coie (eds) *Peer Rejection in Childhood*, pp. 309–37 Cambridge: Cambridge University Press.

Colorado Foundation for Families and Children (2002) *Youth out of School: Linking Absence to Delinquency*. Denver, CO: Colorado Foundation.

Davis, J.D. and Lee, J. (2006) To attend or not to attend? Why some students chose school and others reject it. *Support for Learning*, 21(4): 204–9.

Deffenbacher, J.L. and Kemper, C.G. (1974) Systematic desensitization of test anxiety in junior high students. *School Counsellor*, 21(3): 216–22.

Edwards, A., Barnes, M., Plewis, I. and Morris, K. (2006) *Working to Prevent the Social Exclusion of Children and Young People: Final Lessons from the National Evaluation of the Children's Fund*. London: DfES.

Elliott, J. (1999) Practitioner review: School Refusal; Issues of conceptualization, assessment and treatment. *Journal of Child Psychology and Psychiatry*, 40(7): 1001–12.

Elliott, J. and Place, M. (1998) *Children in Difficulty: A Guide to Understanding and Helping*. London: Routledge.

Evans, R., Pinnock, K., Beirens, H. and Edwards, A. (2006) *Developing Preventative Practices: The Experiences of Children, Young People and Their Families in the Children's Fund*. London: DfES.

Garvey, W.P. and Hegrenes, J.R. (1966) Desensitization techniques in the treatment of school phobics. *American Journal of Orthopsychiatry*, 36: 147–52.

Grossman, J.B. and Tierney, J.P. (1998) Does mentoring work? An impact of the Big Brothers, Big Sisters programme. *Evaluation Review*, 22: 403–26.

Hallam, S. and Castle, F. (1999) *Evaluation of the Behaviour and Discipline Pilot Projects (1996–99) Supported under the Standards Fund Programme. Research Report 163*. London: DfEE.

Hallam, S., Shaw, J. and Rhamie, J. (2006) *Evaluation of the Primary Behaviour and Attendance Pilot. Research Report 717*. London: DfES.

Halsey, K., Bedford, N., Atkinson, M., White, R. and Kinder, K. (2004) *Evaluation of Fast Track to Prosecution for School Non-attendance. Research Report 567*. London: DfES.

Hersov, L. (1985) Refusal to go to school in M. Rutter and L. Hersov (eds) *Child and Adolescent Psychiatry: Modern Approaches* (2nd edition) Oxford: Blackwell.

Kearney, C. A. (1993) Depression and school refusal behaviour: a review with comments on classification and treatment. Journal of school Psychology, 31(2), 267–79.

Kearney, C.A. and Beasley, J.F. (1994) The clinical intervention of school refusal behaviour: a survey of referral and practice characteristics. *Psychology in the Schools*, 31: 128–32.

Kearney, C.A. and Bensaheb, A. (2006) School absenteeism and school refusal behaviour: A review and suggestions for school-based health professionals. *Journal of School Health*, 76(1): 3–7.

Kearney, C.A. and Silverman, W.K. (1990) A preliminary analysis of a functional model of assessment and intervention of school refusal behaviour. *Behaviour Modification*, 149: 340–66.

Kearney, C.A. and Silverman, W.K. (1993) Measuring the function of school refusal behaviour. The school refusal assessment scale. *Journal of Clinical Child Psychology*, 22(1): 85–96.

Kearney, C.A. and Sims, K.E. (1997) Anxiety problems in childhood: Diagnostic and dimensional aspects, in J.A. den Boer (ed.) *Clinical Management of Anxiety*. New York: Marcel Dekker.

Kendall, S., White, R. and Kinder, K. (2003) *School attendance and the Prosecution of Parents: Perspectives from Education Welfare Service Management. First Report*. Slough: NFER/LGA.

Kendall, S., White, R., Kinder, K., Halsey, K. and Bedford, N. (2004) *School Attendance and the Prosecution of Parents: Effects and Effectiveness*. Slough: NFER/LGA.

King, N., Hamilton, D.I. and Ollendick, T.H. (1994) *Children's Phobias: A Behavioural Perspective*. New York: Wiley.

King, N., Ollendick, T.H. and Tonge, B.J. (1995) *School Refusal: Assessment and Intervention*. Needham Heights, MA: Allyn and Bacon.

King, N., Ollendick, T.H., Tonge, B.J. et al. (1996) Behavioural management of school refusal. *Scandinavian Journal of Behaviour Therapy*, 25: 3–15.

King, N., Tonge, B.J., Heyne, D. et al. (1998) Cognitive-behavioural intervention of school refusing children: A controlled evaluation. *Journal of the American Academy of Child and Adolescent Psychiatry*, 37(4): 395–403.

Last, C.G. and Strauss, C.C. (1990) School refusal in anxiety-disordered children and adolescents. *Journal of the American Academy of Child and Adolescent Psychiatry*, 29: 31–325.

Last, C.G., Francis, G., Hersen, M., Kazdin, A.E. and Strauss, C.C. (1987) Separation anxiety and school phobia: A comparison using DSM-III criteria. *American Journal of Psychiatry*, 144(5): 653–7.

Last, C.G., Hansen, C. and Franco, N. (1998) Cognitive-behavioural intervention of school phobia. *Journal of the American Academy of Child and Adolescent Psychiatry*, 37(4): 404–11.

Lauchlan, F. (2003) Responding to chronic non-attendance: a review of intervention approaches. *Educational Psychology in Practice*, 19(2): 133–46.

Lehr, C.A., Johnson, D.R., Bremer, C.D., Cosio, A. and Thompson, M. (2004). *Essential Tools: Increasing Rates of School Completion*. Minneapolis, MN: National Center on Secondary Education and Transition.

McAra, L. (2004) *Truancy, Exclusion and Substance Misuse. Centre for Law and Society, No 4*. The Edinburgh Study of Youth Transitions and Crime.

McCluskey, C.P., Bynum, T.S. and Patchin, J.W. (2004) Reducing chronic absenteeism: An assessment of an early truancy initiative. *Crime and Delinquency*, 50(2): 214–34.

MacDonald, W.S., Gallimore, R. and MacDonald, G. (1970) Contingency counselling by school personnel: An economical model of intervention. *Journal of Applied Behaviour Analysis*, 3: 175–82.

Mansdorf, I.J. and Lukens, E. (1987) Cognitive-behavioural psychotherapy for separation anxious children exhibiting school phobia. *Journal of the American Academy of Child and Adolescent Psychiatry*, 26: 222–5.

Milne, B.J., Chalmers, S., Walde, K.E., Darling, H. and Poulton, R. (2002) Effectiveness of a community-based truancy intervention: A Pilot Study. *New Zealand Journal of Educational Studies*, 37(2): 191–203.

Mize, J. and Ladd, G. (1990) A cognitive social learning approach to social skill training. *Developmental Psychology*, 26: 388–97.

Morris, M. and Rutt, S. (2005) *An Analysis of Pupil Attendance Data in Excellence in Cities (EiC) Areas and Non-EiC EAZs: Final Report*. London: DfES.

Morris, R.J. and Kratochwill, T.R. (1983) *Treating Children's Fears and Phobias: A Behavioural Approach*. New York: Pergamon Press.

Murphy, M. and Wolkind, S. (1996) The role of the child and adolescent psychiatrist, in I. Berg and J. Nursten (eds) *Unwillingly to School*, pp. 129–56. London: Gaskell.

Nardi, E. and Steward, S. (2002) *Attitude and Achievement of the Disadvantaged Pupil in the Mathematics Classroom*. ESRC Final Report R000223451.

National Audit Office (NAO) (2005) *Improving School Attendance in England*. London: The Stationery Office.

NFER (2003) *The Evaluation of the Pilot Devolution of Education Welfare Services to Secondary Schools: Final Report*. Slough: NFER.

Ofsted (2004) *Out of School: A Survey of the Educational Support and Provision for Pupils Not in School*. London: Ofsted.

Ollendick, T.H. (1979) Fear reduction techniques with children, in M. Hersen, R.M. Eisler and P.M. Miller (eds) *Progress in Behaviour Modification*, 11: 127–68. New York: Academic Press.

Pilkington, C.L. and Piersel, W.C. (1991) School phobia: A critical analysis of the separation anxiety theory and an alternative conceptualization. *Psychology in the Schools*, 28: 290–303.

Reid, K. (2002) *Truancy: Short and Long Term Solutions*. London: Routledge-Falmer.

Reid, K. (2003) A strategic approach to tackling school absenteeism and truancy: The PSCC scheme. *Educational Studies*, 29(4): 351–71.

Reid, K. (2004) An evaluation of strategies and professional development needs on attendance issues within an LEA. *Pastoral Care in Education*, 22(1): 15–24.

Reynolds, D., Jones, D., St Leger, S. and Murgatroyd, S. (1980) School factors and truancy, in L. Hersov and I. Berg (eds) *Out of School*. New York: Wiley.

Schloss, P.J., Kane, M.S. and Miller, S. (1981) Truancy intervention with behaviour disordered adolescents. *Behavioural Disorders*, 6: 175–9.

Sinclair, M.F., Christenson, S.L., Evelo, D.L. and Hurley, C. (1998) Dropout prevention for high risk youth with disabilities: Efficacy of a sustained engagement procedure. *Exceptional Children*, 65(1): 7–21.

Spence, S.H., Donovan, C. and Breechman-Toussaint, M. (1999) Social skills, social outcomes and cognitive features of childhood social phobia. *Journal of Abnormal Psychology*, 108: 211–21.

Spence, S.H., Donovan, C. and Breechman-Toussaint, M. (2000) The treatment of childhood school phobia: The effectiveness of a social skills training-based, cognitive-behavioural intervention, with and without parental involvement. *Journal of Child Psychology and Psychiatry*, 41(6): 713–26.

Ultee, C.A., Griffioen, D. and Schellekens, J. (1982) The reduction of anxiety in children: A comparison of the effects of systematic desensitization *in vitro* and systematic desensitization *in vivo*. *Behaviour Research and Therapy*, 20: 61–7.

Wenzel, K.R. (1991) Relations between social competence and academic achievement in early adolescence. *Child Development*, 62: 1066–78.

Wolpe, J. (1958) *Psychotherapy by Reciprocal Inhibition*. Stanford, CA: Stanford University Press.

Zhang, M. (2004) Time to change the Truancy Laws? Compulsory education: Its origin and modern dilemma. *Pastoral Care in Education*, 22(2): 27–33.

Section 4:
Overview

13 Overview

This chapter considers the pressures on raising standards in education in the developed world and issues relating to the intergenerational transmission of deprivation. It summarizes what governments, Local Authorities, schools and families can do to improve behaviour and attendance in order to enhance learning, attainment and subsequent employment and life chances.

Introduction

In a rapidly changing globalized society, education is fundamental to the ability of people to prosper. The shift to a knowledge- and information-based economy worldwide with its concomitant need for a highly skilled and knowledgeable workforce has required that populations have high level skills and a sound initial education. People without skills face increasing marginalization. Particularly vulnerable are those people who, for a variety of reasons, dropout of mainstream education and those in developing countries who do not have access to even the most rudimentary education.

In the developed world, the demands of the knowledge economy, the changing nature of jobs, technological advance and globalization have occurred contemporaneously with changes in society, and in family relationships. The convergence of these factors poses considerable challenges. Of particular concern is the widening gap between those who have the knowledge, skills and resources (financial, personal and educational) to access the opportunities and goods of the knowledge economy and learning society and those whose lack of knowledge and skills and resources place them increasingly at the margins of society. Certain combinations of age, gender, ethnicity and family circumstances contribute substantially to the risk of encountering serious problems.

The children of those who are already disadvantaged are the most likely to do poorly at school. In the UK, Hobcraft (1998), using data from the

1958 National Child Development Study, identified childhood poverty, family disruption, contact with the police, educational test scores and father's interest in school as the most powerful and consistent predictors of disadvantage in later life. Sigle-Rushton (2004), using data from the 1970 cohort, further reinforced the relationship finding that the childhood factors that were most strongly associated with adult social exclusion were academic test scores administered at ages 5, 10 and 16, and parental housing. Cohort members recorded living in local authority housing at least once during childhood were much more likely to be in social housing at age 30. There is evidence that the strength of these relationships has increased. Teenage poverty had a greater impact on later outcomes for those who were teenagers in the 1980s compared with teenagers in the 1970s (Blanden and Gibbons 2006). Disadvantage is transmitted across generations.

A comparison of the intergenerational transmission of disadvantage in Organization for Economic Cooperation and Development (OECD) countries (D'Addio 2007) found relatively little mobility across generations in relation to income, occupations and education. Children largely 'inherited' their parents' socio-economic status, through a broad range of processes including the direct passing-on of wealth and the learning of particular attitudes and behaviours. However, the degree of association between parental and child earnings varied widely between countries. Less than 20 per cent of the difference in parental incomes was passed on to children in some Nordic countries, Australia and Canada while between 40 and 50 per cent was passed on in Italy, the UK and the USA. Earnings mobility was especially low at the bottom of the distribution, strengthening the transmission of poverty across generations. The report stressed the importance of education as a vehicle to increase intergenerational income mobility but noted that educational differences also tended to persist across generations. The range of family characteristics that shape educational mobility included ethnic origin, the language spoken at home, family size and structure, and the socio-economic and cultural background of the parents. Parental education was particularly important in shaping the life chances of children. National educational policies can also impact on mobility, for instance, the early streaming of students based on their ability considerably reduces mobility across generations. Early sustained investment in children and families supporting education, care and health holds the promise of breaking this cycle of intergenerational disadvantage (D'Addio 2007).

Some people overcome the barriers presented by their origins. Pilling (1990) compared those who appeared to be doing well in terms of educational and vocational qualifications obtained by the age of 23 with a similarly disadvantaged group. Social disadvantage in the very earliest years of childhood was particularly significant in explaining the differences. Those who had raised their socio-economic status were more likely than the comparison group to have had good relationships with their parents, a stimulating home background, and a father who played a supportive role in their education. Other protective factors within the environment which have been identified include:

- being female;
- having a mother with some extended education;
- having a father who helps with domestic tasks;
- having parents who are interested in and involved with education;
- being read to on a daily basis at age 5;
- there being four or fewer children spaced two or more years apart in the family;
- being given a great deal of attention in the first year of infancy;
- positive parent–child relationships in early childhood;
- additional caretakers besides the mother;
- care by siblings and grandparents;
- having a wider network of social support (family/community);
- having a good relationship with school;
- the mother having steady employment outside the home;
- having access to special services (health/education/social services);
- there being clear structures and rules in the household;
- having close supportive peer relationships with non-delinquent peers; and
- engagement with formal religion (Schoon and Parsons 2002; Barrett 2003; Blanden 2006).

Next steps

Improving children's behaviour and attendance at school facilitates learning and attainment which impacts on other educational outcomes increasing self-confidence and aspirations. In the longer term employment prospects are enhanced and the likelihood of engagement in antisocial or criminal activity is reduced. It is in everyone's interests to enhance educational outcomes for young people. To achieve this requires that action is taken at the level of each of the interacting systems: community, family, school and the individual.

Policy makers

One of the main objectives of social policy is to break the cycle of disadvantage across generations and prevent the development of a self-replicating underclass which is expensive for society to maintain both directly in terms of the costs of providing financial support and a wide range of services, and indirectly in loss to the economy of a proportion of the adult workforce and subsequent income to the exchequer through taxation. There are also social costs of antisocial behaviour, vandalism and crime.

International comparisons have shown that excellence in education is an attainable goal, at a reasonable cost and that it is possible to combine high performance levels with social equity in the distribution of learning opportunities (OECD 2004). Poor performance in school does not automatically follow from low socio-economic status. High quality teaching is the key to breaking the cycle with well trained teachers working within an appropriate policy framework and institutional context including formulating educational goals and standards, monitoring the extent to which they are being met, feeding back information to schools and teachers, and establishing rewards and support systems as appropriate. Much of the difference in average performance of countries is a result of the extent of poorly performing students and schools. Countries vary much more in the performance of students from disadvantaged socio-economic contexts than in the performance of students from advantaged backgrounds. Raising performance, in part, depends on whether education systems can improve the outcomes for poorly performing students and schools. Variation in student performance and between schools is greater in countries where rigid institutional selection and ability grouping practices are implemented at early ages. High performing countries emphasize mixed ability teaching within integrated education systems with a high level of personalized learning (OECD 2004).

Policy makers in the developed world can take a number of steps to enhance educational outcomes for children from disadvantaged backgrounds, some of which are already being implemented in the UK. At a general level these include:

- reducing child poverty;
- targeting intensive health care and nutrition;
- ensuring that there is good quality care available in early childhood;
- ensuring that there is a wide range of play and extra-curricular activities available for children and young people in deprived areas; and
- developing initiatives within communities which support self-help.

Specifically in relation to education governments can ensure that:

- high quality education is available for all children wherever they live;

- rigid selection and ability grouping processes at an early age are not encouraged and that there is an emphasis on the personalization of learning;
- the curriculum on offer is relevant;
- the infrastructure is in place for ensuring that schools and children have access to ongoing developments in information technology;
- national assessment procedures are motivating and not overly stressful;
- the environment in schools is safe, supportive and conducive to learning;
- appropriate support is available for children 'at-risk'; and
- monitoring procedures are rigorous, able to identify where schools are in difficulties early, and that sufficient support is offered to bring about change.

Policy makers can also take the lead in encouraging society and the media to generate and reward role models who will have a positive influence on young people's attitudes and behaviour. In the UK, most of the role models regarded as having high status by young people do not have high levels of education and are frequently rewarded in terms of celebrity and media coverage for 'behaving badly'. Nevertheless, their wealth and status encourage young people to emulate them.

Policy at the local level

Local Authorities have a crucial role to play in facilitating those living in disadvantaged communities to develop initiatives which will improve the quality of their lives. The evidence from the Children's Fund initiative and the OECD 'Overcoming Exclusion through Adult Learning' programme suggests that multidimensional approaches developed at grass-roots level in local communities are often the most effective in bringing about change. Those initiatives which most motivate participants are perceived to have clear benefits for meeting practical needs and offer the possibility of transforming lives, individually or collectively. Projects need strong local leadership, and should empower and build individual and community strengths, enhance employment opportunities within the knowledge society, encourage other opportunities (self-employment, community enterprise), develop human capital (knowledge, skills, competence), and develop social capital (networks).

Local Authorities are uniquely placed to ensure that all children have access to a high quality education and that they and their families receive appropriate support to enable them to make a long-term contribution to society. To these ends they need to ensure that:

- appropriate systems are in place to monitor school performance, provide feedback and offer support where it is needed;
- schools are encouraged to work collaboratively;
- a range of alternative curricular is available for children at risk of exclusion or dropping out;
- a wide range of extra-curricular activities are available locally for all children;
- appropriate provision is made to ensure continuous education for excluded children;
- support is available for persistent absentees to return them to full-time education;
- multi-agency support is available for 'at-risk' children and their families;
- there is good communication within multi-agency teams and clearly defined professional boundaries; and
- parenting programmes are available locally, easily accessed and widely advertised.

Schools

Schools in the UK are currently under enormous pressure to raise educational standards. This has created some tensions, in that schools have sometimes found it easier to exclude low attaining, poorly attending, or difficult pupils rather than educating them. If standards are to be raised for all children, they must attend school, be well behaved, and most importantly, be motivated to learn. To achieve these aims schools need to provide an environment which is safe and secure, and which is conducive to learning. The focus needs to be on supporting the students in gaining skills which they perceive will be useful to them in attaining their career, social and personal aspirations.

PISA (2000) indicated that students and schools perform better in a climate of high expectations, high motivation and effort, enjoyment of learning, a firm disciplinary context and good teacher–student relations. Students' perceptions of teacher–student relations and classroom disciplinary climate displayed the strongest relationships with performance across countries. Less strong, although still important were students' perceptions of the extent to which teachers emphasized academic performance and placed high demands on students.

Schools can support the development of such a climate at the level of the whole school, through strong and collaborative management, working with the wider community, ensuring that staff are supported and have opportunities for continuing professional development, and that children have access to appropriate curricula, the opportunity to work in a supportive classroom environment, and receive appropriate support.

The whole school

Creating a positive school climate is crucial in ensuring good behaviour, attendance and engagement with learning. Children need to be the focus in developing such a climate ensuring equity of opportunity and treatment, and eradicating prejudice. Attention needs to be given to:

- the physical environment (making it welcoming and attractive, paying attention to the playground, toilets, cleanliness, safety);
- the social environment (ensuring safety, good staff–pupil, pupil–pupil and within-staff relationships, eradicating bullying, empowering collaboration, rewarding positive behaviour and interactions, being inclusive, ensuring equity of opportunity and treatment for all pupils and staff);
- the learning environment (cultivating a learning rather than a performance culture for all pupils and staff in all areas of the school including the playground and any alternative or specialist provision, ensuring optimum rather than excessive stress, ensuring appropriate curricula opportunities); and
- links with the wider community (other agencies, families, other schools, the police).

In developing a positive whole-school climate the children in the school need to have a voice. This may be through informal interactions between staff and pupils or more formally through School Councils.

Leadership and management in the school

It is difficult to overestimate the importance of the quality of leadership and management in schools. Strong and positive leadership which is collaborative involving all staff, pupils and their parents is crucial. Senior managers need to have a vision of what they wish to attain and the skills to develop policies and practices to achieve their aims while also being engaged with the active everyday life of the school, having up-to-date and accurate knowledge of what is going on in classrooms and at break times, and being willing and able to take action to address arising issues. They need to present positive role models to staff and pupils and have sufficiently clearly defined responsibilities to avoid overload which often results in stress and ineffectiveness.

Policies, particularly those relating to behaviour, attendance, pastoral care, bullying and the curriculum, need to be:

- proactive rather than reactive;
- developed on the basis of evidence and through consultation;

- implemented systematically;
- monitored for effectiveness; and
- regularly reviewed and changed where necessary.

They need to be inclusive, and applied consistently to ensure equitable treatment for all pupils. Systematic and regular communication is also crucial in identifying emerging problems so that they can be addressed before they escalate.

Links with the wider community

Making links with the wider community can add value to the life of a school. Links can beneficially be made with other schools, a range of external agencies, community groups, and families and parents.

Working collaboratively with other schools is valuable in relation to Continuing Professional Development opportunities, sharing practice and developing ideas, offering a wider range of curricular opportunities, developing supportive transition procedures for all pupils and particularly for those at-risk, and making provision for excluded pupils particularly on the first day of exclusion.

Additional support beyond that which can be supplied by schools is frequently necessary to support those children and their families who are experiencing behavioural or attendance difficulties. Developing good working relationships with a range of educational and social support agencies, voluntary and charitable institutions, and local religious and community groups can provide schools with valuable additional resources. Schools can be proactive in developing these relationships and those with families. To do so they should provide a welcoming environment and appropriate facilities for outside agencies, community groups and families. The provision of workshops, social occasions, formal and informal opportunities for families to engage with school staff, and the development of effective communication systems (website, email, text messaging, telephone, newsletters, meetings) are all important. School Councils also have a role to play. Parents in particular often do not know how to support their children in their education, and schools can be proactive in arranging opportunities for them to learn how to do so.

The school staff

The quality of teaching in the school is a major influence on children's behaviour and attendance as are staff–pupil relationships. Schools need to value and invest in all of their staff. This is reflected in the way that staff are empowered, consulted and develop ownership of policies and practices, and the opportunities they are given for training collectively and individually. Important is a school climate which has an open culture which allows staff, particularly newly qualified teachers, to admit to difficulties and provides support and mentoring. In addressing issues of behaviour and attendance staff training is particularly important in relation to:

- inclusion;
- pupil well-being (being receptive to changes in behaviour which may indicate problems); and
- pastoral care (the roles and responsibilities of form tutors, key workers).

Curricular issues

The introduction of the National Curriculum in the UK took away from schools and teachers much of the freedom that they had previously had to determine what was taught, although they maintained control over the way it was taught. Recently schools have been given more freedom to offer alternatives to the National Curriculum particularly for older students. Schools need to be proactive in tailoring the taught curriculum to meet student needs. In addition, there needs to be recognition that learning is not confined to the classroom. Children learn in the playground, at break times, on school trips, through links with industry and the wider community (work experience), at home, through extra-curricular activities at school, local or national levels, on holidays (particularly extended ones to other countries), and through the hidden curriculum in schools (values, attitudes, staff models and behaviour). These sources of learning can have a greater impact on children, their aspirations, behaviour and attendance at school than the formal school curriculum. Schools should encourage students to engage with such opportunities for learning and teachers should utilize them in the classroom as a means of making the National Curriculum relevant and increasing student engagement and motivation.

The classroom environment

To support learning, classrooms need to be orderly with a positive, tension- and stress-free climate. The focus needs to be on learning for all pupils, with behaviour seen as a prerequisite for this rather than an end in itself. Teachers need to acknowledge that they cannot learn for their pupils. To facilitate learning teachers have to motivate their students. If students are motivated learning will be supported by the clear communication of aims and objectives; explanations which are interesting and have clarity, well designed tasks making good use of resources, and constructive and formative feedback on work undertaken. In support of this teachers need to:

- value all pupils;
- be inspiring;
- make the curriculum relevant;
- value the learning experiences that students may have had elsewhere;
- develop good relationships with students;
- offer a variety of activities and pupil groupings to meet pupil needs;
- be positive role models for pupils (no bullying or sarcasm);
- treat pupils equitably;
- offer praise for good or improving behaviour and work;
- be supportive when pupils are experiencing difficulties; and
- accept that pupils may become frustrated and offer them time out opportunities to regain control of their emotions.

Support for individual pupils

Even when schools have exemplary policies and practices relating to behaviour and attendance, individual children from time to time may experience difficulties. Schools need to make provision for this. There is a tendency when pupils experience difficulties at school to label the child as the problem rather than the specific behaviour. Once a child is labelled as difficult any behaviour that they exhibit is interpreted accordingly and behaviour which in another child would be perceived as trivial is viewed more seriously. It is extremely difficult for a child once labelled in this way to change staff perceptions. For most children difficulties are transitory and schools need to acknowledge this. Children need to be provided with a range of skills and strategies for coping with the problems that they are facing. Working with other agencies or providers, for example, Behaviour and Education Support Teams, Educational Welfare Services, with school learning mentors or home- –school links workers, schools can offer a range of support including counselling, training in anger management, and mentoring. It is also important for schools to recognize problems before they become entrenched. If they are not addressed early on, the school sends a tacit message to the child and his/her family that they do not care. Speedy action signals that the child is valued. When issues have been resolved schools need to have mechanisms for formally signing off a problem providing closure for children and their families.

Families

Families play a crucial role in their children's education. Parents' aspirations and expectations, the discussions that they have about educational issues at home, and the support that they offer all play a part in the extent to which children are successful at school. Parents, and the extended family, can undertake a range of activities to help children succeed educationally. These include:

- supporting the development of spoken language skills through positive communicative interactions;
- playing games particularly those which involve numbers and language;
- reading to and with children;
- encouraging activities which involve drawing and writing;
- encouraging active participation in a range of interesting activities outside school;
- having high aspirations, showing an interest in their children's education and discussing issues arising from it with their children;
- modelling good behaviour, self-control, responsibility;
- rewarding good behaviour and minimizing the attention given to poor behaviour;
- reducing stress and anxiety; and
- being unafraid to seek support when problems arise.

The extended family has a role to play in supporting children in all families but this is particularly important in single parent families, especially when there is a lack of suitable male role models.

The responsibilities of children

We should not underestimate the capacity of children to take responsibility for their own behaviour and learning. Some children are highly motivated to succeed in their chosen area of expertise from a very early age. While they may require adults to provide them with resources and support, it is their determination to succeed which is of crucial importance. To maximize their potential and create an environment conducive for doing so children need to:

- take responsibility for their learning and behaviour;
- take advantage of every opportunity in and outside school to develop their personal, intellectual and social skills;

- have high aspirations and set themselves interim goals to attain them;
- be proactive in engaging their parents in supporting their educational and career aspirations;
- take a stand against bullying, engender positive peer relationships, and offer support to those who need it;
- act as positive role models to others; and
- make a positive contribution to their school and community.

Endnote

While it is hard to break intergenerational cycles of deprivation, the differences in levels of intergenerational mobility between countries demonstrate that it is possible to develop systems which support individuals in raising their aspirations and changing attitudes and behaviour increasing mobility. Poverty is a key cause of disaffection and under achievement and requires intervention at the highest levels in government but there is much that Local Authorities, schools, teachers, groups within the community and families working together can do to bring about change. Focusing on motivating students to learn and achieve in school and in informal settings should be a major priority for all. The consequences for individuals, families and society of school failure have been well documented over the years. Globalization and the changing nature of employment means that it is no longer sufficient to acknowledge the problems. It is incumbent on us all to take action.

Chapter summary

- The shift to a knowledge- and information-based economy worldwide requires a highly skilled and knowledgeable workforce.
- Education is fundamental to the ability of people to prosper in this rapidly changing globalized society and economy.
- People without skills face increasing marginalization. Particularly vulnerable are those people who for a variety of reasons dropout of mainstream education.
- Economic changes have been accompanied in the developed world with changes in society and the breakdown of the family. This presents considerable challenges.
- Disadvantage is transmitted across generations. The extent to which this occurs varies between countries. The UK has one of the highest levels of intergenerational transmission of poverty. It is possible to change this.
- Government, Local Authorities, schools, families and children all have a role to play in this process.

Further reading

Centre for Educational Research and Innovation (CERI) (1999) *Overcoming Exclusion through Adult Learning.* France: Organization for Economic Cooperation and Development.

D'Addio, A.C. (2007) *Intergenerational Transmission of Disadvantage: Mobility of Immobility across Generations? A Review of Evidence for OECD Countries.* Paris: OECD.

References

Barrett, H. (2003) *Parenting Programmes for Families at Risk: A Source Book.* London: National Family and Parenting Institute.

Blanden, J. (2006) *Bucking the Trend: What Enables Those Who Are Disadvantaged in Childhood to Succeed in Later Life? Department for Pensions Working Paper No 31.* A report of research carried out by the Department of Economics, University of Surrey and the Centre for Economic Performance, London School of Economics on behalf of DWP. Norwich: HMSO.

Blanden, J. and Gibbons, S. (2006) *The Persistence of Poverty across Generations: A View from Two British Cohorts.* London: Joseph Rowntree Foundation.

D'Addio, A.C. (2007) *Intergenerational Transmission of Disadvantage: Mobility of Immobility across Generations? A Review of Evidence for OECD Countries.* Paris: OECD.

Hobcraft, J. (1998) *Intergenerational and Life-course Transmission of Social Exclusion: Influences of Child Poverty, Family Disruption and Contact with the Police, CASE Paper 15.* London: London School of Economics, ESRC Centre for the Analysis of Social Exclusion.

Organization for Economic Cooperation and Development (OECD) (2004) *Learning for Tomorrow's World: First Results from PISA 2000.* Paris: OECD.

Pilling, D. (1990) *Escape from Disadvantage.* London: Falmer Press.

Schoon, I. and Parsons, S. (2002) Competence in the face of adversity: The influence of early family environment and long-term consequences. *Children & Society*, 16: 260–72.

Sigle-Rushton, W. (2004) *Intergenerational and Life-course Transmission of Social Exclusion in the 1970 British Cohort Study, CASE Study Discussion Paper No. 78.* London: London School of Economics, ESRC Centre for the Analysis of Social Exclusion.

Index

UNDERSTANDING EFFECTIVE LEARNING

Strategies for the Classroom

Des Hewitt

Within education, concepts such as learning styles, learning strategies and independent learning are often cited as important areas for development in schools (DFES 1998, 2001) but these are rarely satisfactorily defined. It is essential for teachers to develop a detailed understanding of learning across the curriculum, as well as appropriate strategies, if children are to learn effectively.

This book explores these important concepts by examining learning in a range of classroom settings and drawing on evidence from teachers and pupils, through interviews and observations. The focus is two-fold: to understand learning in the classroom, and to develop practices which will support learning. Topics explored include:

- Models of learning
- Learning strategies and the teacher
- Learning strategies and the learner
- Assessment for Learning

The social dimension of children's learning

The book provides a rich mixture of examples, reflection points, case studies and strategies for the classroom to provide the reader with a wide range of ideas to encourage more effective learning in their classroom.

Understanding Effective Learning is key reading for student, beginning and early career teachers in primary education.

Contents: *List of activities, strategies for the classroom and case studies – List of tables and figures – Preface – Introduction – Overview: what is learning? – The problem with learning – The competing social settings of learning – Learning strategies and the individual learner – Learning strategies and the teacher – Whole school approaches to learning strategies – Standards: developing the debate about independent and effective learning – Glossary – Bibliography.*

June 2008 192pp

978-0-335-22237-7 (Paperback) 978-0-335-22236-0 (Hardback)

DEVELOPING THINKING; DEVELOPING LEARNING

A Guide to Thinking Skills in Education

Debra McGregor

'This highly informative book provides a comprehensive guide to the teaching of thinking skills in primary and secondary education.'

Learning and Teaching Update

It is now recognised that thinking skills, such as problem-solving, analysis, synthesis, creativity and evaluation, can be nurtured and developed, and education professionals can play a significant role in shaping the way that children learn and think. As a result, schools are being encouraged to make greater use of thinking skills in lessons and the general emphasis on cognition has developed considerably. This book offers a comprehensive introduction to thinking skills in education and provides detailed guidance on how teachers can support cognitive development in their classrooms.

Developing Thinking; Developing Learning discusses how thinking programmes, learning activities and teachers' pedagogy in the classroom can fundamentally affect the nature of pupils' thinking, and considers the effects of the learning environment created by peers and teachers. It compares the nature, design and outcomes of established thinking programmes used in schools and also offers practical advice for teachers wishing to develop different kinds of thinking capabilities.

This is an indispensable guide to thinking skills in schools today, and is key reading for education studies students, teachers and trainee teachers, and educational psychologists.

Contents: *List of figures and tables – Acknowledgements – Introduction – What do we mean by 'thinking?' – What kind of thinking should we encourage children to do? – Thinking and learning – The nature of thinking programmes developed within a subject context – The nature of general thinking skills programmes – The nature of infusing thinking – Effectiveness of thinking programmes – Development of creative thinking – Development of critical thinking – Development of metacognition – Development of problem solving capability – Synthesising the general from the particular – Professional development to support thinking classrooms – School development to support thinking communities – References – Index.*

2007 344pp

978-0-335-21780-9 (Paperback) 978-0-335-21781-6 (Hardback)

BEHAVIOUR IN SCHOOLS

Theory and Practice for Teachers
Second Edition

Louise Porter

Behaviour management in the classroom and playground is one of the most challenging aspects of teaching. The new edition of *Behaviour in Schools* offers a comprehensive overview of the major theories of behaviour management in primary and secondary schools, illustrated with detailed case studies.

The theories covered range from teacher-dominated methods to more democratic approaches. They include assertive discipline, applied behaviour analysis, the new cognitive behavioural approaches, neo-Adlerian theory, humanism, Glasser's control theory and systems theory. The emphasis is on proactive approaches to discipline which allow teachers to achieve their educational and social goals for their students and themselves. Porter also shows how to enhance students' motivation and help students become confident and independent learners.

Maintaining the balance of theory and practice, the new edition has been fully updated in light of recent research, including a strengthened discussion of inclusion and anti-bias curricula, and sections on motivation and self-esteem. References have been also been updated, making fuller use of UK research.

Behaviour in Schools is a textbook for education students and a reference for experienced teachers who want to improve their ability to cope with disruptive behaviour.

Contents: *Part one: The theories – Introduction – The limit-setting approaches – Applied behaviour analysis – Cognitive-behaviourism – Neo-Adlerian theory – Choice theory – Systems theory – Critique of the theories – Part two: Motivating students – Safeguarding students – Meeting students' need for autonomy – Fostering competence – Meeting students' social needs – Part three: Beyond the classroom – Collaborating with parents – Formulating a discipline policy – Bibliography – Index.*

2006 368pp

978-0-335-22001-4 (Paperback)